AF619792

12th Man: The MIND & METHOD

of an ELITE cricketer

OrangeBooks Publication

Smriti Nagar, Bhilai, Chhattisgarh - 490020

Website: **www.orangebooks.in**

© Copyright, 2020, Author

All rights reserved. No part of this book may be reproduced, stored in a retrieval system, or transmitted, in any form by any means, electronic, mechanical, magnetic, optical, chemical, manual, photocopying, recording or otherwise, without the prior written consent of its writer.

First Edition, 2020

ISBN: 978-81-947079-8-1

Price: Rs.650.00

The opinions/ contents expressed in this book are solely of the authors and do not represent the opinions/ standings/ thoughts of OrangeBooks or the Editors .

Printed in India

12th Man: The MIND & METHOD of an ELITE cricketer

20 chapters of cricket talk every serious cricketer MUST KNOW...all secrets revealed, GUARANTEED to improve your game OVERNIGHT!

Nikhil Jain

ACT state rep – bowler

Mark Heading

ACT state rep – batsman

James Ndlovu

Zimbabwe, Midlands state rep

OrangeBooks Publication

www.orangebooks.in

Dedicated To The

- Aspiring youth of their country

- Minnow cricketing nations – USA, Kenya, Zimbabwe, Bangladesh, Afghanistan, Ireland, UAE, Nepal

- Junior state level cricketers to senior international level players, who should consolidate their understanding of the theory behind the game

Guarantee From Author

If you find that upon reading the contents of this manual that you did not learn anything or did not see an improvement in your approach, temperament and skills as a cricketer in live match conditions to the order of 20% - 50%, then please email us on elitecricketer100@gmail.com with your account details and we will give you a full refund of the price you paid for it minus printing and postage cost. Any profit or proceed we received from your order will be refunded and returned in full.

Use This Manual

Use this book as a reference guide and manual – skim over the table of contents page and only read what you need to. You don't have to read the whole book or the introductions to get the most out of the book. But you DO need to read the chapters relevant to you and you DO need to have your cricketing cap on and absorb as much knowledge and teachings as you can. The book is intended to take an already decent player at what so ever level of cricket and turn him/her into a better one if not a great one, OVERNIGHT!.

Foreword by 'Rajinder Goel'

Highest ever wicket taker of Ranji Trophy – State competition India

I am excited to be a part of this new instruction manual – a book, a coaching manual on the game of cricket designed to give aspiring cricketers a good understanding and grasp over the fundamental and necessary science, method and technique involved in the game and playing on turf, in a short space of time.

By educating youngsters on the game's theory and method early and encouraging them to learn their cricket the right way from the beginning, this manual provides some very interesting insights and tips in regard batting and spin bowling especially. The cricket playing community of not only India but the world, particularly the minnow nations, are encouraged to reap the clinical insight and expert guidance this manual offers to the elite or aspiring cricketer. By encouraging the playing of a brand of cricket based around correct education on the game's theory and method, the manual advocates the changing of a mindset and approach to cricket to one which is more clinical, professional and mentally tough.

I am sure that via the confronting and insightful issues in regard mental toughness raised in the book as well as biomechanics, a mentally tough and hard-nosed cricketer will be a reality for everyone including and especially the upcoming minnow nations. I support Jain and the book's purpose of changing the game from the grass roots level up and molding the youngsters and future of tomorrow into more mentally astute and shrewd athletes, and am excited about standard of cricket rising both in India and worldwide through this manual.

This book is the ideal education on the science and method behind cricket and mental toughness aspects and will take you through the art of batting and spin bowling in a novel manner which you will find very readable and user friendly. Theory and tips for captaincy are also provided.

Biomechanics and finer points of spin bowling is discussed and all spinners regardless of your current level of competency will learn something new and be well guided via the book's spin bowling chapters.

A very thorough yet concise manual on cricket, interesting to read and not just a novelty on the bookshelf but perfect for serious learning and reference purposes. In light of India's loss to NZ in semi-final WC2019, Jain writes the perfect manual which cracks down on athletes and teams who let their talent down due to mental toughness. Physical skills are also discussed at length, and I rate it a must that all serious cricketers have an exposure to the contents of this exciting new manual.

Raman Garg

Dedication

This book is intended to be a concise manual designed to share the knowledge, understanding and training of the game which we received, with other aspiring cricketers who may not have been fortunate enough to pay coaching fees, play on good pitches, may not have the right guidance or education about the game at the right time, or just may not be learning or improving fast enough at their current coaching academy – trust in this book to teach you the basics you'll ever need to succeed as a budding cricketer. It is a book of a very high standard and is also directed at the first class and international level cricket community, and men's level cricketers who are already playing a high standard of cricket are encouraged to consolidate their skills and understanding of cricket via this in depth analysis of the game. Not to mention the female contenders of the sport also!

We can't guarantee to make you a Tendulkar or Kumble overnight as this requires not only ability but many years of monitored dedication, but you will see a marked improvement in your physical skills as well as your temperament, **I GUARANTEE,** overnight! All the knowledge and guidance you may need to become a great player is presented in an easy to follow format. We are confident that with the teachings presented in the book that you will improve your cricket by as much as **20% - 50%** within just a short space of time (given that you properly absorb and understand the more difficult chapters within the book).

If we write something in this book please try to understand it as this book is intended to be in a sense the one and only definitive textbook of cricket or bible of cricket – there is nothing we are going to talk about here which does not have any benefit to its reader, so don't despair if the reading gets too much, we have tried to make it as compact and to the point as possible and as beneficial or worthwhile as possibly can be to bowlers and batsman alike. There is more to cricket than meets the eye so there is a lot to learn if we want a complete scientific education on the game to guide us in our dreams of one day being a great cricketer ourselves, so just hang in there if the reading gets too much it will not go to waste.

.

We want to help produce the stars of tomorrow and help mold the youngsters of the future, and hopefully by reading this book, anyone who takes on board its advice will have a head start before they begin their work as a bowler or a batsman or even a captain, and before they even set a foot onto the practice field.

This book is written purely in the interests of the reader with the sole intention of improving your outlook, approach and skills as a cricketer – not as a reader. You don't have to read the whole book if you don't want to – you don't need to, the chapters relevant to YOU are outlined as follows:

BATSMAN: Chapters –1,2,3,5,6,7,8, 9, 10, 11, 12, 13, 14, 15, 19, 20, 21, 22,24, 25

BOWLERS: Chapters – 1,2,3,5, 6, 12, 13, 14, 15, 16, 17, 18, 19, 20,21, 22, 24, 25

CAPTAINS: Chapters – 15, 21, 22, 23

COACHES: Recommended read whole book

Remember, this work is more of a coaching manual than a book and is more about quality than quantity, and has been kept compact and concise as possible, without neglecting any topics important to a complete and thorough understanding and guidance on the game, which we wish you to have as early as possible. As a source of guidance, inspiration and coaching authority in your cricketing journey, we owe it to you to point you toward other sources of correct and expert guidance on the game. In conjunction to this manual and scientific education on the game, we recommend you watching: https://www.youtube.com/watch?v=HqogQrI6nes. Bob Woolmer's books on batting and bowling may also provide a competent education on the subject, however we don't recommend The Art and Science to Cricket as it is too long and not direct enough to rely upon as a coaching source and one which can teach finer points which we all want to know, and teach them quickly. All you really need is this book you are reading right now and a bit more interaction with your coach in person – excessive reading is NOT the way great cricketers are made but playing the game with an informed and educated approach which DOES.

We want sport science to help develop and encourage the next generation of world class international bowlers and batsmen, and in the mold of cricket's greatest ever – Tendulkar, Lara, Warne, Aravinda, Murali, Kumble, Sehwag & many more. We don't care how you get there and if you resort to reading other literature on the topic of cricketing science, as long as you get there. Virat Kohli, the greatest batsman of today's era committed a big no-no whilst batting in the crucial 2019 world cup semi - final against New Zealand, when he came in to bat against a left-arm pacer bowling over the wicket and swinging the ball into the pads. When he should have taken a leg stump or middle and leg stump guard he took the orthodox and standard middle stump guard and just couldn't get the pads out of the way against a quick in-swinging ball – a mistake which one of the game's most mentally tough, Tendulkar, would never have done. Being mentally alert, astute and tough can make the difference between winning and losing, and that's what we are trying to develop in you by writing this book. It is unfortunate that teams like India and Pakistan have traditionally lacked the mental toughness and acumen to compete in international cricket and win under pressure, despite having decent reserves of talent!

All readers are encouraged to strengthen their understanding of cricket being a 'game of length' and the explanation and science of 'vector forces' behind this, and read the Appendix at the end of the book which gives you detailed background and explanations as to what you need to understand this as a cricketer–not as a scientist!

....through all chances, through possibilities various, we find our way

.....the biggest thing getting in the way of my learning is my education & coaching

....one man flounders under pressure & adversity, another breaks world records – Rohit Sharma

....strength does not come from physical stamina but from an in-dominatable will

....have the drives to succeed – make sure you read this book, with a definitive chapter on how to pick the length!

Preface

We come from a cricket loving nation, perhaps not to the same aura or magnitude of an India or a Pakistan where cricket is the only sport played, but like most kids we were introduced to a few games as children and cricket was the one we pursued till a later age. We were lucky enough to have played till state level where we lived – Australian Capital Territory, U'13s until U'16's level and Zimbabwe U'15s level. Coming from a country with a passion for sports and the resources and infrastructure to provide everyone with adequate training and guidance, sufficient to build great strength and reserve within its representative teams across most sports (bar soccer & basketball), we wish to make this possible for others too, spanning from different age groups all the way to different nations across the globe and even first class cricketers who are already playing good cricket. Through the form of written communication and self-coaching, we wish to share the lessons which we were fortunate to have, with the aspiring youngsters and cricketers from poorer countries whom may not have access to such quality of coaching at the right time. However, the manual is quite detailed and even those who are per say lucky enough to receive expert coaching already are also encouraged to reap the benefit of an unparalleled accurate and scientific education on the game which the book offers.

Unfortunately, myself and others who helped in writing this book were forced to give up the game early, despite good performances at the higher levels, as our family could not afford the costs involved in training, equipment and travel, and studies and working began to take a higher priority. We do however remember all the lessons we were given by numerous coaches, and are willing to share them with other budding cricketers who may need the right guidance in the beginning or intermediate stages of their cricketing journey. However note, this book is quite detailed and is also aimed at the expert cricketer all the way up to international cricketers, and international level cricketers are also urged to reap the wisdom of this concise and user friendly manual, particularly in regard mental toughness aspects of the game which are often ignored and can't be taught via one-to-one coaching and in person.

We urge all parents to first read this book and then translate it to your child orally or if you are a coach first read the book carefully and then translate it to your students orally – remember the book is like a Rig Veda of cricket in a manual like format, it is not intended to be for fun but for serious learning and reference purposes. A minimum age of twelve years old is recommended before reading the book as there are some difficult ideas and theories about science which need to be understood and engrained.

This book is based on the practical understanding we have gained as a spin bowler, top order batsman and wicketkeeper, and the expert coaching we have received in these facets of cricket from a young age all the way up to age 25. We want to help produce the stars of tomorrow and help mold the youngsters of the future, and hopefully by reading this book, anyone who takes on board its advice will have a head start before they begin their work as a bowler or a batsman or even a captain.

This book is intended to teach you or your student enough about cricket and its finer points to get you picked in state level trials or get selected in the major cricket academy of your district, where you will then go and learn/receive more one-to-one coaching about finer points of cricket tailored to YOUR particular game at that moment in time and tailored to what YOU need at that moment in time as a serious batsman or bowler – something which is hard to give through just written word and without observing the player's technique in person. We will however touch upon the topics and make you aware of what you will need to look out for to finally shine up your cricket in the final stages of your cricket coaching/cricket learning journey.

As our experience and understanding of cricket was gained from playing for our state team back in Australia as a leg-spinner, batsman and wicketkeeper in U'13 – U'16 division, we are going to concentrate only on spin bowling and batting in this coaching manual – as that's what we were given coaching in from our team coach, and we don't want to misguide you by talking about fast bowling when we have never done it ourselves. Back then I used to bowl only slow leg-spin like a Shane Warne style during matches, however within a few years by around 17 year of age I was bowling medium pace leg-spin with great enthusiasm. I had bowled off-spin from a young age also but usually bowled leg-spin in games as it is a more attacking option in game situations, but I will still give thorough guidance to the budding off-spinners out there nonetheless.

In this world of computing power and an IT boom, these days computers and programming subjects are studied by younger students also as their applications to the real world cannot be ignored, and cricket is no different. We will show you how computing power in the form of linear programming code and conditional logic can be used to teach and make youngsters to better watch the ball, pick up length, move feet and develop overall stroke play and shot-selection in their batting – via the help of computer science and programming, yes, we can develop our cricketing technique too. We will also discuss how the concept of vectors and vector forces from the sciences specifically physics has a huge role in the game of cricket and how understanding this can benefit us as cricketers to no end, bowlers and batsmen both – hang in there, this book is about to teach you some highly practical things about cricket which you didn't know but absolutely must if you are serious about your cricket. The physics of swing, reverse-swing and drift has been openly discussed before in the cricketing fraternity and coaching arena, but in this book we introduce something additional which has not yet been discussed or taught openly by cricket enthusiasts, sport scientists or cricket coaches.

This will pertain primarily to you batsmen and to the mathematics and physics involved in better seeing the ball, picking it's length and getting into position just that fraction earlier, and the science involved in seeing the ball well and developing the main trait of a successful batsman - a good eye.

Introduction

As the name of the book suggests, we are here to look at the game as methodically as possible and in a manner which allows us to adequately understand it from a theoretical angle, and henceforth improve, modify and make fine adjustments to our movements based on science and not on guesswork from a 'backyard bunny', 'armchair sportsman' or 'make-do-coach' - one who is making out to know everything but is really just out for making business, and may not know enough about cricket and enough about its theory to coach a player to play competitive level cricket, which is our objective, and why you paid for the book.

The game of cricket can sometimes be a very elusive and complex sport at the top level, and certain nations and certain coaches may be especially tardy in conveying vital and key finer points of cricket to their students or team, which you will get a chance to learn through reading this book and through the written word without paying the coach to tell you! Essentially you are picking one of the more difficult sports on the world stage, and there is a lot that can go wrong and there is a lot to learn and being properly coached and educated in regard the finer points of the sport is what we want you to have, that's all we are saying!

This handbook about cricket and it's science and method is not intended to completely perfect your game but to point your game along the right path and correct path early on in your cricketing journey, such that a strong base and good habits are formed for more advanced lessons ahead. The opportunity to learn the remaining 20% of the lessons you need to perfect your game can be facilitated through one-to-one coaching and coaching in person, once the coach has observed your technique and game.

First class and international players who may be reading the book are encouraged to take on board the advice offered and the key concepts and theories, and then cross question their personal or team coaches about as to how to move forward from here – don't just read it and remember it but make sure you present to the coach about actually doing something about it, whatever you discover your weakness to be that is!

This book is not an elaborate coaching manual in the mold of Bob Woolmer's Art and Science of Cricket, rather, it is a concise and to the point coaching manual devised to teach a beginner to intermediate cricketer everything he/she needs to know about cricket in a short space of time and everything he/she needs to know to become a great one. This book is not just a novelty worth keeping on your bookshelf, but a systematic and scientific guide to making anyone and everyone a better more diligent cricketer, and one who bases his movement on the principles of human movement and the widely accepted fundamentals of the game. It only goes in depth where and when we felt it was necessary to your cricketing education, and hopes of rising the ranks as a serious cricketer for your country or state. We have only provided illustrations to help you comprehend ideas which are not common knowledge for a budding cricketer and require more elaboration, and have kept the book as concise and to the point as possible.

In this book, we treat cricket and the science behind cricket as a subject which we encourage to be studied just as any other science subject in your

12th standard curriculum, hence the name 12th man – hopefully by the end of this book your education in cricket and the science and technique involved in the game should be complete.

This book is not only aimed at the student himself but the coach, mentor and parent also. It is encouraged that parents of a boy who shows ability in cricket by the mid-teens to late teens is made to pursue cricket seriously, as it is at the age of 16 or 17 that a boy has the best potential to play like a man – it is now that the mind begins to mature and start following the body to create that beautiful rhythm which we all love to watch in a cricketer aka young Tendulkar, Wasim Akram & Aravinda just to name a few.

And naturally of course the world would love to watch more young Tendulkars and Akrams in action and playing for their country. Unfortunately for the parents out there, this is a tough spot for you because the world of cricket is competitive and boys reach their best playing potential and ability to learn and train at around age 16-17 – the very years of critical value in our 12th standard education, hence the naming of the book ***12th man: The Mind & Method of an Elite cricketer***. We realize studies and science subjects are important at this stage and time but so is your and your child's cricket, so try your best to do both – which is partially why we wrote this book, so that people can self-coach themselves and still remain attentive to their studies.

Take this book as what you would call a pocket guide or short coaching manual for aspiring cricketers – almost sort of like a textbook you would read about cricket, only with more tips and advice about how to improve your cricket and learn your cricket the correct way. It is intended to be more like a novel than a pure coaching manual where unnecessary pictures and details are omitted and something fun and interesting to read on the subject of cricket at the same time as being a serious guide in assisting with your cricketing goals, I'm sure you will find it useful.

I wish you all the best in being part of your state or country's cricketing future, I am sure you will improve your game and learn the necessary science and technique behind the game and as a result of reading this book, have the best possible chance of doing so – all the best in a successful cricketing journey ahead!.

The MIND & METHOD of an ELITE Cricketer

NIKHIL JAIN
With MARK HEADING
& JAMES NDLOVU

Table Of Contents

Chapter One

Is Cricket Really Just A Sport?

So, the first thing we need to know if we are to devote ourselves to a sport is where does that sport fit in in the scheme of sports in general and how does it compare to other sports and what is required of me to succeed? Cricket is a bit different to other sports and is maybe not your typical sport filled with running, hefty guys with muscles, hard-knocks and physical moves, nor does it have the popularity and nor will it ever have but it is a major sport nonetheless and does have certain aspects to it which are very physical also. It is not your typical macho sport or high profile widely followed sport like rugby union, soccer, tennis or NBA basketball, but it is the major sport of the Indian sub-continent and comprises of participants from many 1st world nations alike and moreover, more recently, is the subject of ludicrously large sums of money and IPL player contracts, so don't worry too much about its global image – cricket is still a good prize to chase as far as professional sports goes.

The next thing is, the question arises why is cricket not as popular as the other high profile sports? This is simply because cricket is not just a sport, it is a 'game', it is a 'war', it is a 'story' being written by batsman and/or bowler, with so many undercurrents and overtones happening in the background at the same time. It is a war of attrition, almost a game of chess where each piece is a soldier in battle.

Unlike most games and sports which are highly team oriented, cricket is a game where the bowler and batsman collide in a unique type of battle - a battle which is contested between the two, one-on-one, and a battle in which no other member of the team can ultimately hold a bearing, assist, influence or shape the performance and mind of the two contending. A batsman stands alone against the bowler and 10 other fielders of the opposition team, and as the sole adversary to the opposition's onslaught and game plan, as a weapon all but a piece of willow which he must wield in a way to overcome and defeat 11 members of the opposition unit, all under pressure of match conditions, expectations and run rate pressures. A bowler stands alone against a highly skilled and well prepared batsman with no one to support or help him in his task of removing a batsman from the crease but a red cherry in his hand, which he must propel down a 22 yard pitch in a way which is both skillful and deceptive as well as guileful, and with the sole intent and influence of no one but himself. Cricket is not comparable to the typical sports like soccer, basketball and rugby, in that it is a contest between solely the batsman and bowler, a battle between the two and a battle which requires individual and personal skill alone without the help of team work or assistance from his fellow team mates. Almost like a boxing match or a fight, where there is no team work or luxury of team strategy or team moves or set plays afforded to a batter or bowler. Yes, it is a team sport where one team is contesting against another team and team strategy is almost always of some consequence to the team's performance, but cricket is just that little bit more individual oriented and centered around the individual qualities and performance of a player as opposed to the cumulative or group effort which happens in your usual sports. We can equate cricket as being more of a boxing match than a sport, almost a fight or a war between batter and bowler.

Yes, it is not entirely and not exactly a sport – it is a sport but at the same time it is more than that. Any sport requires 3 basic things to succeed and can be broken down into 3 basic demands or major components:

- **Skill**
- **Stamina**
- **Mental alertness**

In cricket the stamina level demanded is not so high and the skill level demanded is of a relatively 'static' nature. This equates to a theoretical deduction that cricket[in its traditional context, not modern IPL] is more a game of mental power, a war of attrition, and a game of technique as opposed to a sport where stamina, skill and team work is overt and 'slammed' in viewers faces – compare a well strung rugby try score or a well strung soccer goal to a nice well timed cover drive for 4 by a batsman, which one is more athletically convincing? Get the point?

This is a very important point to take on board, the fact that cricket is more a mental game and more a battle of minds and can be a war of attrition at many times, if you are to progress and mature as a cricketer and get serious as a student of the game. This conclusion has been drawn from high level and competitive cricketers who have toiled many a day with each other for little results. For now just accept our word, there will be more proofs and indications as the book goes on. In light of what you have just read, it is obvious and clear that suddenly cricket demands of us that little bit extra mental discipline, acumen and fortitude for it's successful execution than other sports, and that we are foolish to ignore such aspects of our approach whilst preparing to be elite cricketers.

When you first start out playing your cricket and mastering the basics cricket will be a very physical game, perhaps 70% physical and 30% mental; however, as you go on to longer versions of the game and higher level cricket namely Test match cricket, this ratio flips and becomes 30% physical and 70% mental. What an irony and what a bitch, all that practice on our technique and movement only to find that it is now mental aspects of the game we need to master to succeed, once we reach state level or higher that is. For now practice hard on your technique and physical aspects of your game in tandem with the necessary mental components, which I am about to reveal to you later. Let me stress however, if you're serious about going on with cricket that you must not ignore the mental aspects of cricket which I am about to show you when you play in your school or league matches or practice sessions so that you set yourself up for more difficult battles ahead.

Let us think of Cricket Vs Baseball for a minute, the similarities are that like baseball, cricket also uses the strong bottom-hand play to swat or strike the ball hard and long, but unless its 20-20 which is a lesser played version of the game, than this swatting with the bottom hand is only sometimes – most times in cricket we are trying to play 'cricketing' shots because that's what is required of us to stay at the crease, keep our wicket and keep scoring as well as play the pitch of the ball, ie. The line and length of the ball. So just like the multi-billion dollar game of Baseball, cricket is similar in this respect, that strong bottom-hand batting is one part of being good at the sport.

Let's imagine, or rather let us use the word 'equate' for the other example. Equate the bowler in cricket as being a quarter back in NFL – the code of football played in America, probably the biggest and most popular sport in USA for some time now.[1]In NFL the quarter back is required to propel the ball using his hands, arm and fingers in a certain way and certain direction which is advantageous to his team and his team's ability in gaining better field position or even scoring a goal(touch down). He is required to propel the ball at a certain speed and direction and set the ball along a desired and intended path or trajectory. Sometimes this ball may be propelled flat and fast and sometimes it may be propelled slower and higher. These are the exact requirements of a bowler in cricket, the requirement of propelling the ball either straight and fast like a pace bowler, or slower and higher like a spin bowler; only the difference here is that the bowler in cricket is further required to use his run-up and lower body in the form of legs, hips and back to not only create a certain forward force but to disquise the exact forward force the ball he is about to bowl is about to take. So what does all this mean? Well take yourself to be a big athlete just as any quarter back in the NFL, only consider yourself one which is better as you are performing more preliminary and groundwork tasks in the form of your run-up, and are directing the ball using a lot more aim and direction as well as capacity for the ball to deviate and deviate late, than a quarter back. Basically, you are performing the same act as the quarter back role in NFL only using a lot more disguise and variation in your performance. So just another interesting fact to substantiate our theory that cricket truly is a very difficult sport and despite being difficult

---

[11]NFL is the highest paid sport in the world along with NBA basketball, it's players receive the most lucrative and highest salaries of any sport – especially players filling the quarter back position, up to U.S $30,000,000 per annum = 225 Crore rupees per annum

may not get the media attention or fan following it deserves. Often in NFL, the attracting factor is the distance they can throw the bowl whereas in cricket it is a combination of not only speed but accuracy, disguise and deviation or movement a bowler can create to dismiss and remove some of the most well trained and capable batsmen in the world.

So we cannot equate cricket as being for the inept, unfit or girly, it in fact may require greater skill and athleticism than even NFL in certain respects, however it is just that it doesn't receive the same hype and media attention or audience which it might perhaps deserve.

Chapter Two

Cricket: The Unknown – What We Can't See

Cricket is one of those funny sports because it looks so easy to the naked eye and to the spectator, we often mistake it for being an easy sport, hence why it does not have the same media following as baseball or soccer etc, when in fact the opposite is true. Cricket is one of the toughest sports in the world to perform, so beware what you are getting yourself into, but like I said before India has a huge following and lucrative involvement in the game so don't be discouraged, but rather be optimistic of one day yourself making a soccer player fortune out of the game also.

What we don't see as viewers is the new batsman coming in against the new ball, on an uneven pitch against a crafty bowler – the amount of tensile force going through the knees, the wrists, the arms, the hands, all working together to bring the bat down at the right time to defend his stumps, or in combination with sight and timing to play an aggressive stroke all under the pressure of team requirements and nerves. The first 15 balls of a batsman's innings are what makes or breaks his innings, it is at this point where he must concentrate harder than he has ever before – he must have listened to his partner's word about the pitch before taking guard, then he must size the pitch up for himself, then he must slowly get on top of the pitch and the bowling to build an innings. This requires tremendous amounts of concentration on the batsman's behalf, unlike baseball where it is either 6 or nothing and you're done. All this means the onlooker does not always and easily appreciate how tough your job as a batsman or bowler actually is, and that our efforts as cricketers are not lauded and magnified to the extent of other sports, but like we said we don't have to worry about that in this modern era of 20-20 cricket and huge fan followings the world over.

The bowler is bowling well, has rhythm, and accuracy but just perhaps not the variation or the right variation or the right ball at the right time and is struggling to get an in form batsman out – suddenly that bowler is looking rather un-athletic in front of an excited crowd, when in fact it is a small deficiency in his mental cricketing acumen at fault and nothing more.

A great batsman comes in on a low pitch and goes back instead of forward to defend a length ball, perhaps out of laziness, and gets bowled as the ball keeps very low and passes beneath the bat – all for want of not listening to his partner telling him the pitch is keeping low and processing this in 'batsman's talk', he gets out for a duck when he made a technically sound century game before on an even bouncing pitch.

A batsman takes guard at middle and leg as he is a strong offside stroke-maker and late cutter aka SauravGanguly, only to find the bowler is a master of inswing and can make the ball come back in late, he attempts a crafty late cut, the ball comes in at the last second and he chops on to the stumps to get bowled[2].

These are examples of just some of the nuances which add to make cricket a tough sport for one to cope up with and perform well at without full

---

[2] There are yet still finer points of batting coaching we can use to counter-act this as SauravGanguly so successfully showed during his career, and still execute the shot against the in-swing!

concentration and dedication. As you play for hours in high level match conditions you may find 100's of others; but don't despair, like we mentioned, in our era and in today's cricketing world with IPL and commercialisation of the game, your efforts and concentration on the game will not go unnoticed or unrewarded, so hang in there and don't give up yet.

Another difficult thing about cricket is that once we get to higher levels it does to some degree become an easy sport, and you might be saying in light of what you just read that now you are not making sense, but let me explain. The higher the level of cricket we play and participate in, the more countless number of hours players have spent practicing and practicing their basics, this means that we have all learnt and mastered a vast majority of the skills involved in batting and bowling and that simply knowing our own game and knowing how we have to move and knowing what we are good at may not be good enough in a competitive game of cricket – that is we may play well and know full well what we are doing but in a competitive game situation which as I mentioned earlier is like a war of minds and war of attrition and may require certain mental energy and presence, this may not be good enough to get runs or wickets on the day and on that pitch and against that opposition. Now here is the wrap, what these first two chapters have been leading up to and justifying and why you have been reading all this, and here it is:

"If you are serious about taking your cricket to the next level and becoming a competitive cricketer and one day even a representative level one, or you want your son to be one or your student to be one then you MUST put aside your strength and practice your weakness religiously.

Yes, that's right, in a competitive world of highly enthusiastic and committed athletes, you must start plugging your weaknesses from the day one in your cricket journey, so that when you reach representative level you are equipped with the mental cricketing acumen to succeed at that level and the extra 'spark' or extra skills to draw upon in competitive match situations which are contested between others who also have well practiced strengths."

The fact that cricket becomes a tough sport and a mental one at higher levels also leads to another important point to remember and live by whilst taking your cricket journey, and that is:

"Try to enjoy your cricket: find out what aspect of your game you enjoy and try to enjoy this to the fullest and make this as a primary incentive motivating force for your playing the game."

Cricket is too tough a sport and becomes highly mental at the higher levels as all players have good skills. We must focus on enjoying ourselves from the early stages in our cricketing journey so we don't become discouraged about the fact that all players are going to have mastered the cricketing skills commonly discussed in academies and schools and have similar skills to our own. Some batsmen like to drive on the rise, some like to cut and pull, some like to loft the ball, some like to play a long steady innings – find out what gets you 'ticking' and try to enjoy that and look forward to that, take it as a release of pressure and way of letting go the building up of mental pressure associated with competitive cricket. For example, if you get one or two good cut shots for four than you can be happy with yourself and relax a bit for the next two or three overs. That's a long time and could mean you keeping your wicket as your relaxed in a highly pressurised game situation – trust me this makes a difference. Let's make the difference between something which you can do and are good at doing and something which you enjoy. These are two different things. It is the one which you enjoy which is going to help you out the most in a journey which is not easy – the journey of rising the ranks to become a useful competitive cricketer. For myself, I am a good cutter and late cutter but I don't enjoy them, I enjoy the drive on the rise and the lofted stroke even though I am not so good at it – enjoying and being good at, these are two different things. Enjoying the cricket is just as important if not more important than actually being good at cricket.

For all the coaches and Dads, try to observe your son or student carefully not just for weaknesses but for the shots or deliveries which he enjoys and try to make this as a type of incentive/reward for him sacrificing studies to play the game, almost like giving the baby his candy – find the shot he enjoys the most and make him practice this one so he can play in different conditions and have best chance of enjoying his cricket through this shot. Make it harder and vary the line/length slightly and make him master at his beloved reason for cricket. Reward him when he masters or gets better at this particular stroke with money or extra batting time, etc. But please, don't be discouraged by the fact that cricket is a tough sport – focus on your student enjoying a particular aspect of cricket first and foremost and make cricket as a personal journey and personal learning curve no matter how good the other players appear.

Conclusion:

Many a fine/talented cricketer has fallen away or failed to reach his full potential or failed to perform under pressure or even failed to play for their state or country at all when they could have due to the two points aforementioned in bold in this chapter. Don't let it happen to you or your son/student, cricket is a tough sport and requires of you proper consistent practice and conditioning to get the results you want. You can't play and practice cricket blindly if you want to reach the top and perform at the top level, you have to improvise with your routine and train yourself new things as opposed to just building upon your strengths. Here are some examples of some players whom this phenomenon of 30/70 ratio flip affected and hard hit the most:

Mark Waugh: very talented, all the shots – low concentration, unable to build an innings and go on with it.

Sanjay Manjrekar: Great defence, great technique & cricketing shots and use of top hand – just minimal to no use of bottom hand to pull and cut and play big-drives

Mohammed Azharuddin: Great player of pace and spin, very wristy, great timer, great stroke maker in the mould of Chappel/Gower – defensive technique against pace not stable enough and so unable to build an innings

Steve Waugh: Great concentration, great fighter, great innings builder – just lacks quicker footwork to play big shots in one-day cricket

AjitAgarkar: Great bowler, gifted with pace and swing, can be fiery and match-winner at full rhythm – just did not have the stamina required of a fast bowler and upper body conditioning to bowl quick for long spells. As high level cricket became more mental he was unable to focus on his physical aspects of cricketing fitness[3]

On the contrary, some players who flourished and thrived as cricket became more competitive and mental are:

- Tendulkar[4]
- WasimAkram
- Shane Warne
- AravindaDeSilva

---

[3] He can and can frequently clock 140 - 145km/hour

[4] Notice how Tendulkar was always able to pace his innings even under pressure of run-rate of one day cricket – this is because he was always mentally in control and had great understanding of mental aspects of cricketing technique*see: 1996WC Aust vs Ind Tend:90stumped

Chapter Three

Introduction To A Tough Sport

So, before we move on let's just recap what we have learnt and what we need to remember.

1st: Cricket becomes very mental at the top level – make sure we practice this at the same time as we are learning our technique and action and variations.

2nd: cricket is insanely competitive at the top level and it is important and critical we enjoy our cricket and at the same time plug our weaknesses while we are in the learning stages.

3rd: Cricket has similarities with the multi-billion dollar sport of Baseball being the use of the bottom-hand, so this must be an important aspect of the sport to master.

4th: Many a talented player has failed to reach their true potential at the top level for want of plugging a few small weaknesses.

Unlike Baseball, in cricket the ball is ideally intended to and made to bounce by the bowler in an advantageous way to the bowler and fielding side and the batsman is then made to *'play'* or *'answer'* this proposition by the bowler using his bat without getting out, and at the same time asked to avail opportunities to strike the ball and score runs. So what does this mean? It comes down to the fact that cricket is a *'game of length'*. The bowler is trying to use the length and obviously the line also, but lets ignore this for a second, to make life difficult for the batsman and prevent scoring, and the batsman is trying to read the length as best as possible to create scoring opportunities as well as knock the bowler off his length. We usually say the length ball is the ideal ball for a bowler and this is true – the length ball at pace is one of the hardest things for a batsman to play. The entire body and tremendous exertion is required in playing this shot as it is in that awkward position and puts the body under pressure – the body must position and move in an unnatural way to successfully ward off danger and execute the stroke. Moreover, there is a subtle change in your back lift which is required and 'softhands' must come into play and the body is fooled into not knowing whether to go forward or back, but we'll talk about this in the batting section in depth. So cricket is basically a *game of length* and nothing more – this means suddenly the pitch you are playing on becomes hugely critical to each and every player batsman and bowler on the field which would not have been the case in baseball or in street cricket or cement pitch cricket. But note, from a cricketing angle cricket is still a game of length no matter what the surface, but becomes just that little bit more harder and more centered around length when we play on turf pitches. We often hear of praise aimed at batsmen in the form of "picks up the length" well and we hear it by almost every player, ex-player, commentator and coach, because that's all cricket is essentially – a battle and game of length! We will talk about what this actually means and what YOU need to know in regard this critical observation about picking up the length in a separate chapter as it draws upon ideas of Physics and requires diagrams to understand – you will even find out why the turf pitch was invented and why we are made to play on turf at all.

Playing Straight Vs Cross-Batted Shots:

Playing straight means playing with the bat vertical or perpendicular to the pitch and usually means driving or 'playing in the V'.

<u>DiagramI:</u>

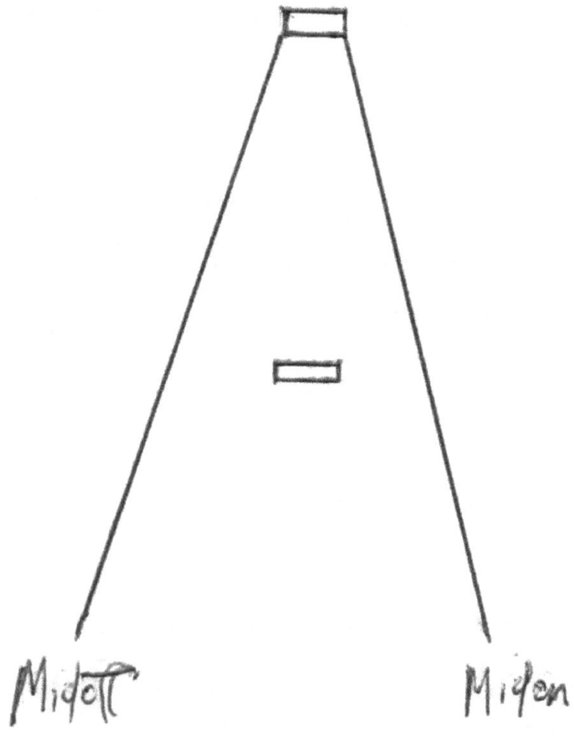

Playing cross-batted shots comprise of cuts, pulls and any shot where the bat is horizontal to the pitch.

Diagram II:

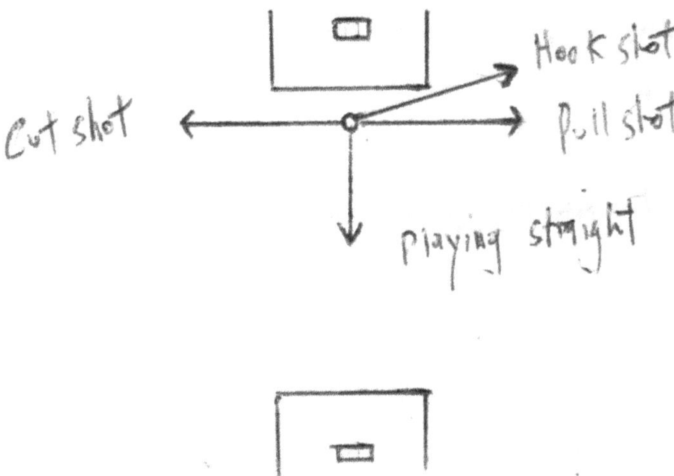

Then there are shots which are a combination of the two. These are usually only played by in-form and better batsmen and include the square-drive, straight batted swat & square cut off front-foot.

Diagram III:

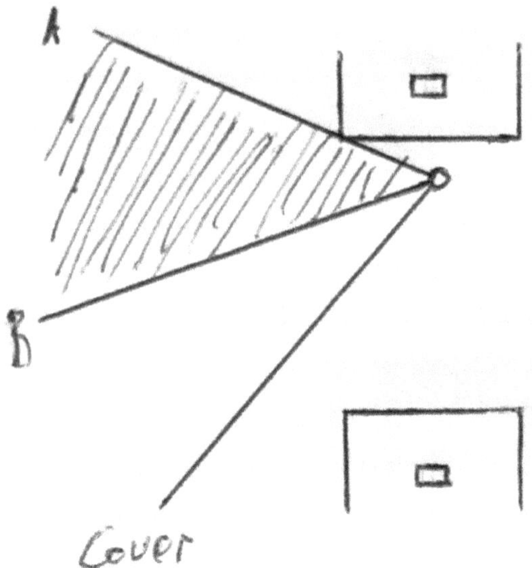

The square drive is an example of a shot which is the combination of the two – is generally played with weight steadily balanced on both front and back foot, as opposed to a shot which is either back or front foot or horizontal or vertical. Another example is the cow/slog shot, these shots are neither straight bat or cross bat shots but in between.

What does it mean by 'rhythm'? The bowler is bowling with good rhythm. Rhythm is referring to the overall biomechanics of the bowler and his action and his movements prior, during and post delivery of the ball. When everything is gelling and in sync and the bowler is bowling fluently and the ball is coming out as intended then we say he has good rhythm. So it would include all the components of the delivery being performed in perfect form and in perfect speed and in perfect timing with the other including the run-up, the release, the follow through and the arm coming down with the other arm coming down in tandem, all happening in perfect harmony – usually this thing called rhythm is harder for spin bowlers to strike than for faster bowlers as the biomechanics is a bit more complicated and it is difficult to strike an overall or perfect harmony.[5] Rhythm is when the perfect combination/permutation of the biomechanical components of the bowling action and delivery stride happens and the bowler is bowling as intended. Some bowlers naturally have good rhythm whereas some have to 'find form' – Murali from Sri Lanka always seems to have a good rhythm or we can reasonably say that his rhythm is consistently good and up there, whereas Wasim Akram's rhythm is often good at times and on big occasions or when he is in the mood for a fiery spell or a big match occasion – he can sometimes be just an average bowler when his capacity hovers upon greatness, as he may be a rhythm bowler and may not have perfect rhythm at all times.

Ok now let's talk about perhaps one of the most important theoretical facts about cricket that you may or may not know and may ever know, but should know especially if you are a batsman but important for you bowlers out there too. Well you've heard the saying a million times that batsman win one-day matches and bowlers win Test matches, so what does this mean and why is this so? What is the reasoning for this? The fact about this game called cricket is that the batsman has an advantage over the bowler – yes that's right cricket is not a fairly contested game between bat and ball, the batsman has an advantage, and your job is slightly easier if you are a batsman than if you are a bowler. At a high-level or professional

---

[5] Shane Warne: 1996WC Final; SriLanka psychologically destroyed Australian team's moral and Shane Warne just could not build any physical rhythm to his bowling whatsoever

level it is preposterous to assume that a batsman who has practiced that hard and is that skilled in the basics of batting technique cannot sit there and defend his wicket for an entire innings without getting out – there are thousands of batsmen out there who you could bowl to and not get out in a million years if there were no pressure to score runs at a certain rate or if there were no anomalies in the pitch.[6] So if we take Test match cricket as the natural default form of the game, then we take one-day matches and shorter formats of the game as attempts to put the batsman under pressure, create a fairer contest between bat and ball and ultimately balance the uneven scale and tilt it slightly toward the bowler to create a more even contest between bat and ball – 20-20 cricket is just the extreme of this theory or idea in action, the idea that the batsmen have so well-honed skills and defensive techniques that the bowlers have little chance of defeating them in a competitive one-to-one, and that more pressure should be put on the batsman to score faster and faster to bring the bowlers back into the game. Perhaps twenty-twenty is taking it a bit to the extreme but the Boards were only working off this simple theory when they decided to popularize and commercialize this form – they perhaps could have made it 25 overs a side or just let it remain at 50 over cricket as even 50 over cricket overcomes this problem of cricket lending an advantage to the batsman, but that's not our business nor our job so prepare yourself to take 20-20 format seriously also.

So what does this mean to us as cricketers, well firstly to bowlers it means we shouldn't get discouraged because the batsmen have an advantage but

---

[6]Mathew Hayden: big, tall batsman has a huge test best score of 335 which not many batsman have – very hard to get out with those long legs and reach and superior capacity for defensive technique.

rather we should build our repertoire of attacking bowling options and work on our variety and deception – this is the key for you bowlers, even if you are a pacer but especially if you are a spinner, the only way you are going to beat these guys who have practiced for hours and can bat all day is through deception and disguise – we will talk about exactly how in the bowling chapters coming up. For you batsmen, well you must not abuse your advantage that this game of cricket has given you if you want to be picked and succeed and help your team win – you must aim at becoming an attractive stroke-maker in all conditions and not just someone who can bully the bowler and not get out. Set standards and goals for yourself and don t just try hang around at the wicket and not get out because there are thousands of batsmen trying out and anyone can do that – this is your mantra to take out of this chapter for you batsmen out there, that you must:

"set standards, expectations and goals for yourself and your batting or you will never succeed in the competitive world of quality batsman-ship and the modern era of limited overs cricket."

Cricket is basically an off-stump or off-side game, that is the bowler is trying to focus on and test out and probe the off-stump of the batsman and the batsman is trying to look for any weakness or looseness in the bowler's accuracy or off-stump line. Generally leg-side shots are not as difficult to play as off-side shots, so you should really try to practice your drives, punches and cuts as much as you can, especially your square drives and late cuts also.[7]

---

[7]SauravGanguly practiced and mastered the harder aspect of batting that is offside play to perfection and to great success first – he learnt to play off his legs second and after his inception into international cricket and had no problem playing all around the wicket within due time. However he would not be where he is today

Generally batsmen take guard at middle but some who are especially good at off-side strokeplay and cutting like Ganguly or Ranatunga, may take legstump guard or middle and leg, to give that fraction of width to glide the bat through offside.

When first coming into bat, usually recommended to take middle in case the ball is moving in late. However, if the bowler is for example a left arm over the wicket and moving the ball in to the pads, then remember to ALWAYS take middle and leg or even leg such that your pads don't get in the way and you reduce your chances of getting an LBW.

---

nor even have been picked, if it weren't for his mastery over the harder aspect of batting – offside strokeplay.

Chapter Four

Some Of The Harder Things To Do In Cricket

This is a list of shots or deliveries which have been performed by cricketers in the past and still are performed today and which are considered the difficult aspects of the sport – that is the hard parts of the game which really 'pull the crowds' and can turn you into a big name. Just for information sake, an interesting bit of information for any serious cricketer and one dreaming of playing for the country.

- Defend the length ball – can be played off both front & back foot
- Drive the ball 'on the rise' or 'on the up'[8]
- Square drive
- Lofted shot over in-field
- Inside out cover drive
- Inside out lofted shot
- Reverse swing – pace bowling
- 'dusra' – off-spin bowling
- 'flipper' – leg-spin bowling
- 'bouncer' – medium pace leg-spin bowling[9]
- Bowling to a right hand/left hand combination
- Spin bowling in general – rhythm is not easily found

[8] We note that Virat Kohli the batting great of our era plays all these strokes on a regular basis, even in Test Matches

[9] Only possible by the shorter spinners as right trajectory is required to generate flight and dip and bounce – even Kumble could not bowl it he was slightly tall, his strength was more sideways movement

- 'slider' – leg-spin bowling – is an advanced ball only bowled when ball is coming out well and bowler has good rhythm
- 'drifting' the ball by a spin bowler – requires a perfect seem position during flight
- Loft/flick the ball off the pads

These are the more advanced aspects of cricket, don't worry too much if u can't do them yet, but make it a part of your practice routine to practice one or two of these difficult things each week for just 20minutes or 30 minutes at a time. These are techniques and shots/deliveries developed by cricketers in the advanced stages of their professional careers, so no wonder you don't have a good grasp over them yet, but the point is why delay now that they are known to us we may as well practice them sooner rather than later – these are techniques used in highly competitive high-level games of cricket, something you are also gearing yourself up for, so try them out slowly and gradually, you have to learn them eventually.

Attention all Coaches:

"Amongst the signs of a good batsman and one who shows true potential to be given greater attention is the one who is able to play the square drive along the ground and the lofted flick off the pads with confidence, when a batsman can do this we know he is not just playing around and means business!"

- aka young Tendulkar, Azharuddin & Mark Waugh just to name a few

"Amongst the signs of a good fast bowler is the raw pace and bounce accompanied with swing through the air – the movement off the pitch is merely a grip thing whereas getting consistent swing both ways means the bowler's action demonstrates potential, he is ready to be further trained and ready to be picked for higher level cricket"

- *Aka young WasimAkram, AjitAgarkar & Bhuvneshwar Kumar just to name a few*

"Amongst the signs of a good spinner are the ability to bowl a big top-spinner and vary the side-spin and over-spin ratio on the ball – this is what creates that dart like line which also turns upon pitching and is a hard ball for even the best to play"

- *Aka Kumble, Murali & Chahal just to name a few*

Attention all batsman:

Assuming that Test Match cricket is the most natural and purest form of the game and that bowlers win test matches, it would make sense to conclude that bowling is harder than batting – and this is true. But if you are a batsman let it be clear that at the same time batting is not all so rosy and easy either, it takes great concentration, technique and a degree of athleticism also, just like bowling and athletes from other sports.

If you are a batsman, just cut this little fact of cricket out of the equation and out of your mind and approach to the game. Make it your goal to play your absolute best, dominate the bowling and continue to surpass your personal goals. It is not your problem as a serious contender of the sport, and do not feel any mercy for the bowlers you face in your formative and junior cricketing stages as this will catch up with you soon and it is important you have played, trained and practiced to the best of your ability. When you play higher levels of cricket and you meet the more guileful and skillful bowlers you will need to draw upon all your experience and resources to compete under pressure so it is important you continue to practice hard and with all your concentration and spirit whilst the bowling is not so threatening or mighty.

Attention all bowlers:

Remember what we said before, being successful at cricket and rising the ranks is not about building your strengths but developing and plugging your weaknesses. Start practicing your variations and how best to disquise these variations immediately, do not delay. By the time you are done practicing you will have developed your weaknesses whilst still retaining your strengths for competitive game situations.

Generally, in Test match cricket or higher level cricket, the medium pacer is often predictable, easy to read and easy to score runs from. It is an observed phenomenon that bowlers are most effective and dangerous when they are bowling either slow or fast, but not at medium pace. Bowling at 60 – 75 miles per hour is considered medium pace, and is not so effective against good batsmen. It needs to be slower or faster than this range.

Chapter Five

Seeing The Ball

What does it mean to watch the ball, to see the ball and to have a 'good eye', as we often hear people say when speaking of a batsman in awe – "he has a good eye". Well it has little to do with our vision and our eyes in fact, but more to do with our mind and body and the way the two co-ordinate with one another and the speed at which they co-ordinate with one another, also maybe our ability to keep our head still whilst waiting for and whilst playing the ball – so basically let's say for simplicity sake, technique and hand-eye co-ordination related factors as opposed to the quality of our eyesight.[10] Whether one has a good eye or not so good an eye is more so about the way and style in which his mind and body reacts to the visual input going into the eye, which is the same for every batsman facing that same bowler, so let's focus on this to help us improve our ability to see the ball in a cricketing sense. What we need to learn is how to see the ball, how to watch the ball and what to watch for what to look for and how to move accordingly, including moving our feet, arms elbow, hands and the whole ensemble and bells and whistles which comes with playing a proper cricketing shot safely and correctly.

Ok let's take this from a 'top-down approach', as you may have heard in computer programming subjects, as in the next coming chapters of the book we are going to talk about how with the help of linear programming

---

[10] Later we will talk about this thing called 'foot-eye' coordination as opposed to 'hand-eye' coordination

and conditional logic we can help batsmen to be more technically sound and organized in their stroke-play and technique. I will show you the protocol I use and I believe in in regard to how best to see and watch the ball whilst batting. You can try it see if it works for you if so than yes if not then maybe try your own or another coach may be able to show you a few pointers about how best to watch the ball, but here is my method anyway, which I think is going to help you most particularly in your shot-selection:

Watching the ball or seeing the ball is not as simple as just waking up in the morning, opening our eyes and remembering to see a little red ball in our sight – it requires a lot more discipline and concerted effort than that and in the context of cricket being a side-on sport and a game of length, watching the ball must be aligned with our future movements and potential stroke-play of the batsman which is about to happen. It's not just about looking out for a red spot in our vision.

There are different theories here. Some say to watch the ball from the bowler's hand and some say to watch the ball off the pitch, and different players have used either of the two strategies successfully to amass runs and be successful stroke-makers in international cricket. In cricketing jargon, batsman who see the ball out of the bowlers hand are said to be good at 'picking up the length' whereas players who are good at seeing the ball off the pitch are said to be good at seeing the length. Who were the best five batsman of world cricket in Tendulkar's era and prime – Tendulkar, Lara, Steve/Mark Waugh, Sehwag, &AravindaDeSilva. Of these greats, Steve Waugh was the only one who really used to use the strategy of reading or seeing the ball off the pitch, and despite his great achievements and record, he just never was the great one-day batsman in the league of the other four. Why is this? Because by seeing the ball out of the bowler's hand and picking the length as opposed to seeing the length off the pitch, we give ourselves extra time to position ourselves and get our feet ready to play the ball, and it is no guess that that's why the other four had better one-day records – they had more time up their sleeve to get feet in position and more time to wind up their back-lift and strike the ball harder and longer, that's why.[11]

So let's assume we want to be trained in this particular method of seeing the ball and further discuss and elaborate on how we also can bat like these one-day batting greats one day too. Now this is the hard part of the book so put your cricketing caps on and hopefully you will understand enough about its science to make a significant difference in your ability to see the ball, and play all the shots in the book like the greats mentioned above.

But first let's look at some more general tips and guidelines about seeing the ball, before we delve into the hard stuff, and this talk of picking the length Vs seeing the length.

Now the very first thing our eyes pick up is the general vicinity of the ball. Is the ball heading toward the sky, is it heading toward the stumps or is it heading down the leg-side or off-side as a wide or is it heading straight down the center at the stumps? – once we spot the little red cherry is far away off the pitch our body relaxes and we don't worry about it at all, or

---

[11] Try watch some videos of these batsmen and see if you can notice the differences in batspeed, backlift and footwork between the two styles of seeing the ball contrasted – compare the batspeed of Lara & Tendulkar to the others who were not so good at picking up the length.

if it is going wide we stop at our backlift position and don't bother bringing our bat down to try hit the ball.

When we get the 'length ball', that is the ball which is on that difficult length not full or not short AND it is directed at our stumps, this is where we suddenly have to switch into defensive mode and try to bring our bat down straight down vertically and not from 1st or 2nd slip – why you might ask, why is this so important? Well, the reason is we need to protect ourselves from any late deviation which might happen at the very last fraction of a second before the ball hits the bat – this is when we suddenly have to be prepared to slightly open or close the face before we play our defensive shot. Bringing our back-lift down from 3rd slip won't allow us to do this properly and safely and may result in an edge or bowled, so this ball is the one we need to look out for and prepare ourselves for if we are serious about building an innings and keeping our wicket.

<u>DiagramIV:</u>

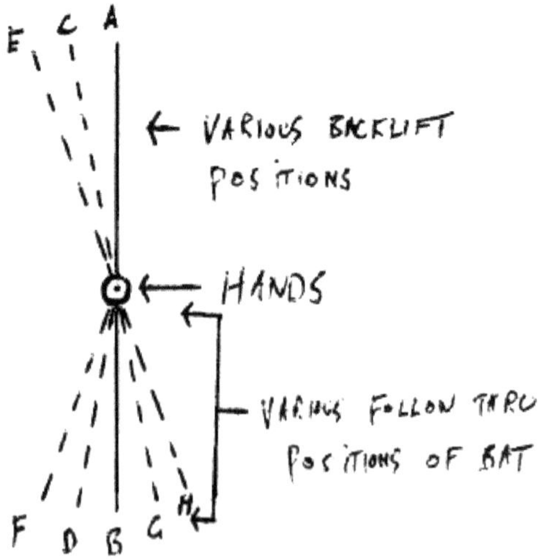

AB or in the worst case CB or EB is the back lift we want, but it is definitely preferable if we bring our bat down straight early on and stick with follow through position B. Just avoid following through with D or F, at any cost whilst defending the good ball early on.[12]

So, when training ourselves to watch the ball and see the ball, we must first scan our vision for the length ball which is on the stumps, and be fully prepared for this – remember this requires us to be prepared to bring our bat down dead straight and open/close the face at the last second with soft hands. We will get into the technical side of it later and how we change our technique for different balls, but for now just remember to scan your vision for the length ball on the stumps as the first step in our batting and in watching the ball – this is the hard part of batting which looks easier than it is to actually do in real life as we must do it in concurrency with leaving our attacking scoring options open also, so just hang in there if you're not perfect at it yet![13]

There is more to batting than just defending the length ball, as important as it is, so let us move onto the next part of seeing the ball and how we train our vision to dictate or control our bodily movements to finally play the ball.

---

[12]Rohit Sharma in WC2019 semi final Vs NZ made this mistake. His follow through was more CD or CF rather than a beautiful AB

[13] Watch the Indian batsman Ravi Shastri& Graham Gooch – these guys based their technique around contending with the length ball and were always prepared to bring their bat down straight, so much so and didn't want to lose their wicket that their back-lift was ALWAYS coming down straight even when receiving a 'loose' ball

The next thing is going forward Vs going back, and getting inside the line of the ball Vs getting outside the line of the ball, pretty straight forward. So let's get out of defensive mode now and start scoring runs!

So once we see the ball is not on our stumps at a length, we can open up a bit and prepare ourselves for an attacking shot. We must essentially decide after seeing the ball what feet movements are required – this is the first part of executing good stroke-play, getting our feet into good position. Most batsman have their own methods about footwork but let's follow the method of the world's two best one-day batsmen, Tendulkar & Mark Waugh. We want our first foot movement to put us in a neutral position so we can either take off forward or take off back or likewise get in-side the line of the ball or get outside the line of the ball. This is best done by taking a small step forward, whereby you can either move further forward or you can transfer weight off your front foot, which has taken a small step forward, and transfer all your weight on to the back foot for a back foot scoring shot.

The trick is to put our foot in a neutral positioning which then too puts our body in a neutral positioning, until we pick the line and length, and then in a fraction of a second make a more decisive committed movement with our foot and make it go forward or back or left or right. The best example of this approach was Ravi Shastri – his foot was always in a neutral position before the ball was even bowled and was always ready to bring the bat down straight for the length ball defense as well as move the foot either way from the neutral grounding position of his front foot in order to play his attacking shot. So if we see the ball pitched up we go further forward and if we see the ball pitched short we bounce off our front foot and go back – not so hard, the best batsmen's footwork is the most uncomplicated.

"You bowl – I Hit"

….. VirenderSehwag

The vast majority of balls you receive will be in that zone where a front foot shot is required as opposed to a short or very short ball – that is why we use this method of foot work because it allows for shot maximization and our ability to play the vast majority of balls/deliveries which are pitched up or relatively pitched up and get into position early and precisely. It is not usual in high-level cricket for bowlers to give anything too short and too loose, so we best to have an initial movement which goes forward!

What does this mean? Sehwag was a very uncomplicated player and apart from the forward defense, often used little footwork in a lot of his big attacking strokes. As we discussed before, the batsman has an advantage in cricket, and Sehwag in respect of this fact, had aimed to develop an attacking spark to his batting and especially one-day batting, and concentrated on timing and simply seeing the ball well and early. He had such confidence in his ability to see the ball well and pick the length that he had the full backing in himself to hit the ball hard no matter where the bowler pitched and no matter how good the ball was. So there are many methods of footwork, just find one which works for you and allows you to stroke the ball and time the ball to the best of your ability, as afterall hitting the ball is the main aim and objective of us as batsman and not always our processes or methods but the final result which counts.

Now, after taking a small step forward and one which faces straight down the line of the pitch preferably down middle stump or close, we must see the ball's positioning in regard its line – whether it is to the outside of middle and our front foot or whether it is to the inside of middle.

So let's keep it simple for now, hopefully you will have more confidence in your ability to see the ball after this chapter and confidence in how you will react depending on where the ball is pitched. But remember to be a good stroke-maker all around the wicket, we need to see the ball well and get our feet in position as quickly and decisively as possible whilst maintaining our balance and still head-position – to do this we must become expert at seeing or reading the ball. Some days you might see the ball well straight away and others you might need to play yourself-in or spend more time trying to 'get your eye in'. One of the keys to great batsman-ship is being light footed or nimble on our feet and that is why I am teaching you this method, as it allows for shot maximization and optimization as far as playing the different deliveries you will receive, hence why the two greats aforementioned use it.[14]

When you are seeing the ball well and your feet are moving in tandem with your eye and the visual input of the ball coming down the pitch, we say

---

[14] Compare the light-footedness of Mark Waugh & Tendulkar against some of the other batsman – these two had such good foot positioning combined with head positioning whilst playing the ball that they were in a league of their own, skill wise

the batsman has a 'good-eye' or has 'played himself in' or 'is seeing the ball like a football'. As you will see in the chapter about starting your innings, usually give yourself a few overs to start seeing the ball satisfactorily, after which you should start seeing the ball better and better from there on in.

In the beginning we must concentrate on our first two movements and concentrate predominantly on seeing the ball as opposed to attempting to strike the ball. Our initial movements as batsmen are the most important and crucial to our success – hitting the ball or the third and fourth movements of timing and follow through are the easy part.

Like I said different players have different approaches to footwork some have little to no footwork at all – just find what works for you if my method doesn't quite work, but remember to start seeing the ball as though you are a computer scanning for that length ball first, and then go from there.

Think of it in terms of primary vision Vs peripheral or secondary vision. In the beginning we want our primary vision to scan for the length ball on the stumps or any defensive stroke we may need to play, and our peripheral vision to look out for the loose ball for any opportunity of an attacking stroke; however, as we go on, and we get more confident or 'played-in' this reverses and our primary vision is now scanning for the loose ball with the peripheral vision looking out for the defensive shot which could be demanded of us – just like a soccer player where the primary vision is on the ball and his own team mates and the secondary vision is on the other team's players, however once and if the ball gets close to goal and opposition players are clustered in numbers, he may need to change his vision so he can concentrate on dodging or eluding the opposition players and their attempts to gain possession of the ball at the same time leaving his peripheral vision open to possible passing of the ball to his own team mates.

This is something which happens fairly intuitively in most ball games and team sports, but in cricket we just need to be aware of it a little and focus on it a little more diligently, that's all.

"Practice seeing the ball by going to the net and just practicing getting your feet in position as quickly as you can without worrying about the next step of following through with the bat – just practice going forward or back or neutral and inside or outside, practice this for thirty minutes two times a week or fifteen minutes three times a week."

But before you practice, first read the following chapter and the second half of this section on batting and seeing the ball, where we talk about how we can see the ball early, get into position early, and pick up the length of the ball just that fraction earlier – so we are not done yet, now for the interesting part and the part which separates the greats from just the goods.[15]

"This section should almost instantly see a marked improvement in your ability to strike and stroke the ball better and harder and see an

---

[15] This involves some understanding of Physics – but don't panic, there is a scientific brief and introduction to the topic of vector forces in the appendix, you can read this first or read the chapter content first it depends on your current understanding!

improvement in your scoring rate. If you are serious about limited-overs batting, make sure you understand this next chapter well – good luck!"

……. see the ball well and have the drive to succeed!

Chapter Six

The Physics Of Seeing The Ball: Pick The Length Like Vivian Richards & Virender Sehwag

Who were the most ferocious and destructive batsmen in one-day cricket and that the world has ever seen, a game where only the fittest, sturdy and high performing of athletes survive and prosper? It would have to be and that too unanimously Vivian Richards of West Indies and Virender Sehwag of India.[16] Who could hit the ball as long and hard and that too consistently and score at such a rate – almost as if they were ALWAYS in attacking mode and didn't have a worry in the world about getting out! Why? And what made these two giants of one-day cricket so good? Quite simply, it was their ability to see the ball, pick the length early and be in good position earlier than their counterparts which made them stand out and gave them this ability. So if we were to devise a training protocol for how to bat in one-day cricket situations, shouldn't we be looking to aspire towards and emulate these two giants of the one-day game, and learn from their approach and mentality toward batting? Of course we do, and that is what we are about to show in this chapter so just hang in there, this chapter could be a huge help in your maturing as a one-day batter!

---

[16]Dean Jones of Australia was also a quality one-day batsman deserved of world class status along with Kohli and Tendulkar, but neither were so brutal and destructive as compared to batters in the league of Viv and Sehwag who were able to pulverise the bowling consistently. But why?...their mind!

Sehwag truly was in the league of some of the greatest batsmen ever to play the game, and for him to have been that good and consistently scored at such a high rate up above 100% and picked up runs at will and that too in boundaries, he must have been a master and adept at picking up the length and seeing the ball well and early – this is the only explanation! With a fast scoring rate both in test and one-day cricket, a calculative mind and good use of the bottom hand to cut and pull, it is almost fair to claim that Virender Sehwag along with Vivian Richards were the best batsmen ever to play the game, perhaps even surpassing the little master Tendulkar. These two guys were truly match winners for their respective teams and may never be replaced. Yes there are several others who are quite adept at picking the length like Kohli etc, however none have the record and statistics to back up, particularly the strike rate.[17]

Back to what we were saying earlier in the previous chapter about 'seeing the length' versus 'picking the length', and how these are two different things and moreover, that we want to be like the aforementioned giants of batting and not just good but great. That we ideally want to be able to pick the length early and get into position early.

Picking the length is basically seeing the ball out of the bowler's hand as opposed to simply seeing the ball off the pitch. Instead of just waiting and seeing how the ball behaves off the pitch, we want to be able to predict and pick how the ball will behave off the pitch, and thereby give ourselves precious and valuable fractions of a second to position ourselves early for

---

[17]Sehwag's strike rate in one-day cricket is 105%, whereas Sir Vivian Richards is 91%. Tendulkar's is 86% and Kohli's is 90% - that's head & shoulders above his counterparts!.

appropriate stroke-play and shot-selection and the task of hitting through the ball and hitting the ball harder.

This is a very effective, advantageous yet simple method of seeing the ball, and can be done and should be done by anyone serious about maximizing stroke-play particularly in limited overs cricket.

All we have to do is basically watch the ball like a hawk as it comes out of the bowler's hand, and not only this, but we have to zone in on the bowler's run-up and pay attention to the momentum or rhythm the bowler is generating or is trying to generate – that's all it is in a nutshell.

So what does it take to do this, to predict the pace, bounce, direction and position the ball is about to take from the very moment it leaves the bowler's hand, and not just wait for the ball to hit the pitch and merely read it's length. What does it take to do this in real life and do it successfully enough to give ourselves a fraction of a second extra time to better see the ball and better position ourselves for our next shot – something which is crucial if we want to be able to play big shots and hit the ball hard and long and with conviction. It all comes down to a simple and basic understanding of a concept from physics called VECTOR FORCES, which this chapter is going to be dedicated to. Remember we mentioned some of the players who can and do use this method as opposed to some players who do not, and that the ones who do seem to have better records in one-day cricket, so if it weren't beneficial and necessary to your cricketing education as a batsman then we wouldn't be talking about it and we wouldn't be devoting a whole chapter of a book on it, so just hang in there and keep learning.

Let’s take this from a back to front approach and talk about the topic assuming you already know what the science behind it is, fill you in on its implications, and then afterwards go back and explain the reasoning and scientific concepts involved.

There are three types of surfaces or wickets as we call it, that cricket is played on both professionally and amateur, and these are: Cement, Synthetic and Turf. Have you ever wondered why all high-level cricket including international level, domestic state level and even serious club level is played on turf and turf only? That’s because as we move up the ranks and progress in our journey as serious cricketers, it becomes a phenomenon that batsmen become so well trained and prepared that they start to develop an unfair advantage over the bowler – remember what we said about cricket being a sport where the batsmen have an advantage and that the bowlers sometimes are left as the saying goes ‘trying to get blood out of a stone’. By playing on synthetic and cement pitches batsmen become so adept at picking the length out of the bowler’s hand and predicting the magnitude, direction and bounce the ball will take, that it becomes almost impossible to stop them. As the element of deviation off the pitch or superior grip off the pitch if you are a spinner, is nullified or significantly reduced, the batsmen have every advantage in keeping their wicket and at the same time maintaining stroke-play all around the wicket. Without playing on a turf pitch and one which offers grip or seam movement off the pitch, and one which will test the batsmen’s technique particularly in playing the moving ball and adjusting his shot, the bowlers seem to be left with no or little hope or at least with a distinct disadvantage – that is why it has become an accepted phenomenon and norm worldwide that all high level cricket where the batsmen are just too good technically, be played on turf and turf only. If they were to be played on cement or synthetic it would just not be a fair battle between bowler and batsman or between bat and ball. By playing on turf this tilts the scale slightly in the bowler's favor and compensates for this advantage which batsmen are afforded in this game called cricket.

We've all heard of pitch laundering and the way especially Indians rig the pitch or prepare the pitch in a certain way. This is generally to give their batsmen the same advantage they would have as if they were contesting the game on cement or synthetic, and at the same time give the bowlers a further advantage in the form of grip and purchase for the spinners – as India traditionally have had a strong spin-attack and weaker pace attack. The same thing happens abroad in places like South Africa or Australia, where the pitch is made to suit their fast bowlers and give a further advantage to their stronger pace based bowling attack. By laundering the pitch, we are trying to nullify or negate the advantages batsmen have, particularly in Test cricket.

We've all heard of Bradman and Ranjit Singh, whom Ranji trophy was named after, and how their exploits as batsmen were simply phenomenal and almost superman like compared to modern players and batsmen of the recent eras – why was this so? How do the greats of yesteryear average twice as much as the greats of today? I mean how do players of today struggle to average more than 50, yet the leading batsmen of yesteryear such as Bradman and Ranjit Singh averaged 100? Is there such a big difference in the bowler's abilities across the two timeframes that you could say that bowlers of the older era were only half as good; or, that batsmen of today are only half as good? Well the answer is no to both of these possible explanations. It is simply because of the pitches being prepared in yesterday's era versus the pitches of today's era, were quite different and did not seek to iron out the unfair advantages batsmen have over bowlers particularly in Test match cricket, and that these guys Bradman and Ranjit Singh and many others, had become so adept at picking the length and reading the vector forces behind the ball that they were just unstoppable. They were comfortably able to keep their wicket and stay at the crease and at the same time score all around the wicket at a good rate.[18] No one can believe that Tendulkar was merely half as good as Bradman or Ranjit Singh and that based on averages that double the accolade has to be given to great batsmen of yesteryear compared to great batsmen of today; in fact, Bradman himself has rated Tendulkar on Public television as not only being comparable in style but comparable in skill and ability to himself – what does it say, well these guys were all about the same and as good as each other, however it is the way that pitches are prepared and laundered in the modern era to suit their own strengths and their own bowlers and to upheaval the advantage afforded to batsmen especially in Test cricket, which is the reason for their averages being vastly different. This and the fact that batsmen can become so good at reading the vector forces behind the ball and picking the length, that they just can't be removed from the crease and stopped from scoring all-around the wicket at a good rate also.

So now that you know the importance and impact to you batsmen of this little thing known as 'picking the length', hopefully you will continue

---

[18]If you look into the scoring rates of Bradman and Ranjit in Test cricket you will see they were quite high. Further they were not-out and undefeated at the end of many innings – the unfair advantage cricket affords batsmen is the reason for their high averages compared to Tendulkars and kallis's and Waughs.

reading and hopefully by the end of the chapter you will be more confident in your abilities to see the ball and pick the length up early, and henceforth see an improvement in your stroke-play and scoring rate.

"Your success as a batsman is determined by two things – what's in between the ears, and your ability to pick the length or read the vector forces behind the ball"

……. Nikhil jain

So let's get you ready for this and talk about vector forces and what they are and what you need to understand about them as a budding and serious batsman who wants to keep his wicket and at the same time score at a good rate. To best understand this, we will talk about vector forces in the context of fast bowling and medium pace bowling first. Once you have a better grasp and understanding of the topic, we will introduce how it applies to spin bowling also.

A vector force has two dimensions, firstly magnitude and secondly direction, both of which combine to form what is known as a vector. A vector is simply the sum of two scalars, the scalars being magnitude and direction respectively. So a delivery or ball bowled by a bowler in cricket can be take to be a vector – the pace, speed and force of the ball coming out of the hand being it's magnitude, and the height of the bowler and where he is aiming to bounce the ball on the pitch being it's direction component. If we were to be secretly told or knew these two scalars which the bowler's delivery will consist of before the ball was even bowled, we would be able to immediately know where the ball will bounce and how high the ball will bounce and where the ball will be positioned as it comes forward and closer to us and our bat – imagine if you could do that, wouldn't it in a sense almost be like cheating. Well we are not cheating as the bowler is not secretly telling us what is about to come out of his hand, what we are doing is perfectly legal, we are merely trying our best to foresee and predict the length by watching the ball hard out of the bowler's bowling hand. However, often even just by doing this we are successfully able to predict the ball's position, speed and direction almost as if someone were telling us what is about to be bowled – no wonder they say that cricket is a batsman's game and that the batsmen have the upper hand or advantage against the bowler. As we progress in our cricketing journey and play more competitive and higher levels and beyond street cricket or club cricket, the bowlers are consistently required to have more guile and artistry in order to beat, contain and remove the batsman. Subtle variations and deception become the cornerstones of a good cricketer suddenly as opposed to blatant expertise or skill, just as we spoke about earlier that cricket becomes a more mental proposition as we move up the ranks, especially for you bowlers.

So all vectors are in layman's speak are the ball's speed and direction – nothing more! The speed is the force and pace on the ball, and the direction is simply where on the pitch the ball will bounce and from what height is the ball being released – or simply the bowler's physical height. Exactly where on the pitch the ball is forecast to land comes from watching the bowlers hand and observing the initial or first half of the ball's trajectory or as you will become soon in the chapter – the Z-point Don't be discouraged or daunted by our elaborate details as we try to make you understand this idea and an idea which is what you could say the essential 'crux of cricket', but have your cricketing cap on, study it a few times and then go to the net and really put our theory to the test – is it right or is it wrong and how useful could it be in my batting?

Let's picture two separate and different deliveries bowled by the same bowler – let's say he is about six feet tall. Both will bounce on the same position or length on the pitch but one will have more pace on it and the other will be slower. What do you think is going to happen? Well they are two different deliveries and two different vectors with different vector forces being imparted, so they will have two different paths, even though having the same length. The direction component of the vector will be same for both but the magnitude component will be different as the strength or forward force being put on the ball will be more. What happens? Well it is common sense but that's all vectors and vector forces are.

Diagram V:

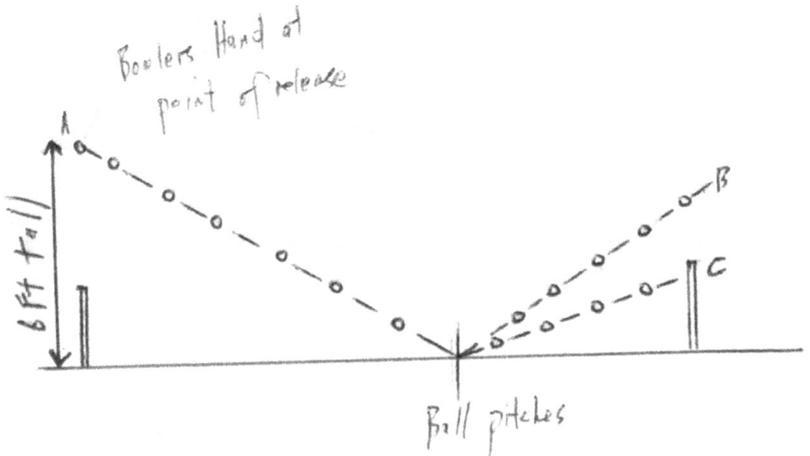

So path AB is our normal or fast ball and path AC is our ball with less pace on it or slower ball. Because there is less pace on the ball with path AC, it does not bounce as much or as per 'normal'. If we were able to read the force component of this vector as the ball was being bowled, we would immediately be able predict that it will reach our bat at point C, and get ourselves in position to play a hard attacking stroke, but if we didn't we might even risk our wicket via a miscue and get out or even bowled and what's more, not be able to hit the ball hard and with conviction.

Now let's take two separate deliveries by the same bowler with the same pace and forward force being put on the ball, but with different directions – one is pitched up and one is pitched short. What do you think will happen? Where will the ball be by the time it reaches your bat? In this case the magnitude of our vector is the same as the pace is the same, but the direction of our two vectors or two deliveries is different – so obviously the ball will take different paths and be at different positions by the time they reach our bat

Diagram VI:

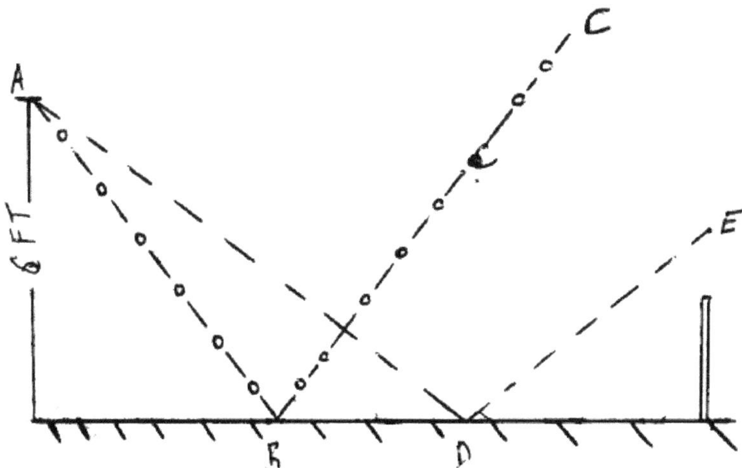

Now let's take two different deliveries by two different bowlers, one is 6 feet tall and the other is 5 feet tall. Both are bowling at the same speed and pacelet's say 150km/hr, and so we assume the vector's magnitude to be the same, only it's direction component which we assume to be the height of the bowler's hand, is different. What would happen or what would be the resultant vector if both bowlers were pitching at the same length?

Diagram VII:

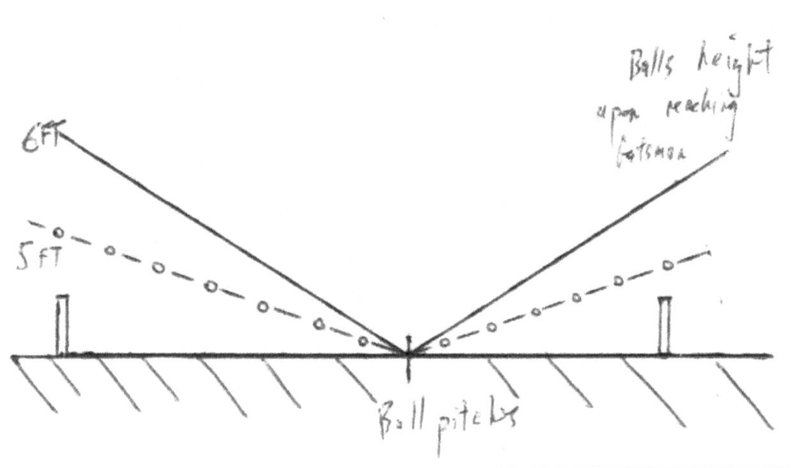

Notice how the taller bowler or the line in solid black is bouncing the ball higher off the same length – this is what we want, however, the shorter bowler is not generating as much bounce.

So we see now that picking the length is actually about predicting the shape of the ball and where exactly it will reach, how high and at what pace, by the time it reaches us and our bat. It is not simply just picking the length it will land it is more than that. Hopefully after you study the given examples and the appendix at the end, you will have your head around this concept and understand it well and well enough to improve your 'eye', the way you see the ball and your ability to 'pick the length' and get into position early.

Now let's consolidate our understanding by going backwards and ask ourselves, in order for the ball to be in the same position or height as each other, or the resultant vectors height to be the same upon reaching the batsman, what is the initial vector force required to be. That is what is the required vector for each of the two bowlers one shorter one taller, and what is the required initial vector force required to obtain the same resultant vector.

Diagram VIII:

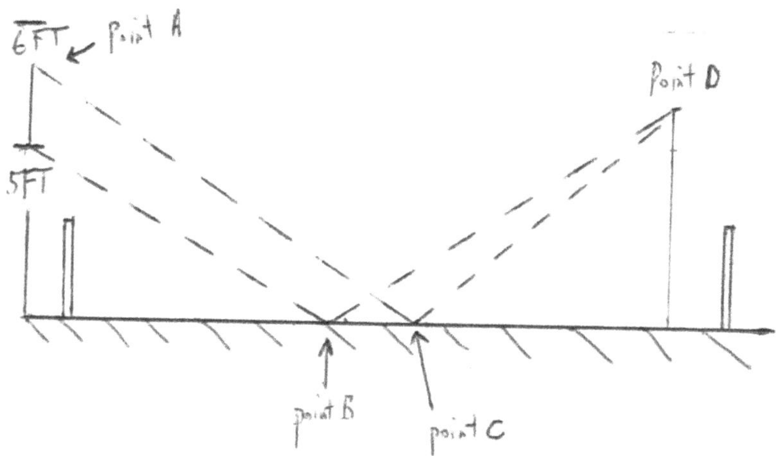

So in order to attain the same height or position by the time it reaches the batsman, namely point D, the 5 feet tall bowler has to pitch it shorter whereas the taller bowler has to pitch it up. This is consistent with Snell's Law which states that a vector or an object in motion which hits something, i.e. in this case the pitch, always deflects at the same angle at which it hit. There is nothing we can do about this and this may be a problem if we are too tall and must pitch the ball up or we are too short and must pitch short. However, being shorter is the problem here as we will never get the right bounce unless we pitch short, which is just a 'gimme' for the batsman.

So, in a cricketing sense and cricketing context, we are simply using our understanding of physics and Euclidean geometry to predict the shape of the ball and predict its bounce and positioning by the time it reaches our bat. By doing this we can sum up where the ball might be by the time it reaches us, and get into position early. That's all we as cricketers need to know about vectors. Practice your understanding of vectors and Euclidean geometry on paper by drawing the paths of different vectors and how the path of the vector will vary depending on it's two component scalars of pace and direction being varied. You don't need to draw diagrams which are mathematically exact in terms of geometric units used in the strict sciences, but you do need to know how the vector's paths differ and that their resultant paths are dependent upon the two initial scalars of magnitude and direction. Remember as we said earlier in cricket and in bowling we take each ball as being a vector whose magnitude is the pace, speed and force of the ball, and direction being the aim or target or length of the ball which he is or is trying to pitch at and from what height the ball is being released. This is what creates the different final shapes of different balls, and what we are trying to be good at predicting before the ball hits the pitch.

What we are doing basically is intuitive and many of you are probably doing this anyway, watching the ball out of the bowler's hand that is, and trying to predict it's position by the time it reaches you; however, it is the mental calculation of determining the vector's resultant vector – its final shape that is, depending upon the initial vector or it's starting position which we need to practice, both on paper and in real life.

So there are two elements to this style of seeing the ball, one which we labelled 'picking the length', one is estimating and determining to the best of our ability the initial vector force out of the bowler's hand and the second which is purely a matter of consequence and mathematical reality – calculating or estimating the vector's shape, which we call in physics the 'resultant vector'. Practice on paper drawing the resultant vector for any particular and different initial vector forces and try to appreciate how each vector has a varying resultant vector, or simply as we have been calling it, a different resulting shape. This is really not a hard concept of physics to understand and remember what we said earlier, we are not asking ourselves to make a mathematical and exact calculation of our resultant vector, but merely a rough idea of it's final shape and an appreciation of how different deliveries and vectors have different shapes and that the ball may have a different height by the time it reaches us.

So remember, we want to be in the league of the greats and get in position early and improve our stroke-play – hopefully by consolidating and practicing your understanding of this idea from physics and Euclidean geometry, you will have more confidence in your ability to see the ball well and early, pick the length and final positioning of the ball and give yourself a better chance of playing better and bigger shots. Like I said it really is not that hard an idea to grasp it is merely coated in a daunting and pragmatic scientific notation – but remember we do not have to perform the calculation mathematically and on paper, we are merely interested in it's real life application which to us as cricketers is estimating the resultant shape of the ball and final positioning as it reaches the batsman and how quickly or slowly it will reach our bat too[19]..

You need to practice four or five vectors and their resultant vectors on practice in real life by simply watching the ball and predicting what you think the balls final shape might be based on your estimation of the force and direction put on the ball. I'm sure with a bit of practice both on paper and in the net, that your estimation as forecasted from your watching the ball from the bowler's hand like a hawk, will very quickly become accurate and that your mental calculation will be in alignment with it's actual shape.

So after studying these examples of vector forces you may encounter in the form of deliveries faced, you should by now appreciate that 'picking the length' is not necessarily predicting the length the ball will pitch at, but knowing where and how high and at what speed the ball will actually reach you and reach your bat by the time it ends it's path of motion, for any given delivery.

Before we move onto the physics and vector forces involved in spin bowling and how to improve your vision and ability to 'pick the length' against spinners, we must introduce one more important concept of physics which will help you against the pacers and that is called the law of

---

[19] The pace or speed at which the bowler releases the ball dictates exactly the speed at which the ball will reach your bat – it could be slower or it could be faster depending on the vector's magnitude component which call simply it's speed!

reflection by Greek mathematician Euclid – the same inventor of geometric vector forces previously discussed within this chapter. So let's label this physics of predicting and picking length and path of the ball before it has hit the pitch or just as it leaves the bowlers hand, which is imperative for you batsmen, as Euclidian physics.

The law of reflection basically states essentially that the angle of reflection is equal to and the same as the angle of incidence. Study the provided diagram and illustrations to better appreciate this law by Euclid, and a law which has enormous importance and relevance to us as cricketers contesting a game of cricket over a 22-yard-long pitch.

Diagram IX: 5'6" tall pace bowler:

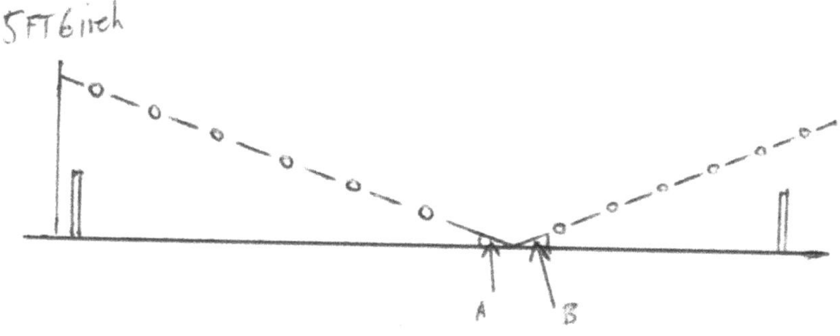

Angle A is strictly equal to angle B according to Snell's Law of incidence and reflection. Notice how this pace bowler being only 5'6", is only getting a very modest or meagre bounce by the time it reaches the batsman – just above stump height only.

Diagram X: 6'6" tall pace bowler:

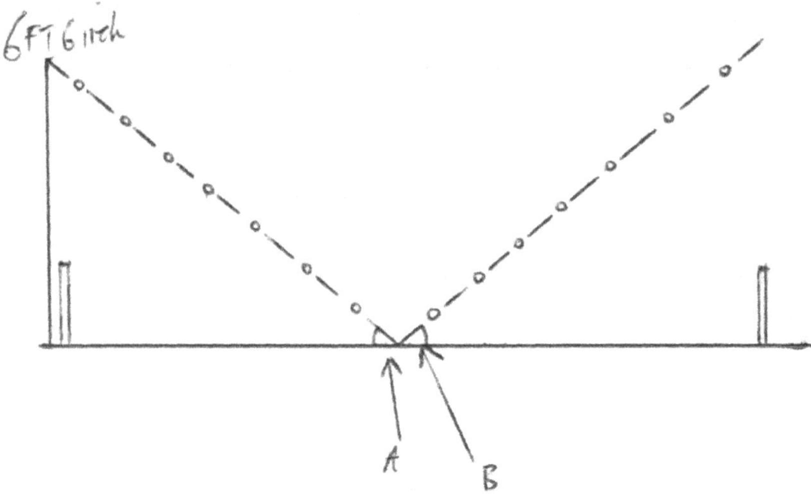

Again angle A is strictly equal to angle B. Notice how the taller bowler is getting the ball to bounce up to shoulder or head height as opposed to waist height in the previous example.

So what we can see from these two diagrams and our law of reflection which is not just a theory but an observed fact of physics and scientific reality, is that the ball will behave and can only behave in a predicted manner according to and dictated by the angle of it's path from bowlers hand to hitting the pitch – there is no refuting or scope of argument about this as it is science and has been observed to be correct for thousands of years over thousands of industrial applications, including ball games and ball sports also (so why not cricket?). The only way that the path of the ball in cricket, can feasibly differ from this law of reflection, is due to the pitch and the way the pitch is prepared – it might be slightly faster or slightly slower, but even then the resultant path of the ball once it hits the pitch will still in most cases be at the same angle or very close to the angle that it hit the pitch upon delivery and release by the bowler. Now that's the path side of it which we can depict on paper, but you need to also practice the speed side of it – that is will the ball reach me slower or faster and at what speed and when. This should be practiced in the nets whereby you practice simply picking the length and speed of the ball quickly as humanly possible and don't bother about the hitting the ball part so much. Practice acting upon this theory and science behind cricket and using it to your advantage in a game of cricket – that's how the greats' mind works too and your's should too!

What does this mean? Well, it may sound cruel, but in view of scientific reality and what you have just seen in previous two diagrams, it may not be a good idea to pursue fast bowling unless you are a minimum height. The shortest fast bowler ever to have produced good bounce and the right bounce, as and as is dictated by Euclid's law of reflection, was still 5'7" – AjitAgarkar of India. If you are not 5'7" or more than it may be a good idea to simply be a 'chorr' pace bowler or become a spinner instead, and there is always batsman-ship to be pursued which actually lends advantages to those who are under 5'7" in height, yes, batsmen actually have a distinct advantage in facing and scoring off quality bowling when they are 5'7" or less.[20]

Often when the bowler is short or less than 5'7", suddenly the batsman is able to bully the bowler, that is even good length balls and short balls can

---

[20]Bradman, Tendulkar, Aravinda, Lara, Gavaskar&Miandad, were all around 5'7" or less in height, and were some of the most successful Test Match batsmen ever.

be played comfortably off the front foot. Pay attention to the height of the bowler when you first come into bat against that bowler – if the bowler is short it is contra-indicated that you should generally get onto the front foot and play most your shots off front foot, however, if the bowler is very tall it is contra-indicated to play off back foot while you can.[21]

Now on to the vector forces involved in spin bowling. There are two types of vector forces at play here depending upon whether you are a 'chorr' bowler or whether you are a front line spinner trying to achieve that beautiful flight, dip and loop, that traditionally spinners are out to master and employ in their bowling. The first is similar to a fast bowler where the vector is a straight line, as it does not have any loop or flight or very little even if it does, and can be taken as a simple straight line vector where the resultant vector is equal to its initial vector and follows the law of reflection just as we illustrated previously. The chorr bowler is not flighting the ball in any way but rather is simply banging the ball into the pitch, so its resultant path is basically in line with the resultant paths of pace deliveries which we diagrammatically illustrated prior. Study this example and illustration of a typical chorr bowler's delivery. While the ball does have spin imparted on it, its point of bouncing and its resultant path is very much just like a pace bowler's.

---

[21] Watch Tendulkar play the taller bowlers and the precision of his footwork to play attacking shots to semi-lose balls.

Diagram XI:

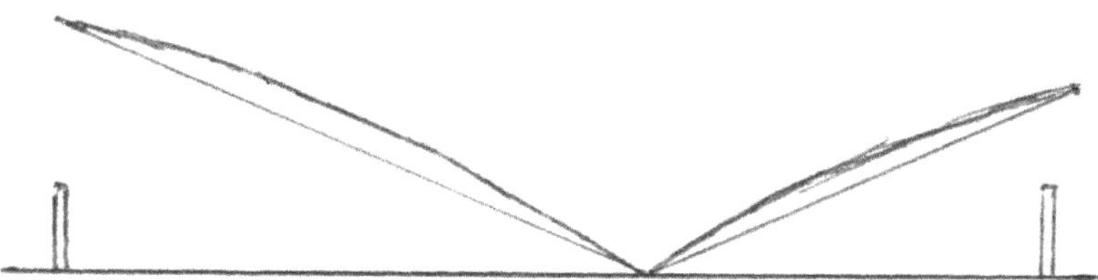

The straight lines would typically illustrate a medium pace or pacer's ball and the curved line is illustrating the 'chorr' bowler or part time spinner's delivery, which does not have the flight usually associated with spin bowling. Notice how the paths are almost identical meaning batters can play this type of spin bowling with ease and just like as though facing a pacer.

In essence, by understanding all this speak on vectors and 'picking the length', we are trying to train ourselves and our vision to pick up the ball's final path and position upon reaching our bat early. Somewhere around point Z on the diagram – fancy that would not that be nice. Well if you understand the chapter well and re-read and revise it and practice in real life, this is a certain reality – it has been done by the greats and can be done by you too!

So point Z on the following diagram is the time where we want to predict the final position, shape and destiny of the ball the bowler has bowled and the vector force which has been imparted. The vector force has been imparted and nothing but little things like air resistance and minor aspects of the pitch can change its path and change it significantly by now – the path will always be 90% in line with Snell's Law of incidence equals reflection and vector forces which we have now discussed in detail. We should have our feet in position by this time – point z on the diagram that is. So now you are ready to start picking the length like a master, start seeing the ball and predicting it's shape at point Z and start hitting the ball better and getting into position earlier, especially for your defensive shots.

Diagram XII:

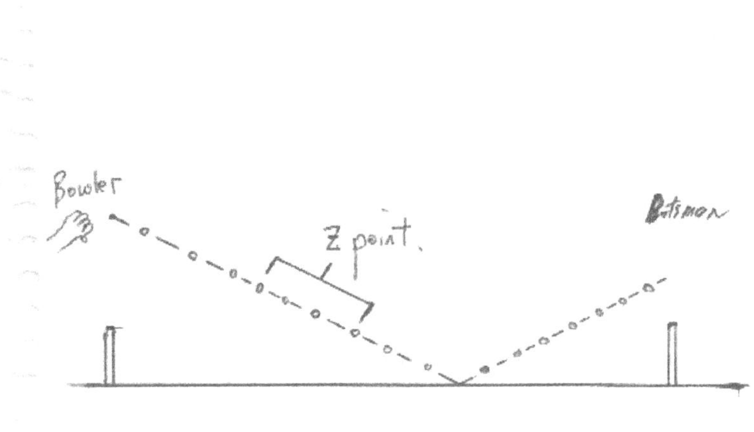

One more finer point whilst reading vector forces of pace bowling is to watch out for the bowler's hand in in particular watch out for if he is trying to ball with a high arm action or high hand action or if he is trying to ball with a low arm action – this will consequently change the bounce and direction component of the vector as the height of release will be lower or higher and the ball will either bounce a little more or bounce a little less – just another aspect of picking the length we need to look out for whilst playing quality bowling

Vector forces involved in Spin bowling explained:

Now let's get to the harder bit where our delivery is by a frontline spinner, and one who is aiming for flight, dip and loop, what will its resultant path be and how do we pick it and prepare for it? Well explaining this and breaking it down scientifically and according to exact geometric vector forces involved from release until the point it reaches the bat, basically incorporates everything we talked about before about vector forces only we will introduce one more concept of science and mathematics and that is 'parabolic motion' and the way objects given an initial vector force in the skyward direction behave and what path they take. Moreover, we will account for the topspin put on the ball and illustrate how this too is incorporated within the parabolic motion created and how it contributes to the object's final path and resultant trajectory. Note, here with spin bowling that is, we are now talking about a ***resultant trajectory*** as opposed to ***resultant path*** we talked about earlier with pace bowling and picking the path of pace bowling. So an understanding of parabolic motion, which you have studied in math classes anyway, is required. For those who do not remember the ideas and mathematics behind parabolic motion or would like to recap and revise or just have a better chance of understanding what we are about to talk about in regard how parabolic motion applies to all spin bowling, then it is advised to read its scientific explanation within the appendix at the end of the book first. It is advised you read it anyway first before we get down to the mathematics and physics you need to know as a bowler or a batsmen trying to bowl or trying to play pick spin bowling –note we have not got down to and explained how to play the ball from a spinner, but we are first and primarily showing you how to 'pick its length' and how to determine and predict it's path or trajectory as the ball approaches the bat. This in itself is 80% of the task done anyhow for you batsmen, knowing how the ball will come and where it will land and how it will behave that is, the remaining task of playing spin bowling is the easy part and only requires some simple coaching tips which you can easily learn from a local coach or the likes.

Ok, so hopefully you have studied briefly the appendix and the definitions in regard projectile motion, and have a fair idea of what we are talking about and why we want to talk about it in picking the paths of spin-bowling. So let's get explaining this physics and mathematics of projectile motion in context of cricket and spin-bowling and how we can use our understanding to be better cricketers.

Note that the second half of the projectile's path – once it reaches its vertex or highest point and then begins to descend and come down, is exactly the same, that is just as if it were being mirrored, and obeys thelaw we spoke of earlier that the resultant vector is exactly the same as it's initial vector.

Also note the quotes:
'except for how the air affects it'; and
'if the effects of air resistance are assumed to be negligible'.

This is where we bring in the second element of accurately tracking the projectile motion and path of a parabola or in our case a spin bowl – yes, in cricket and spin bowling, a simple parabolic motion and simply assuming a perfectly symmetrical path and one which obeys the laws of projectile motion, is not good enough. What if the ball, as is a cornerstone of good spin bowling remember we explained and all spinners are trying to do, what if it has topspin on the ball in addition to being lobbed in the air by the bowler along a certain angle and certain path? What will happen? Well of course the path will not follow a parabola strictly and according to laws of projectile motion! Well topspin creates air resistance so the path is not parabolic in the strictest sense, but is slightly deviated from this. Study this hypothetical scenario of two balls, one with know topspin and one with ample topspin – remember the simple theory we spoke about in spin bowling chapters about the topspin creating greater loop and dip, well we are simply explaining and justifying WHY through this discussion on parabolic motion and science behind it, that's all!

<u>DiagramXIII:</u>

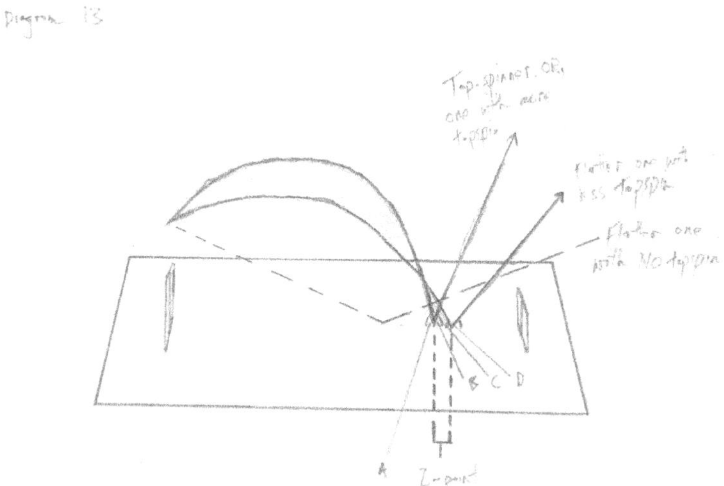

In consistency with Snell's law of incidence and reflection, angle A = angle B and angle C = angle D, however the thing to note here is that the path of the ball WITH topspin is different to the path of the ball WITH LESS topspin, and that the one with topspin hits the pitch at a sharper angle and deflects at a sharper angle, creating more bounce by the time it reaches the bat.

Due to the topspin on the ball the air resistance increases and the ball curves a little more sharply than the standard parabola or standard ball with no topspin and subsequently the angle of incidence as it bounces on the pitch is increased therefore increasing the angle of reflection and henceforth creating a bouncier ball – pretty basic stuff. We see something called the z-point on the diagram also and we see that it is a very narrow distance. This is the critical factor in playing spin bowling successfully and playing more attacking shots – the mental visualization on the pitch of where exactly this z-point is and what is the exact distance of this z-point. Once we get a 'sighter' and begin judging where and at what length the loopy one bounces and at what length the flatter one bounces, we can immediately estimate the z-point in mathematical or geometric units and upon visualizing this or marking this on the pitch, we can start estimating where each delivery by the spinner will bounce and where exactly within the z-point it will bounce.

Cricketing instinct tells us that if we estimate and visualize a mathematical middle or centre line, we can then start deciding which foot to play the ball off. If it is forward of the center we can play off front foot if it is backward of the center we can play off back foot, but just remember to use a visualization on the pitch of the z-point and the center of the z-point whilst playing spin bowling – this will be a huge help and guidance in you playing spin bowling properly and preying upon tiny and slight margins or variances in the bowler's length.[22] See the following diagram:

Diagram XIV:

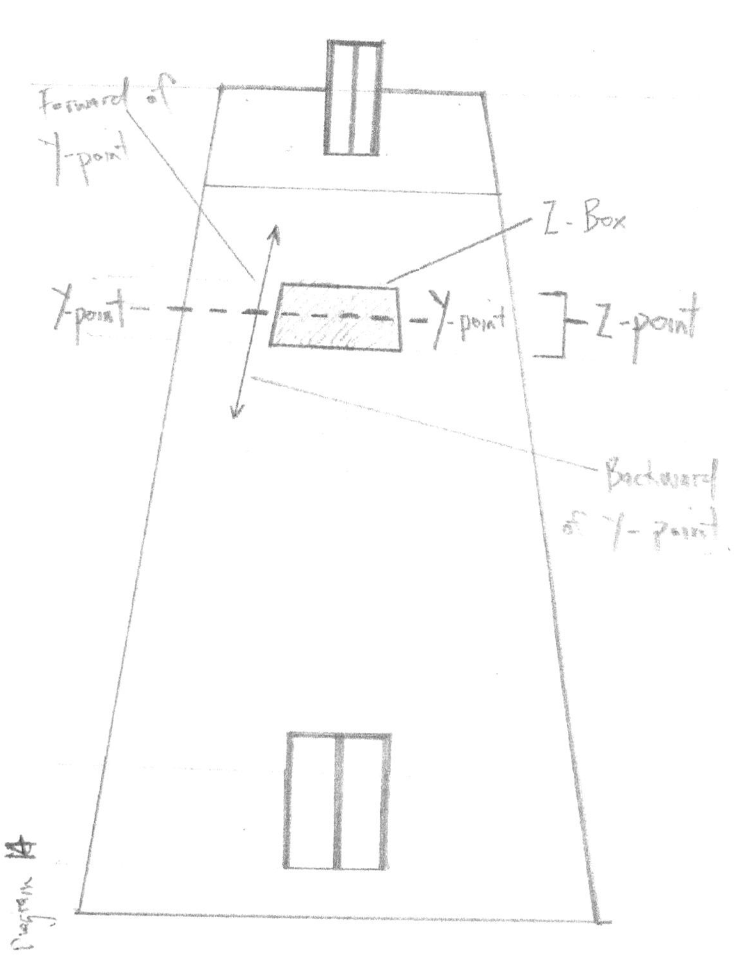

[22] The centre of the Z – point is labelled as "Y – point" in the diagram.

If the ball is at or forward of the y-point we try play off back foot, however, if it is marginally forward of y-point we can lunge out onto front foot or we can use the feet to dance down the track – this is only possible if the ball is expected to pitch only marginally in front of y-point though, as it increases the chances of getting a bat-pad catch. If the ball is backward of the y-point we should play off front foot with confidence, however, if it is marginally backward of y-point only we can still play a back foot flick also. Notice from the diagram, the good ball from a spinner starts just outside leg stump and spans to about a foot outside off stump.

This is just how the greats and professionals do it too, it is the ability to pick the length and not so much the line which helps us in playing spin bowling – that is, when to go forward and when to go back. Unlike playing pacers who swing the ball sideways or get lateral movement, playing spin bowling relies upon the very fundamental crux of batting - the natural impulse to move your feet forward and lean into the ball or go back and wait for the ball to come to you. Unlike playing fast bowling where we said you need to get moving forward as your initial movement or impulse, the same is not true for playing spin bowling – we must keep still and neutral until the ball is released out the hand and stay as still as possible before moving forward or back or using the feet to advanced down the wicket.[23]

---

[23] The box which appears on the diagram represents those deliveries on the pitch by a spinner which are in that good zone and are hard to play and may be considered accurate or a threat to the batsman's wicket – labelled "z-box".

A similar diagram showing the z-box or rectangle of uncertainty as we can call it is shown for pace bowling below. The same premise as to using the y-point to decide on footwork applies, that is going forward or back.

Diagram: XV:

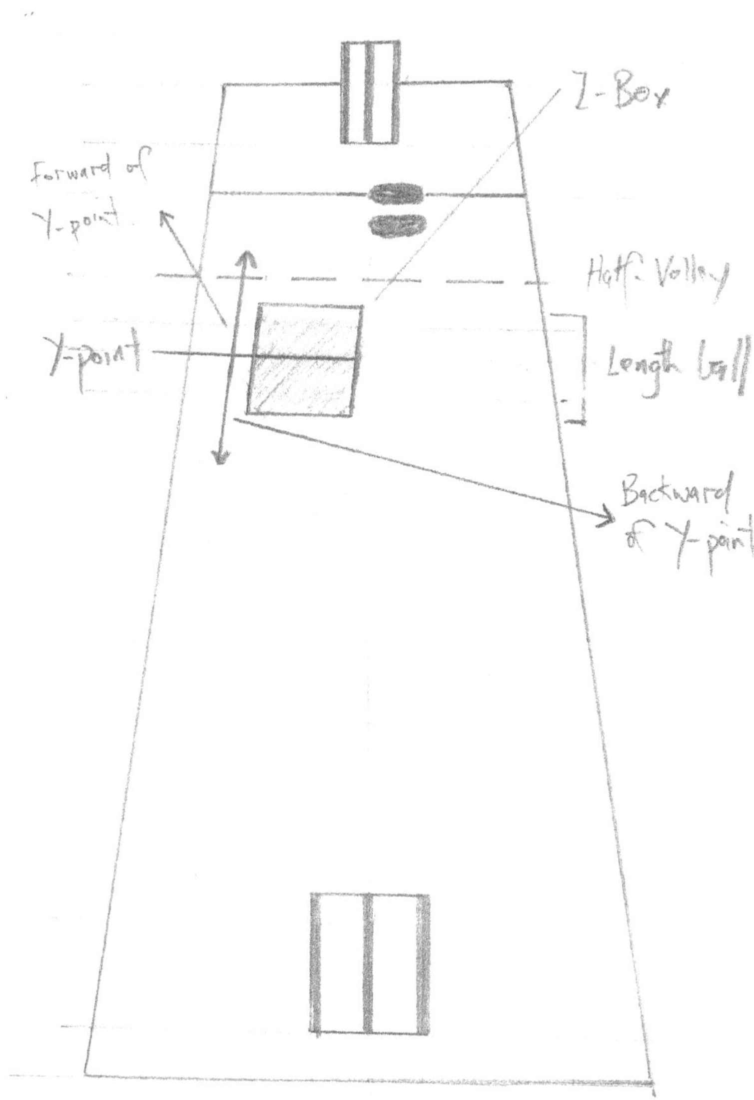

We notice that our z-point is quite narrow in the case of spinners as batsmen can successfully prey on anything shorter or fuller than the y-point and the margin for error for spinners is very low, whereas the pacer's rectangle of uncertainty or z-box or just known as the length ball, is bigger and longer with slightly more margin for error available or tolerable to the pacer. The pacer's good ball starts from middle stump to about half to three quarters of a foot outside off stump. Anything within the z-box is considered accurate and should be approached with caution and a sound defensive shot on behalf of the batsman. We will show you how in the next book, soon to be released, how to turn good balls into scoring opportunities and delve into the mathematics of playing calculated attacking shots to balls which lie within a z-box or accurate range.

Well that's the physics explained and all you need to know really, study the diagrams above and just remember a standard parabolic delivery and one with greater topspin and how the projectile path changes, and try to use this in your batting to quickly and decisively position your feet and go back or forward.

What can we gleam from this speak of flight and length balls or balls which fall within the z-point or z-box?? Well all this means is that we should learn to prepare for both the flatter one and the loopy one and use different footwork for each. For example if the bowler is getting good flight and more over spin then maybe play off back foot and play late; however, if the spinner is bowling flatter ones maybe try play off front foot and use your feet to dance down the pitch – this is the principle which elite batters use anyway.[24] For more advice as to how to negotiate balls falling within the z-box in a more attacking and one-batting mode, watch out for the next book soon to be released "the linear code and logic of one-day batting". But for now you can now appreciate the process and mathematics deployed by elite batters against elite bowling and the advantage of using mathematically correct and geometrically accurate estimates of anticipating variation in line and length and deviation of the ball whilst batting at a higher level.

So a perfectly symmetrical parabola is purely academic and hypothetical in spin bowling as we are almost always aiming for greater dip via imparting over-spin on the ball and aiming for a greater forward force on the ball through putting over-spin revolutions in addition to sidespin revolutions on the ball. So all deliveries we will ever bowl as a spinner will fall in between the following two resultant paths shown in the previous diagram, a perfect parabola that is one with 100% sidespin and a skewed or in-symmetrical parabola which is one with 100% top-spin, remember we talked about the ratio of overspin and sidespin and how we should be adept at varying this in good spin bowling and if we want to be a great spin bowler. Like we explained, why Murali is so good is because his 100% topspin is so ferociously packed with topspin and well disguised, that the path of the ball is not a typical parabola which the batsman would predict and pick, but follows a drastically different path consistent with the one illustrated in the above diagram.

---

[24] Watch Azharuddin and notice how even when the bowler bowls a good ball with flights and more overspin, he was able to play the flick through midwicket off the BACKFOOT for a single or two.

Conclusion:

So as you can see, all this speak about vectors and mathematics is not a fallacy or a fictitious concept trying to lure you or misguide you or giving us a 'big head', but it is scientific reality, and a scientific reality which you absolutely MUST know as early as possible before you begin your training and practice as an elite batsman. This is, as we mentioned earlier, the 'crux' of cricket and the whole backbone upon which playing and succeeding in cricket is based. Re-read these chapters on vectors many a time so there are no ifs and buts in regard you grasping this idea and the physics behind batting.

Chapter Seven

Understanding Batsman's Talk

How many times have we as batsman walked out to the middle and asked our partner "how is the pitch playing?" only to get a response, "its keeping low", and get bowled off one which kept low – you would think what was the point of asking in the first place if we are just going to get out first ball anyway!

Well what we have to try to do is understand batsman's talk a little better – that is we need to extract meaning out of what was just said and make a cricketing interpretation out of it before we even start to take our guard or do anything else. We need to just listen, listen to our partner or wicket keeper or fielders to pick up any clues we can. Now this may be a skill which is new to some of you and may take some conscious effort to learn and apply, but I will teach you mostly what you need to know as a batsman and what batsman talk you need to understand and interpretations you need to deduce, after that it is up to you to apply it in real life..

It all pertains basically to how the pitch is playing and how the bowler is bowling so it is not that hard and doesn't have that many combinations/permutations to know really. Here is a list of common 'batsman talk' and their respective meaning and cricketing interpretation:

Firstly, here is a list of the main 'batsman' talks you will probably hear – we will get into the interpretation after:

1. Its playing low
2. Its Moving around a bit
3. Its Bouncy
4. Its seaming
5. Its Gripping

You may also hear things like:

1. He's bowling well
2. He's bowling to his field
3. He's all over the place
4. He's tossing it up
5. He's zippy or he's zipping it through

Now for the important bit, what do we think when we ask our partner about the bowler or the pitch and hear the above comments or observations? What do we make of it and what do we think in a cricketing sense? What meaning do we draw from this little piece of wisdom being confided to us and how do we allow for this as a fresh batsman who has yet to face a ball and one who has no idea what to expect – whether the ball will come at your head or at your feet, at a million miles an hour or just 10, dead straight or like a curved banana?

"We are foolish if we don't listen and take this on board and adapt our technique accordingly, at least for the first 15 balls of our innings – the crucial part".

Here are some guidelines in regard how best to interpret batsman's talk:

"Its playing low":

There is nothing much the bowler can do to make the ball bounce low except the flipper, that's if he is a leg-spin bowler only. When it plays low this means the ball is skidding and keeping low due to the pitch and the way the pitch has been prepared – as most pitches do in India and subcontinent. This means there is less bounce on the pitch and you can afford and sometimes even must try get on the front foot where and when possible – this is important so the ball doesn't skid underneath the bat. Often these pitches are dry and hard. We can begin playing the drive on the up once we are played in very nicely on these pitches, also square drive off front foot.

"Its moving around a bit":

This could mean and imply a series of different things. It basically means there is significant deviation happening or the bowler is extracting significant deviation. This could mean through the air as in swing or it could mean off the pitch as in greater bounce, also it could mean deviation off the seam – which one is it or is it all? When we hear this we need to stop and clarify with our partner for a moment and ask simply: " *in the air or off the pitch*?". Be prepared for the moving ball and the one on the stumps which moves, so get ready to defend the good length ball with all your experience and also watch the ball a bit harder for the first few balls and maybe even let a few balls pass bye until you see how the ball is behaving.

"Its bouncing around":

Usually a characteristic of foreign pitches and ones in Australia or South Africa. Usually this happens because of the pitch and its preparation but there are some bowlers who can get the ball to bounce more than it normally does, however just assume in 99% of cases that the pitch is bouncy and you have to bring your back foot shots into play, also there is no need to reach or hurry at the ball you should just let the ball come to you and play with soft hands especially when playing forward defence. These pitches are good for drivers and cutters/pullers as the ball is coming on to the bat. Look out for the ball short of a half volley to execute drives and in generally be prepared to drive on the up only once you are played in as the extra bounce may lead to a spooned catch, also look to leave or let go some balls on a length or short of a length until you observe the bounce properly, as sometimes bounce off a length can cause nicks and edges to slips – protect yourself from this in particular on bouncy pitches and get your body right in behind the ball when you play shots. Leave good length balls go if you can.

"Its seaming around":

This means the pitch is offering good assistance to the seamers in the form of consistent movement off the pitch. Be ready to play the ball late and open/close the face of the bat late in case the ball deviates late off the pitch. Do not go for drives on the up on these pitches unless fully confident and try to play good length balls with soft hands. Be fully prepared for the death ball in the first fifteen balls of your innings by bringing the bat down dead straight and adjusting your backlift to do so.

"Its gripping":

Usually said when the spinners are bowling and there is considerable grip and purchase/turn from the pitch. The pitch is assisting the spinners and the ball is gripping and turning sharply. Get pad and bat close together and try to get to the pitch of the ball before attempting drives. When the ball is gripping do not play drives on the up early on in your innings until confident enough or try lofted shots until confident enough. Be cautious in regard using the feet to come down the pitch.

"He's bowling well":

This generally implies that the bowler is bowling with accuracy and not giving too many loose balls. That he is bowling an offstump line and is bowling a good line and length. It means he is making the batsman defend a lot of balls and work hard for runs. Be prepared for the length ball first up if your partner says this, and get yourself into 100% defensive mode for the first few balls.

"He's bowling to his field":

This usually means the bowler is making an attempt to choke the runs and is bowling to for example a 6/3 on-side or off-side field and bowling a leg-side OR off-side line only. This may mean you have to alter your guard from middle to leg or middle to middle and off, or try play inside out shots. Also you may have to start playing the flick from outside off-stump more often to get runs. Just use your cricketing brain to work around this once you figure out what field and what line and length he is bowling to. Just try adapt your shot making and your guard accordingly – the most typical example is provided as aforementioned, there may be other fields or examples of tactics of bowling to the field used by the bowler, just figure out what it is and adapt accordingly to get runs

<u>"He's all over the place":</u>

The bowler is struggling for accuracy and rhythm and is giving away a lot of loose balls – be prepared to put away the loose ball outside off-stump particularly and anywhere for that matter – but still watch out for the length ball in first 15 balls.

<u>"He's tossing it up":</u>

A tactic used by spinners which equates to slower and higher as opposed to faster and flatter, which is meant usually to entice or lure the batsman into driving or even driving on the up and thereby miscue or get an edge. Only drive if confident and can get to the pitch of the ball, also be careful about the use of the feet and coming down the pitch as this is the whole idea of the tactic on the spinner's behalf.

<u>"He's zippy or he's zipping it through":</u>

If the bowler is a spinner well then this implies he is bowling faster and flatter as opposed to slower and higher as we just spoke about. This means he is usually bowling with more accuracy and pace and you should be careful about your shot-selection and when you choose to cut and pull in particular in case you get a bowled while cutting or a top edge while pulling – be careful about picking the length of the ball in general especially. The bowler may not be getting much turn but is cramping the batsman for room and making scoring difficult – be judicious about horizontal bat stroke-selection.

If it is a pace bowler, then it means he is bowling at a decent pace and is quite zippy – that is the ball is almost hurrying on to the bat. This is what we want when we are played in the ball coming on to the bat as opposed to holding up, but what if we are in the initial stages of our innings? We need to protect ourselves from the extra pace and the caught behind so try get your body right in behind the ball and get your elbow up whilst playing defensive and attacking shots. Imagine yourself playing on a synthetic pitch in this scenario when the ball bowler is zippy and account for a little extra bounce also.

Remember to do your bit as a fresh batsman to the crease by asking and clarifying with your partner about the pitch and how the bowler is bowling. Especially if you get a response of ***he's bowling well***, try get in pure defensive mode for at least 3 deliveries.

What's in between the ears is 80% of batting, so you should read this chapter twice and study it carefully to increase your chances of making it through your warm-up period whilst being a new batsman at the crease.

Chapter Eight

Starting Your Innings

So a wicket falls and it's your turn to walk out to the middle, as you walk out stretch your arms and jump as you walk to get blood flowing, or you can wait to get to the crease and then jump on the spot a few times just to get the blood flowing. Remember what we said earlier about the length ball being so hard to play sometimes as the feet don't know whether to go forward or back - this is the one we need to prepare ourselves for, it sounds silly but every little bit helps and we need blood flowing to our left thigh and left foot in case we need to play this shot first up. Just jump on your legs a few times just to make sure they are there and let your brain know they are there in case it needs them and that they are there to serve you if you need them. Don't worry about your arms or hands or shoulders as the movements required in batting are not that explosive or demanding – they will warm up and stretch as you run and as you stay at the crease for a few overs, you can do a quick stretch if u like. Try keep the animations in front of the field to a minimum as we don't want to give away a mental advantage in the form of firing the other team up or stirring the bowler up when we are just new to the crease, or looking as if we are inviting a challenge – just a quick stretch and jump of your thighs and feet is all you need.

Remember what we said in the previous chapter about batsman's talk. It is important you conference with your partner at the other end quickly, not just to say hello or to get some morale boost, but to exchange his experience with the bowler and with the pitch – this is a big help for you as a new batsman coming in fresh with no knowledge of the pitch or bowler and can't be stressed enough. As you get experienced and older in playing cricket obviously your application of batsman's talk will get better, anyhow there is not much to know, but for now we just need to be warned about any abnormalities in the bowling or the pitch which we may need to look out for as a new batsman, that's all.

If it is a test match or a limited over match, your approach to starting your inning should be the same or similar – you should allow yourself a few overs to settle in before you expect to score more freely. In a one-day match, you should allow yourself 15 balls to settle in during which time you should size up the pitch, the bowling and expect of yourself maybe around 5 runs – that's about 1 run every three balls. The first 15 balls of your innings are the most crucial and are the 'make-or-break' of your innings, that is if you are out in first 15 balls then your back in the pavilion, but if your still there after 15 balls then there are good chances you'll still be there after 115 balls or 215 balls and have a good score also. You have to use this time period as a learning curve or an investment for the rest of your innings, it can't be stressed enough that you don't get impetuous and try play big shots or risky shots early in your innings – just play in the V and maybe cut out the square drive or drive on the up until your settled in. The aim is to get your eye in whilst at the same time being mentally present enough to play straight and put away loose balls either short of a length or full tosses – that is all you should expect of yourself in the beginning of your innings.

Just like placing a bet or gambling on a mediocre horse and betting too much money and taking too much risk, as opposed to betting less money on an experienced and in form horse – you are that mediocre horse and you don't want to take too much risk by betting too much money and playing too many risky shots. We are better off picking up runs the less risky yet guaranteed way early on and sacrifice the 'big win' early on for the sake of not losing out altogether and getting out cheaply.[25]

Remember to tap the pitch just at that spot around a length and there abouts, especially if it's a medium-pacer or a pacer you're about to face, and look around basically that little spot for broken bits or divots or indentations and just slightly give them a few taps to flatten them out – remember we said before it sounds silly, but every little bit counts, and quite often even the best in the game like Tendulkars and Kohli's get out to length balls or good balls, so don't feel embarrassed, it's your wicket on the line and being back in the pavilion certainly isn't any fun.[26]

Ok so now we're ready to take guard. Find out what guard is best for you according to the strength of your off-side play – yes, the guard is usually dictated by your propensity and capacity for off-side mastery especially cuts and late cuts. Either way, it is advised to take middle at the start of your innings in case you're not at full-form and in case the bowler produces an in-swinger or in-dipper which comes in late – you can always change your guard once you are comfortable with the pitch and the bowler and your stroke-play begins to flourish a little more, but for now take middle.

---

[25]We call a batsman a mediocre horse in the beginning of his innings as he is not played in nor knows anything about the pitch or the bowling yet

[26]Often despite how good the batsman is, the length ball is just too much to handle early on – see Allan Donald Vs Tendulkar: one-dayer

Now we are finally ready to take stance and face up to the bowler. Everything about this is as per the coaching book and what your coach taught you, only we are just going to add to this one more super important finer detail – and that is related to the position of our back lift, and specifically our back-lift early on in our innings. The usual back-lift starts at 1st slip and can go all the way around to 3rd slip. This is the optimal back-lift for stroke-play, generating maximum bat-speed and playing square of the wicket, however may not be the optimal back-lift for defensive strokes and particularly the one we keep talking about – the forward defence or defending the length ball, which is what we are weary of in the start of our innings.

The whole concept and idea of 'playing-in-the-V' early on is so that we can concentrate our efforts on defending the 'death ball' or 'rattle ball'[27] early on when we are most vulnerable and have no idea of the pitch, the bowling nor have ourselves played in nor are seeing the ball satisfactorily yet; and at the same time score runs and not stagnate into scorelessness and keep the score ticking whilst not giving our wicket away cheaply.

The biomechanics of bringing our bat down dead straight and not from the slips is not a natural nor biomechanically easy motion to get used to but then again so is the whole act of batsman-ship in general, so just try your best for the sake of the rest of your innings and not getting out to the death ball early on and try to make it a part of your overall batting technique. When we don't yet have our eye in it becomes easier and more effective to play the death ball with a straight bat and soft hands whereby we can

---

[27]From here on in throughout the book, the good length ball will be referred to as the death ball or rattle ball

play late and bring the bat down straight and with soft hands to prevent any edges from carrying to slips or any edges from happening altogether. When we do get the opportunity to drive the ball the emphasis is on making contact with the bat in the middle and not the edge, seeing the ball right on to the bat and stroking the ball with timing with less follow through – yes, early in your innings concentrate on timing the ball out of the middle as opposed to hitting the ball far or following through, and watch the ball all the way on to the bat with your head down and over the ball.[28]

The purpose of our restricting ourselves to playing in the V early on as every coaching manual says, is so that we give ourselves a short time to get played in and start seeing the ball and get used to the pitch – it is like an investment for the rest of our innings and the main thing we are trying to do here is start seeing the ball well and protect ourselves from the death ball while our bodies and minds are not yet warm yet.

Think of it like investing in a stock or a share – in the beginning we invest in multiple low-return stocks until we get enough money together then we invest in a more high-return or high performing stock. Because we are new to the crease we don't have much resources up our sleeves in the form of hand-eye-coordination, knowledge of the pitch & bowling and ability to see the ball early so we invest in multiple cheaper or low-return shots until we do and then buy a bigger or high-return stock or in this analogy high-return shot.

---

[28]So far what we have discussed is ditto as per the coaching manual – only we have explained the reasoning for playing in the V early on, that is all

During this get your eye in phase, we are trying to do what is called *'make the bowler bowl to you'*. We are effectively almost cutting out all our stroke-play, leaving good balls not on the stumps go and only playing in the V, all for the sake of defending ourselves from a good ball early while we are not warm, and aiming to successfully get our eye in and begin to start seeing the ball well and early enough to set ourselves up for a big innings. By making the bowler bowl to you we are cutting out the other 99 ways of being dismissed, as we have cut out all our shots, and reducing it to just 1 – the death ball on the stumps. Even then there is a 60% chance that you will successfully negotiate even the best of death balls, making it a 99.6% chance of keeping your wicket in the first fifteen balls. What can the bowler do in this situation? Well this can't last for too long as we discussed earlier in the book about the batsman must sooner or later start playing strokes all around the wicket – but we are still collecting runs from playing in the V remember AND by making the bowler bowl to us we have reduced our chances of getting out to just 0.4% for the duration we need to properly get ourselves played in. Now what would happen if we did this for the whole innings, play in the V only that is and just practice seeing the ball well and early, like we mentioned earlier in the book – well the batsman does have an advantage and we wouldn't have a very competitive total to defend and give our poor bowlers to defend that's what. So that's why we can't do this forever, we have to get ourselves played in as soon as we can and start playing all around the wicket and start trying to actually hit the ball as soon as we practically and physically can.

So, playing in the V is a good way to give ourselves a bit of practice at seeing the ball well and early, defend ourselves from the death ball and at the same time pick up a few runs also. The main reason is however based on high level cricket and the quality of pace bowling encountered wherein we are often required to play the ball late and account for the moving ball particularly on a length – if we knew there was no length ball or that there was no length ball which was going to move or deviate, then we would not find a need to adjust our back-lift and play in the V early like we have just advocated, but then we are training ourselves for higher level cricket and that too on turf pitches so we DO need to worry about it and DO need to make it a part of our technique.

While the length ball is something to be weary of early on and we DO have to look out for it, it is not everything and after all the very reason you are there, the reason you are there is to score runs, but what if we get out how do we score runs then? Of course the other batsman will score the runs but then what if all the batsman thought this and we all got out cheaply to good balls early on – we would all be out for a meagre and measly target and give our poor bowlers nothing to defend. Obviously this preparing for the length ball is critical more so for you opening batsmen or whilst the ball is still new and shiny, however, all batsmen regardless of what position they bat at and when they actually come into bat are urged account for the good ball or length ball early in their innings.

Think of it this way, imagine you are at a crowded venue a concert or a sporting match and it's a packed house with a lot of people. While you are walking around you see so many people and so many faces, lets imagine each individual face in the crowd as being an individual ball a batsman faces from the bowler. Now while we are not looking out for the faces of our friends and family emphatically and consciously, when we do see someone who resembles them, we immediately take more notice, look closer, ensure it is them and not just an illusion and then we prepare ourselves to say "hello mate, how are you, I thought I might see you here, or I knew you would come here also". This is the exact same rationale for our playing of the length ball – we are not looking out solely and solely for it but we are aware it may be there, and when we see something resembling it, we tighten up, look a little closer and then say "hello good length ball, I knew you were coming", and greet it with a dead straight bat and soft hands. When we go to a crowded venue we do not consume our entire mind and concentration looking for and scanning for the faces of our family or friends but we are as human beings looking out for them in the back of our minds and we do sub-consciously awaken and pay attention if anyone who passes bye resembles them – this is the same for batting, we are preparing for anything and everything all around the wicket, but especially prepared for the death ball, as subconsciously we know how important it is to our wicket, and we know we should be able to greet it with a nice straight bat and soft hands.

As we spoke about earlier you may also choose to make the bowler bowl to you and play only with a dead straight bat for 15 balls and play only and in anticipation only for the death ball, or you may choose to play according to our natural instinct which is to seek scoring opportunities first and foremost - these are two different ways and methods in regard seeing the ball early in our innings. It all comes down to how well and how quickly the batsman is picking the length, batsman who are a bit unsure prefer to play in the V only and concentrate for the length ball whereas more confident batsman may be able to click into second or third gear from the ball one and start playing all the shots – see what works for you and just how important your wicket is at the time.

Rely on your strengths and strong shots, whatever they might be, to pick up runs safely and easily whilst still new to the crease. We must try to play percentage cricket while we are new to the crease, and cut out any risky shots and possibilities of getting out cheaply and unnecessarily in the beginning of our innings when we are not warmed up or played in yet.

The most important lesson in batting you will ever get:

As we spoke about earlier in regard our backlift and playing dead straight in defence, one more point needs to be conveyed, and that is in regard our foot work. Whilst playing defensive shots off front and back foot it is advised to get your foot to the line of the ball. That is get your foot moving so that your body and weight is directly behind the ball and you can bring your bat down straight to defend. We must get our body right in behind the ball so that we are not caught fishing or flirting for the ball and playing away from our body – something which leads to edges and caught behinds.[29] We want to be tight whilst defending and play close to our body and not be caught playing away from our body whilst simply defending a good ball. The trick to this is getting our foot to the line of the ball and having our body and our entire weight directly behind the ball before we poke our bat out to hit it with soft hands. So all we have to do here is pick up the line once it hits the pitch and get either our front foot forward in line with the ball or our back foot back in line with the ball's pitch or line, and simply use our bat and hands to open or close the face if the ball deviates from this line and deviates late. The key is to make up your mind

---

[29] KL Rahul was guilty of this not only in WCsemifinal vs NZ but afterwards against WI in test match series – don't repeat this mistake if you are a serious batsman.

early whether you are required to attack or defend depending on the ball's accuracy. If it's a good ball and we feel the need to defend we must wholeheartedly get our body right in behind the line of the ball and play with soft hands, but try in any cost to not be poking or fishing for the ball outside off stump and playing your defensive shots away from the body where your bat is fishing or flirting for the ball. This is the single most important thing that you should master as a batsman and the skill which is going to help you stay at the crease and make big scores – getting in behind the ball in defense that is, and bringing the bat down straight as possible. Sometimes you will be required to open/close the face and sometimes you will be required to move the bat out of the way and leave the ball go. But remember the process outlined above in negotiating accurate good balls, and you will be well on your way to doing something even the international players struggle to do.[30]

Diagram XVI:

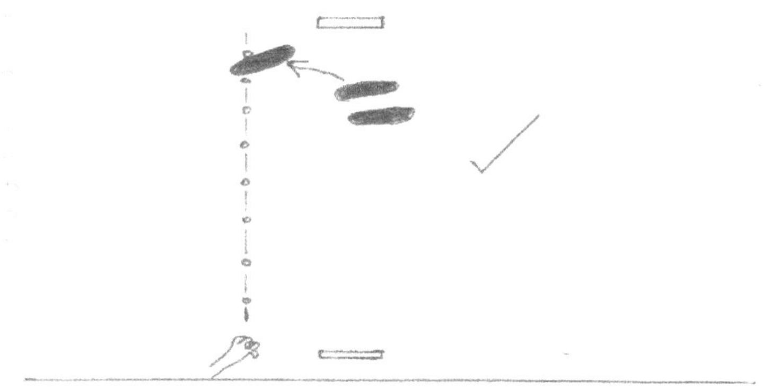

[30] KL Rahul is not the only one who has not mastered this skill there are so many, but majority of batsmen do know it

Important lesson on batting continued: Front foot defence

Both backfoot and front foot defence is required when the ball is well directed and pitched on a length which is hard to score off, however there are criteria as to how to play them and which foot to play them off.

Diagram XVI:

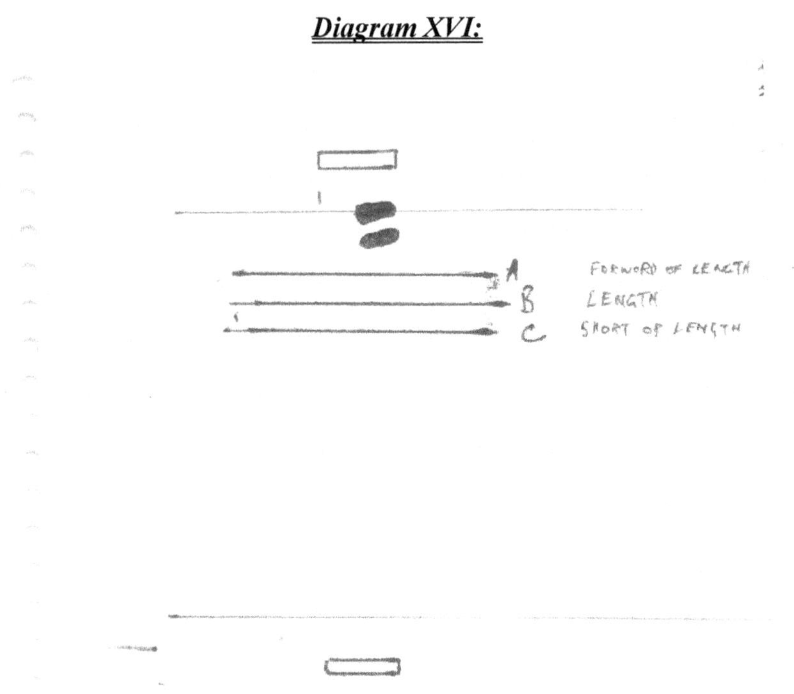

When the ball is pitched up at point A, we play off front foot always but we play off the toes of our leading foot and play with soft hands and a dead bat. When the ball is at point B, we also play off front foot but not so much the toes but with our foot grounded normally and slightly more harder hands. When the ball is at point C, we either lunge out onto our front foot with front leg stretched and play with a solid face and hard hands, or we can go onto back foot and play with soft hands. This is dependent upon whether the bowler is getting movement off the pitch and there are two ways to play this ball in order to protect ourselves from this tough 'rattle' ball. If the bowler is getting inswing and incut or outswing and outcut, we can opt to play the ball late and off the back foot so as to protect ourselves from the ball cutting in and going through the gate and in between bat and pad and giving a bowled, or moving out and catching the outside edge for a caught behind. If the ball is swinging out we should lunge out and play off front foot with hard hands and full face of bat so as to avoid getting an outside edge and caught behind.

Our defensive technique is 70% of our game and technique as batsmen, and it is our defensive technique which should preoccupy 70% of our energies and thought processes early in the beginning of our innings. The defensive aspect to batting can be said to be more mental and our attacking shots or scoring shots can be said to be more physical –consistent with what we opined in earlier chapters about the challenge of cricket being 70% mental and 30% physical at the higher levels.

As far as vision and seeing the ball goes, in the start of the innings try zone in on the off stump and offside as opposed to the middle or leg side, and prepare yourself for the deliveries aimed at the offside which may swing or be very accurate in regard length.

In the beginning, until you get your 'eye in' that is, try use your strong shots to get runs and if you are weak in certain shots just try cut them out. For example, some players like Ganguly are strong at offside play but not so good in leg side play – wedon't want you to cut out legside shots for ever but just in the beginning of his innings in case you mis-time it or mis-hit it whilst fresh at the crease. Generally, as batsmen when we start our innings we don't want to miscue and give a catch, so we must look out for and store in our minds where the close in fielders are in addition to memorizing where the big gaps in the field are. As batsmen, ideally we want to be looking out for where the empty spaces and gaps are, however early in our innings we must look out for any close in in-fielders or any peculiar field positions, particularly in-close. Once you are played in, we tend to memorize the empty spaces and nothing else, but we must guard from the miscue early on and at any stage of our innings for that matter.

Chapter Nine

Choosing Your Bat

It looks so daunting, when we first walk into a sport shop and see hundreds of bats and are forced to decide on just one, the one which is right for us and our game – how do we choose? How do we know? Who do we ask? Well it all comes down to a few basic things, most bats only come in a few different styles and shapes the rest of the variation is just in brand and make etc.

Well the trick is to decide on the right bat suited best to the style of your batting and the style of your game, also to your height and build as well. Here are a few general rules of thumb which players use to customize their bats for match conditions according to their style, strength and physique and sometimes even according to the pitch but this is not so important.

- If your stocky and well-built you generally have more tensile property in your body and your body withstands movements and stress in any direction without jolting or jerking, especially stress forces which batting is full of – this person can afford a heavier bat as the body can withstand the stress forces going through the body

- If you are a strong bottom-hand player often known as someone good at the all-or-nothing shots, the big shots or the cross-bat-shots, then this person often requires and prefers a heavier bat – these players are good enough and prepared to commit in their footwork early enough to give a good wield of the bat and want full value in the form of a heavy powerful bat

So as far as weight of the bat is concerned, this equates to strong cutters, pullers & drivers on-the-up demanding a slightly heavier bat as opposed to touch-players or wristy players wanting a slightly lighter bat – one which allows for adjustment of stroke and footwork at last second as well as creation, generation and perfection of timing certain wristy shots and getting their timing going. [31]

- For those who like playing-in-the-V, you are presenting a straight perpendicular bat to the ball most of the time as opposed to a cross bat, so your bat can maybe be a bit longer than normal in case of any deviation up-and-down ways.

- For those who like driving, playing in the V and especially driving-on-the-up, you can maybe even consider having a higher sweet-spot or middle to help you middle those drives on-the-rise.

- For those playing on low pitches – have a lower middle or let the meat of the bat start lower down so you can middle your drives

- For those playing on bouncy pitches – have a higher middle or sweet-spot and maybe consider dropping the weight slightly

---

[31]Note Tendulkar is a strong bottom-hand player and also stocky build – he uses a heavier bat, the heaviest in the game in fact; Azharuddin is lean in build and also more a touch/timing player – he uses one of the lightest bats in the game

- Shorter players may need a higher middle – but not necessarily

- Lean, lanky and thin people are advised against a bat on the heavier side – you may not get the right batting rhythm and forces going for yourself if the bat is heavier proportionately to your body

So we can opt for a shorter or longer bat known as the long-handle or short-handle, depending on our regularity at playing in the V, our height and the pitch being bouncy or keeping low.

Use these criteria as a way of analyzing and appraising yourself as a batsman and your style and just use your common sense, based on the afore-mentioned theories about how you would customize a bat for yourself. Even the greats do it that way, so just use your cricketing brain a little bit, have a think about it and decide on a few options before you decide on the absolute final option for yourself – don't just walk into the bat shop before you have done your homework about what bat is right for your technique and build etc.[32]

Just a small note on the curve. Well, all bats have some curve but some have a more pronounced curve than others and some are more on the straighter side. While the curve is not such an important factor in helping you play your natural game to your best ability, we will just talk about it briefly to help you decide which way you want to opt – greater curve or lesser curve, either way it is not a significant determining factor in defensive technique and your ability to perform 90% of shots anyway.

---

[32]Note: Tendulkar is also a strong player in the V and on the up – he uses a short-handle, that is where the blade is longer and the handle shorter

The curve is designed for two things, apart from overall weight-distribution and the way the bat feels – known as 'pick-up', the functionality of curved bats has two main advantages. Firstly it is usually sought by players who like to flick or scoop the ball with the wrists from around or outside off-stump to mid-wicket or even behind square-leg, the curve assists in generating this scoop motion which the batsman is trying to make with the use of the wrists at the last second[33]. Secondly, for off-side players and cutters the curve gives the batsman a fraction of a second extra so that even if he is late playing a square-cut and might have played a late-cut for the ball hurrying onto him, because of the curve he can still comfortably place the ball toward point and play a square-cut like stroke. The disadvantage of the curve is you really must get your head down and on top of the ball whilst playing straight drives or you might scoop it up for a catch, especially off slow bowlers – some batsman like to change their bat when a spinner comes on to a straighter bat, but then the same advantage of being able to scoop the ball with the wrists from outside off is lost.

So unless we are a Tendulkar, an Azharuddin or a Kohli, then the curved bat may not offer any advantages for us until we actually reach this level in our game and start playing these particular shots both off pacers and spinners – but by all means buy a curved bat if you are more a wristy player so that you can develop these shots.[34]

---

[33]This shot was best played by Azharuddin and Tendulkar – their bats also have a slight pronounced curve as opposed to being just straight like other players
[34]These days you can have a bat custom made, just like the stars and pros do, within a reasonable cost - there are places online, they do it in UK and I am sure if you find out maybe India also.

COACHES:

"Always keep a well curved bat in the kit and make students practice their straight drives off pacers with this bat – this is the best way to learn to keep the ball along the ground whilst driving!...especially whilst practicing the drive on-the-up along the ground and the back foot punch"

Chapter Ten

Batting Technique: All The Shots In The Book

In this chapter we detail all the different cricketing shots we need to know how to play in order to be a good batsman, and the nuances and technical finer points to remember whilst playing them – hopefully with this basic guide and the basic tips provided, you will see an improvement in some or all of your cricketing shots and improve your all-around-the-wicket stroke-play, whilst being able to defend the good balls also. We are basically following the coaching manual and what our coaches are saying in this section about playing good cricketing shots whilst batting, but we have added any extra or finer detail we think you need to be aware of and which could help you as an additional guide to your existing understanding of good cricketing shots from your coach or existing knowledge.

Here is a list of the typical cricketing shots which we often speak of in cricket and in batting:

- On-drive
- Off-drive
- Straight-drive
- Cover-drive
- Square-cut
- Late-cut
- Leg glance
- Pull-shot

- Hook-shot
- Square-drive
- Drive through mid-wicket
- Flick off the pads
- Cow-shot
- Drive on the rise
- Back foot punch

There are obviously more shots including lofted and inside out and flick shots, but almost all shots in batting are a derivative or a combination of the above-mentioned typical or standard ones.

Before we begin, let us outline and stress some of the hallmarks or cornerstones associated with a good batting technique and one which is considered 'correct' according to classical Test match cricket guidelines, and highlight the main points to remember whilst batting in order to conduct our work as a batsman in the best possible way and one which is going to give us a strong foundation upon which to build on for more advanced batting techniques and strategies down the track. These are listed as follows:

- Elbow up
- Head down
- Bat-speed whilst playing attacking shots
- Straight bat in defence
- Foot to the pitch of the ball
- Bat and pad close together
- Good temperament

- Shot-selection
- Playing in the-V
- Eye on the ball
- Good timing
- Use of the wrists in 'flicking' the ball to onside
- Playing through the ball with the hands
- Use of soft hands whilst defending and playing late cuts
- Picking the length and seeing the ball well – having a good eye
- Playing on both sides of the wicket
- Let the ball come to you
- Make the bowler bowl to you[35]
- Building an innings through patience, shot-selection, concentration and a sound defensive technique

Along with keeping our eye on the ball, keeping our head down and accounting for the length ball early in our innings by playing with a dead straight bat, these are just some of the things which come to mind when we think of good batting and correct batting technique.

Now that you have read the chapter on seeing the ball and vector forces, now is a good time to iterate the fact that it is impossible when bowlers are bowling at that speed and ferocity to watch the ball entirely from release and on to the bat – that is to watch the ball all the way on to the bat. We must detect the vector force on the ball as it comes out of the hand and keep our head down and elbow up. Once the vector force has been imparted and the ball has been delivered from the hand, we must then keep

---

[35]Play ball close to the body only and don't flirt or chase the ball outside off stump

the focus of our vision on the pitch and where exactly on the pitch the ball is predicted to land – this is what is known as keeping our head down. We don't want to be watching and keeping our focus of vision on the bowler and his hand the whole time, once it has been delivered we must get our head down and get ready to position ourselves to play the ball as it pitches, bounces and approaches our bat. As the saying goes, 'playing the man and not playing the ball'; we do not want to commit this mistake. We do NOT want to watch the bowler and his hand the whole time and allow our head to be floating in the air, instead we want to predict the ball's trajectory or path or as we mentioned, it's resultant path, and then do our best to get in position and play the ball – we DO NOT care who the bowler is and do not want to keep our focus of vision on the bowler, we want to prepare for the resultant path the ball will take once it bounces according to our judgement and get our feet moving accordingly and get our head down as soon as we can.

Whilst facing pacers and that too fast ones and good quality ones, it is imperative that we keep our focus of vision on the pitch and where the ball is about to pitch. Going back to the technique we theorized in previous chapters about secondary vision versus primary vision and the way to see and keep our eye on the ball, we must apply a similar method here also. We must watch the ball like a hawk to at least mostly if not entirely and correctly pick up the vector force being put on the ball, but we must also watch the pitch too so we can actually see where the ball is landing and prepare to play a shot – remember we have already picked up and predicted the ball's speed and to a greater extent it's landing position, now its just a matter of actually getting in position and playing the ball. How would we do this with our head still up waiving in the air and watching the bowler or man once the ball is delivered and is now about to take its resultant path by first bouncing somewhere on the pitch and then rising up there afterwards – we couldn't, we must now get our head down and shift our vision to the pitch and seeing the ball bounce and subsequently playing the ball. Now, both these aspects of playing the ball are equally as important, seeing it out the hand whilst our head is up AND seeing the ball off the pitch whilst keeping our head down – how do we decide in regards our primary vision versus secondary vision in this case?

Well we don't take our stance with our head down do we? We bring our head down after the ball is bowled and is about to pitch, so lets just follow our instinct here. As 90% percent of our task is to actually predict the ball out of the hand and the vector force's initial or starting vector, it makes sense to concentrate our vision on the ball upon release, out of the bowler's hand that is, and devote the majority of our watching and seeing energy towards doing this well. So we want to be watching the bowler's hand like a hawk and let this be the focus of our primary vision, and allow the act of actually 'picking the length'(predicting the length and position of the ball, as previous chapters opined) to be of primary significance. Once we have picked the vector force and the rough path the ball will take, we want to THEN and only then focus on seeing the ball actually bounce and get our feet into position. That is our footwork, keeping our head down and watching the ball hit the pitch after delivery is what we can say the secondary task in our visionary task or sequence of events in our task as batsmen.

Now that you know why it is important to get your head down let us talk about why the coaching manual advocates to get our elbow up whilst playing both off the back foot and front foot. Well the main reason is that it helps give our shots direction and helps us to not only put more batspeed and force into our shots, but allows us to place the ball and pierce the field and find the gap whilst batting – something which is imperative to you batsmen in actually scoring more runs. That is why we must practice using our elbow as a power generator and a director or field piercer in our stroke-play.

Ok, so now that you have a better overview of batting let us get down to coaching you on the major cricketing shots. Try to read this carefully and study it on paper, and try pick up and study the different techniques and tips suggested for different shots and how they vary from shot to shot and their subtleties.

Straight-drive: played when the ball's line is on the stumps anywhere from leg to off, and the ball is pitched up at a half-volley.Sometimes a full follow through with elbow up is required and sometimes a mere 'punch' with correct timing is all that is required. Foot is placed inside the line of the ball usually and bat and pad are close together.

Offdrive: Played when the ball pitches on off stump or slightly outside off-stump and on a half volley. Almost always is guided by the elbow up and full follow through with the elbow and bat through the line of the ball. Foot is placed inside the line of the ball usually and bat and pad close together.

Cover-drive: Played when the ball pitches outside off-stump but not too wide, and on a half volley. Almost always is guided by the elbow up and full follow through with the elbow and bat through the line of the ball. Foot is placed inside the line of the ball usually.

On-drive: Played when the ball pitches on middle or leg and a half volley. Guided by the elbow like the other drives, only here we almost square up and play the ball with our head over the ball and over our feet, and timing as opposed to full follow through. Just a little well timed punch is usually required here and stay on your toes during execution and not your full foot grounded.

Square-cut: played when the ball is short and outside off-stump. Usually the tiny movement forward with front foot and then launch back off this foot to transfer all your weight onto your back foot, get your head over the ball and strike with the elbow pointing toward cover and guiding the placement. Either roll the wrists to keep the ball down, or slightly raise elbow and try get under the ball to loft it or hit in the air.

Late-cut: same as if playing a cut shot in the air with the elbow slightly higher and slightly higher than the bat. Play the ball late and concentrate on timing and making contact with the ball late but off the middle or sweet spot still. We can hit through the line of the ball with an opened face, or we can just let the ball come to us and use a deft touch to deflect the ball behind point.

Leg-glance: Get in position exactly as if you were playing an on-drive with weight on your toes of front foot, and follow through straight, only here we flick and close the face of the bat at the last second. Lead with your elbow as if you were playing a straight drive or on-drive and flick with the wrists at the last moment or roll the wrists at the last moment.

Pull-shot: don not go forward with your front foot, instead go all the way back and across onto your back foot, and try get outside the line of the ball as much as possible. Then hit through the ball with a horizontal bat and twist and swivel through your back and hips to generate more power. Roll the wrists over the ball.

Hook-shot: Exactly the same as the pull shot, only try get underneath it and loft it if you are playing in the air. If playing on the ground the same technique of rolling the wrists over the ball is all that is necessary.

Square drive: Weight is on the front foot but we do not want to lean into the ball, instead we want to keep our feet position still once we have brought our front foot forward, and stroke the ball through covers and point with a slightly angled bat and on the rise with timing. This is a hard shot to play and teach – seek further coaching if necessary.

Drive through mid-wicket: played when ball is pitched up and on or around leg-stump. Get your feet slightly forward or even just in a neutral position, keep your weight on the toes and punch the ball with timing and again use elbow to place and direct your shot. Play ball along ground usually.

Flick off the pads: can be played off front foot or back foot, and requires you to get your head down and elbow up also. Usually played to ball on a length or just short of a length – watch Tendulkar against fast bowlers when in form to learn this stroke. It is a hard stroke and an attacking stroke played to a relatively good ball, but requires the elbow and head over the ball for its direction and execution. Relies heavily on the flick of the wrists at last moment – again it's a hard shot watch Tendulkar to learn this shot

Cow-shot: does not require raising your elbow or using the elbow in creating direction, but does require you to watch the ball well and keep your head down. Create room for the big wind and follow through of the bat aiming at midwicket. Usually try to hit it for six or four – it is not an accumulating shot but one of the most attacking and ferocious shots in cricket. Make room for the big swing by placing left foot wide of leg-stump and to the left as much as you can, that is place your front foot to the most leftward position possible to give the bat which is coming from the right side and give yourself maximum room to swing through ferociously. Try hit as hard as can yet place the ball too.

Drive-on-the-rise: Played to a ball which is not that full and not a half volley, usually around a length or just above or short of a length. Best played with elbow taking the lead and generating all the force. Hands and back lift are brought higher so as to follow through the ball just like any other drive and keep the ball along the ground. Best played by Aravinda DeSilva. Can be played to spinners or quicks, can be played straight or square and through point. This is essentially what a square drive is – a drive on the rise.

Back-foot-punch: played to a ball on or outside off stump and either on a length or just short of a length. Elbow is used heavily to generate power and direction. Get elbow up nice and high and lift hands and backlift a bit higher just as in playing on the rise. Jab at the ball with timing yet still follow through with the elbow and bat too. Main thing is to punch the ball with timing and with a short sharp strong jab like motion.

As we are training ourselves to first be a classical text-book batsman in the mold of a Test-cricketer, we are not going to talk about the other shots which we mentioned are usually a derivative of these main ones. We want to build a strong base and learn and engrain the fundamentals of batting first before we begin practicing advanced one-day cricketing shots.

The physical aspects of batting are not so hard and are relatively concrete or 'set in stone', and are learnt and practiced as per the batting textbook and as per our coach's instruction. We are only helping you notice the differences in the various cricketing shots you need to master, and helping you notice and pick up on the differences in technique and footwork required. Hopefully you will have an appreciation of the subtle differences in technique for different shots – batting truly is a science and you have to get used to implementing this idea in your quest for better batting and a better all round game and scoring rate – the fact that batting is a Science more so than an Art!.

If you do wish to be coached on the nuances of batting technique and stroke-play, and can't afford joining an academy or getting coaching, we recommend reading 'The elite batter', which is available from Amazon E-Books store for under 4USD. However this book is all you should really need as you are probably already a good if not intermediate level cricketer to begin with.

The number one thing which will advance your technique and batting prowess is footwork, timing, picking the length and having a sound defensive technique, especially playing the good length ball which may deviate late; and so appropriately, this is what we have focused on in the batting section of this book. Being able to adjust your backlift according to the situation also plays a big part in our keeping our wicket and hitting the ball with power and timing.

The ideal back-lift and the one which generates the most power and bat-speed in our shots comes down from first or second slip or even 3rd slip, but we must first negotiate the good balls if we are to even keep our wicket. So what do we do? We basically have to have a straight backlift early in the innings and slowly bring it around to 1st or 2nd slip as we get more confident. We can't be expected to hit powerfully and score fast and hit across the line toward the end with a straight back lift, but we are only asking you to do this in the start of your innings when you are not seeing the ball quickly enough.

Chapter Eleven

Computing & A Scientific Approach To Shot Selection

"The mind is an athlete"

— Bryce Courtenay, The Power of One

Imagine your body as being the computer or even a robot and your mind as being the programmer, your body is acting like a puppet at the strings and whims of what your mind is instructing it to do, and even better, what we are aiming for here and through this approach to batting, what it has been pre-programmed to do. We want to pre-program your body through a specialized and specific training/practice regime to automatically re-act to the ball in a game situation without our mind even thinking – would not that be a dream and would not that be nice. Well with the advent of computer programming in the form of computer code which is being used throughout millions of industries and applications, this is no longer a dream within the grasps of mere mortals like Tendulkar and Kohli when in form, it is reality and if you master this chapter you can too!.

If we can successfully start thinking and playing like a pre-programmed computer in our daily and everyday batting routines, we suddenly raise our playing potential and capacity to 'play big' substantially, and we too can have the flourishing stroke play of the aforementioned greats when in full flight. We are about to teach what is considered the most crucial component of good batting in this chapter – prudent shot selection, so put your cricketing caps on and try to challenge what we are teaching you in your mind and study it carefully so that you slowly start understanding the what and why of this model we are making you read, and why we are even making you read it. This is the best way to learn something new and something hard to grasp - by being critical and questioning why!

Picture the greatest batsmen of the world, the Tendulkars, Laras, Mark Waughs, Sehwags and Kohlis. They do everything right from seeing the ball, picking the length, moving the feet, adjusting the back-lift to timing the ball to using the wrists and elbows in their shots – as if it were poetry in motion. Don't we also want to one day have great stroke-play, technique and stroke-selection and be great like them too? Of course you do! Well what these ultimate performers and athletes in their field are doing is not so much poetry in motion or art or individualism in a strict sense or any sense, but more a scientific approach to their batting, and this will be the focus of the chapter – how we too can accomplish the great technique and superb shot-selection almost as if you were watching a perfectly programmed robot in motion which can make no mistake, and all through a specialized approach to batting incorporating linear computer programming and **CONDITIONAL LOGIC**.

Like we said earlier, the greatest talent a batsman can have is what's in between the ears and through the application of this new and revolutionary approach to looking at and practicing batting, hopefully we can not only improve our stroke-selection but perfect it and give ourselves a significant advantage in our overall technique.

What makes these guys the top of their field are a multitude of factors but the greatest is ultimately stroke-selection – that is to play the right shot to the right ball, and that is what batting is afterall, right? Or better yet, that is basically and essentially all batting is! Well at the highest level it may involve a certain degree of improvisation or art and being able to be flexible in regard which shot you are playing to which ball and being able to play many different shots to the same ball, but this stage of batting is the very last and most advanced stage of batting – this stage of batting is not reached even by international batsman as perfecting the first stage, the one which we are talking about currently, is a hard enough task and hard enough journey, so don't worry about the final stages just yet lets focus on developing our stroke-selection abilities from scratch first and developing them correctly. We are laying the foundation for all you aspiring batsman out there and batsman who have ambitions of sailing the deep ocean or rocking the boat so to speak, and ambition without knowledge or understanding is like a boat in no water, so try your best at perfecting your stroke selection – hopefully this chapter will see a marked improvement in your footwork and ability to pick your shots and pick your balls and you will be on your way to sailing the deeper oceans.

Once we have a good system and program for overall batting technique or what we would call textbook batting or classical batting, we will develop a more refined and more detailed program for batsman-ship in limited overs cricket and one which contains more attacking and improvised shots, and one which is based on and designed for more advanced stages of batsman-ship.

We will be using a simple construct of linear computer programming known as **IF; THEN; ELSE or IF; AND; THEN; ELSE**, and the basic notations and layout used in linear programming code. However, we will present this in what is known as pseudo code, that is a code which is comprehendible to the layman and does not require an understanding of the syntax of the language you are programming in, and can be easily understood by all. When we get into and write pseudo code for the more advanced stages of batting which as we talked about earlier centre around improvisation and being able to play multiple shots to the same ball or so to say 'think outside the box' and play more creative shots, we will introduce and use what are known as NESTED statements and LOOPS. These serve to add detail and more possible actions to the already existing action suggested to be taken, which in this case is the particular shot you will be playing to that ball and how you ultimately 'compute' this decision, and will teach you to play and bat better in one-day cricket where we sometimes need to play attacking shots no matter what the ball is or where it is pitched. We could present our model, our model of stroke-selection that is, in a more formal and standard syntax or language used in programming languages such as C# or JAVA, but this is outside the scope of its practical application which in this case is to simply select a shot according to the ball, and is not necessary and may not be understood without a deeper understanding of computer programming. So we have kept it pretty simple and comprehendible and the nested statements and loops will be omitted for now, as we want you to master the fundamentals of orthodox batting stroke-selection first and foremost and before we take you through the advanced stages of one-day batsman-ship which can become a little more complicated and a handful to handle to someone just learning this computer-based model to developing good shot-selection. In the next book, ‘The algorithm and logic of one-day batting’, we will delve into the mastery of shot-selection, but just get used to understanding our introductory model first.

Let’s get you introduced to the basic IF, THEN, ELSE statements through some simple examples so we can begin using it to improve our batting technique.

IF: time is = or < 9.00am

    THEN: “continue sleeping”

    ELSE: “wakeup”

ENDIF

IF: it is raining

    THEN: “take umbrella with you”

    ELSE: “leave umbrella at home”

ENDIF

IF: ball is on pitch

    THEN: “prepare to bring bat down & play at ball”

    ELSE: “stop at back-lift and do not play at ball”

ENDIF

These are basically testing for a condition and if it is true then a certain action is taken, but if it is false then another action is taken. But what if we want to test for two conditions before we decide to take an action? Well then we need to use what is called the IF; AND; THEN; ELSE programming construct.

IF: it is raining

AND: decide to go outside

    THEN: "take umbrella with you"

    ELSE: "leave umbrella at home"

ENDIF

IF: it is not raining

    THEN: "go outside"

    AND: "leave umbrella at home"

ELSE: "do not go outside"

ENDIF

So it is not that hard to understand I hope, and hopefully now you have an idea of how we can take a computer to be our mind and our body merely a puppet acting according to its computed course of action and that we can run certain logical tests to make it generate an outcome or a particular instruction or set of instructions for any given condition. We want to pre-program your mind to give your body a certain instruction or set of instructions based on the occurrence of a condition or a true or false logical test, and we want our mind and our vision of the ball and the way we see the ball to work like a computer and generate the necessary action we should take in the form of our response or stroke-selection to a particular ball, all in the space of milliseconds – yes it is possible and this is how the great batters' mind also works when they are in form it's just we can't see it.

Let's take it step by step and suggest some possible pseudo code for batting in it's most fundamental or elementary form, that is going forward or back with our feet, playing an attacking shot as opposed to a defensive one& position of our back-lift, just to mention a few of the very basic decisions or computations required in batting.

By thinking in terms of computer code and thinking like a computer, we want to better train our eye to see the ball, pick up the length, get into position and choose our stroke to any particular ball. Through this exercise, we are essentially trying to build our skills in stroke-selection and seeing the ball, such that we too can bat and play like a pre-programmed robot which makes no mistakes. As the saying goes computers are always right and never make mistakes, whereas humans do!

Here are some logical tests we want our mind which is working like a computer by now I hope, to perform before we decide to play at the ball. By reading these examples, thinking them over and studying them on paper, you will no doubt become more adept at seeing the ball and developing a good sound fundamental batting technique, and one according to the textbook.

IF: ball is pitched on a length
AND: is coming on the stumps
AND: you are in the first 15 balls of your innings

> **THEN:** "play forward defense, soft hands, straight backlift"
> **ELSE:** "leave ball go through to keeper"

ENDIF

IF: ball is pitched on a length
AND: is coming on the stumps
AND: you are past the first 15 balls of your innings
    THEN: "play flick off the back foot through mid-wicket"
    ELSE: "play drive on the rise or on the up"
    ELSE: "play forward defense, soft hands, straightbacklift"
ENDIF

Note, through this last example we are coming closer and closer to detailing the full and complete computer code which applies to batting, however we do not want to do this, at least not in this edition of the book, as documenting the linear code and conditional logic protocol used in batting would be like revealing the cure to cancer. It is a very complex algorithm which would be generated and would obstruct your ability to understand and master the base code – and we don't want to do this, to impede your mastery of the basics that is!

All we want to do at this stage is make you aware of the computer like thinking necessary in good shot-selection, and provide you with the basic and fundamental code required and used in developing classical and fundamental technique and approach to batting. In a nutshell we are trying to get youngsters and beginners to successfully develop sound basic and fundamental technique and make those who are already quite decent in shot-selection to further consolidate their fundamental approach to batting and shot selection such that it just clicks into gear on match day.

If we were to reveal this elixir of batting, the exact and mathematical decision process involved in shot-selection that is and for every possible scenario, we would be overloading you with too much too soon and we don't want to reveal this to the world just yet. Essentially all it takes is someone who has an understanding of computer programming and knows enough about it, or someone who studies the subject for 2 days and reads this code, and suddenly they have the entire act of batting mapped out and before their eyes almost like mapping the cure to cancer. We want to allow you sufficient time and opportunity to practice and gain a personal understanding of batsman-ship and shot-selection and this introductory version of our model of shot-selection, such that there are no ifs and buts in developing correct technique early on.

However, cut to the point, we just don't want to bombard you with a detailed and thorough algorithm or linear code designed for the most advanced stages of batsman-ship and developing a high scoring rate, as it may impede your preliminary practice and ability to understand our model and develop the basics of good batting technique and shot-selection. It may be too much too soon and we want you to get the best possible practice and preparation first in honing your basics in regard shot-selection and technique advocated by this model of stroke-selection. It is important you get your head around it first and start thinking and moving like a computer to the best of your ability such that you are prepared for incorporating more advanced shots into your technique later down the track.

In the next book titled, "The Algorithm and Logic of One-day Batting', we will give you this code but for now we have given you the very rudimentary and base code used in batting – by all means if you are computer software or computer code inclined, you can develop your own protocol or model of 'batting code' and one which is more in depth.

A world where ingenuity, individualism and creativity is valued and respected is all well and fine, but through this model we wish to build a batsman which is pre-programmed to play like a robot and like a master and one which follows the one and only one correct or ideal way of batting – yes, we want everyone to bat like a master and a robot and according to the one 'correct' way and computational decision process in regard to shot-selection. We want to create a world of Tendulkars and Kohlis and a world of batsmen who are perfect, even if it means corroding the values of fair competition, individualism and creativity generally recognized in sports.

The idea of this approach to batting and the code we are going to generate in order to help us choose our movements and stroke play to individual deliveries, is unlike the conventional section chart which shows corresponding shot selection according to certain areas the ball may pitch. In our model, we use a set of 'linear instructions' to guide our decision process just as if we were a computer being instructed or hand held through each and every mental process involved in seeing and hitting the ball.[36]

As we said before about the approach to effective footwork which we advocate as being best to learn, we need to elaborate a little on this before we proceed. As we begin to take a little step forward with our front foot we want our back lift to be in peak position or at the very top or highest point, or as cricketers often say, in it's cocked position. We want our back lift to be coming down in tandem with our foot moving forward and for these two movements to happen simultaneously. This is so we have maximum forward motion with both, as it is these movements which are

---

[36]You will see an example of this 'section chart' in regard shot-selection, on the NCA's official coaching page website under the batting PDF file.

priming us to position ourselves and ultimately hit through the ball with bat speed and force. Most deliveries you will face let's say around 70%, will be around a length or pitched up and only some will be loose or pitched short – that is why we advocate using this approach to footwork as it allows us to lean into the ball and position ourselves for the majority of balls and the majority of shots which are required to be played off the front foot – no wonder it is a well documented and used technique to footwork.

Offside drive Vs Onside drive

IF: pitched up

AND: on offside

THEN: continue little step forward toward pitch of ball, drive through covers

ELSE: Take only little step forward; get front on; drive through midwicket and mid-on

ENDIF

****Pitched very short Vs less short or pitched up***

IF: pitched short and pick up early

THEN: move back foot back and cut/hook/pull

ELSE: continue with small step forward and prepare for front foot shot

ENDIF

Pitched short offside Vs pitched short onside:

IF: pitched short

AND: on offside

THEN: bounce off little step forward onto back foot(but notback and across, only back!), playcutshot

ELSE: bounce off little step forward, move back foot back and across, prepare to play horizontal bat shot through onside

ENDIF

Backlift during 1st 15 balls Vs post 15 balls:

IF: 1st 15 balls

THEN: backlift/follow through dead straight and play in the V

ELSE: bring backlift from 2nd or 3rd slip and generate batspeed

ENDIF

Primary Vs Peripheral vision:

IF: 1st 15 balls

THEN: primary vision looking out for defensive shot

ELSE: primary vision looking out for attacking shot

ENDIF

So there we have it, through these last six pseudo code examples, we have witnessed conditional logic in motion and developed what you could call the complete decision-process of batting or the top-down approach to batting in its simplest and orthodox style. Sounds pretty simple and too easy to be true, but that's what we want, we want to simplify batting in our early stages of training and train our ability to pick the length and select our stroke, in the most simple and uncomplicated manner possible. That is, we want to make batting and the mental task of shot-selection as clear, plain and uncomplicated as possible, and practice and engrain this in our sub-conscious minds, and then, build upon this base code and add further conditions and further possible options in shot selection.[37]

This is a very important part of your journey as a batsman as you need to really practice this uncomplicated approach to batting well and engrain it into your sub conscious mind – something which we sometimes call 'muscle memory', the ability of our muscles, in this case being our shot-selection decision process, to work according to how they have been trained to work and how our muscles have stored particular actions to particular scenarios within the memory, and can just fire in a certain way in match conditions. Remember, we want our mind to work like a computer and our body to react like a pre-programmed robot, and in order to do this we must pick the length and get into position as quickly as is humanly possible – that is what batting and shot-selection is about. We can't re-iterate, that you must practice according to the training protocol advocated in the seeing the ball chapters and the one presented through our pseudo code examples, and practice them well as this is what is going to help you to be an improvising, exciting and big-name batsman down the track. You can't be a Tendulkar or Kohli who can play all the shots and more and who have taken one-day batting to an entirely different level overnight – it takes gradual and systematic practice and the attaining and

---

[37]Lets take this code as getting you up to the level of a good opening or top order batsmen with classical technique, say in the mold of a Manjrekar, however maybe not with the big hitting or fast scoring potential of a Kohli or Jayasuriya, who improvise and can play multiple shots to the same ball.

surpassing of individual training milestones, and in this case the mastery over grasping and applying our 'base code' to batting.
There are two ways we can achieve this straight back-lift. One is by starting our back lift in a straight position and bringing it down straight upon follow through, and the other is by taking guard with back lift at 2nd slip and then bringing it around to be straight and then following through straight.

Conclusion:

Batting and good shot-selection is merely just conditional logic in motion. Whilst batting, if we think of ourselves as a computer and train our body to re-act as a computer would, then we are well on our way to being a sound, solid and technically correct orthodox batsman. Upon mastering this chapter your batting can only get better and better from here on in and you are etching closer and closer to batting like a Sehwag or Viv Richards down the track.

We come to the conclusion that Tendulkar and Aravinda De Silva were the two most technically correct, mentally astute and mentally tough batsmen ever to play the game. Along with their ability to adjust the technique, backlift and visionary process, these two exhibited a perfect shot-selection process almost as if you were watching a computer which can do no wrong![38] They were the two most capable and astute innings

---

[38] Watch Aravinda's 107* Aust vs SL WC1996final. Watch his playing in the V early and then accelerating once played in and playing on-the-rise, and all via playing good cricketing shots and being adept in picking the length early.

builders and could adjust into batting in cement mode when necessary – something which is critical if the team is in need of big runs and big scores.

50 over cricket Vs 20 over cricket:

Refer to the Gantt charts or schedule charts on the following page as a guide in regards how you should be approaching your batting and how do you determine what your mindset will be. This is just a guide and does not need to be strictly followed but it is basically something similar or pretty close to what a batsman's approach and mindset would be whilst batting in limited over cricket, a mature or calculative approach you could say, and one which wards off the threat of the batting unit having a collapse and posting a sultry total.

We are basically doing the same things in both formats of the game, 50 over and 20 over that is, only in 20 over formats as we see on the gantt we get a much less 'sighter' period to play in the V and be in defensive mode and that we must almost immediately start endeavouring to pick up twos and threes after a few overs. That is the thrill of 20-20 cricket, the fact that batsmen can't afford to have such a lengthy sighter period and that they have to hit the ground running and immediately start playing in cement mode and trying to force the pace – play baseball as we opined in earlier chapters. So if playing 20-20 cricket we need to start attacking almost from the word go and be on the look-out for big scoring shots as opposed to playing in the V in attempt to ward off the 'rattle ball', and need to keep the scoring rate flowing as opposed to keeping wickets intact. This style of cricket, 20-20 that is, is basically like a 50 over game only in 'fast forward', and demands of a batter to have got his eye in or played himself in much before he even faces the first ball. Yes, that's right, 20-20 batting is all about having a good net session prior match day and practicing free-flowing batting shots such that a sighter period is not necessary during the real match..

In contrast, 50 over cricket requires more innings building skills and a lot more defensive technique skills and affords the batter a period to get played in and demands of him the ability to go on and make a big score and anchor the innings. 50 over cricket is won through partnerships, whereby one batter can score big and reasonably fast and the other can just go for it or keep rotating the strike and the team can launch an assault toward the end if wickets remain. Whereas 20-20 game is not about partnerships but how quickly a team's batters can score and what they can reap off of each and every delivery without letting the run rate drop. We anyway explained to you in prior chapters about the whole idea of 20-20 and why it was invented and what its purpose is so get used to clicking into 2nd or 3rd gear if not top gear from the very first ball!

APPROACH & ATTITUDE TOWARD 50 OVER CRICKET

OVER MARK 0-5 5-15 15-40 40-50

MINDSET OF BATSMAN

Play in V pick up 1s &2s(defensive mode: account for rattle ball
pick up 1s&2s(bring backlift around to 1st/2nd slip, look for loose ball
starting 15th push the gaps for 2s&3s(backlift around 2nd 3rd slip now!
Punish loose ball: too short/wide/full
start looking for boundaries(backlift is around to 3rd slip now!)

APPROACH & ATTITUDE TOWARD 20 OVER CRICKET

OVER MARK 0-2 2-5 5-15 15-20

MINDSET OF BATSMAN

Play in V pick up 1s &2s(defensive mode: account for rattle ball
pick up 1s&2s(bring backlift around to 1st/2nd slip, look for loose ball
starting 5th over look for boundaries(backlift around 2nd 3rd slip now!
start looking for 6s(backlift is around to 3rd slip now!)
Punish loose ball: too short/wide/full

What about attacking in the first 15 overs or in the first 5 overs in 20-20, while the field restrictions are in place? This is a time where good batsmen and the better batsmen try to really ‘go for it’ by playing on the rise, playing across the line of the ball and playing lofted shots over the infield for four or six. This is an advanced stage of batting, only add this to your schedule chart above if you have someone on your batting team that is good enough and/or willing to play in this fashion, but especially in 50 over games batsman of the caliber of Tendulkar and Jayasuriya for examples sake are foolish not to take this little gamble in their approach to batting – a gamble which relies on the batter being able to back himself to hit big and not get out or contribute towards a collapse at the top order.

Chapter Twelve

Great Footwork – Big vs Small

"Foot-eye coordination is more of a precursor to successful batting than is hand-eye coordination"

.........12th Men

In this chapter we are going to talk about, teach and advise you in regard the footwork demands encountered in a game of cricket and especially the act of batting. It is observed in all sports ranging from rugby, NFL, soccer and cricket too, that the type of foot motion and amount of the foot movement or size of the foot movement, is not constant, the same or uniform throughout a particular athlete's performance on the field and goal of out playing his opposition. Rather, we see, and especially in soccer most so, that a certain quality and type of foot movement is demanded at different times and in different scenarios, and that an athlete must have mastery and experience over what is necessary and required at any particular moment or situation in time on the field, footwork wise. We look towards and gain insight into this phenomenon of feet work being of utmost importance from key major sports and finally seek to depict the importance and value of precise and quality footwork in the sport of cricket too.

Cut to the chase, we want you to appreciate the footwork component of successful athletes from particularly soccer, rugby, NFL and basketball, and show you how important and valuable it is in a game of cricket too and to someone who is given a piece of willow in your hand and simply told, “get the runs, succeed”. Without this ability to alter, adjust and change our footwork, this ability which great athletes have to score ‘goals’ and score ‘trys’ and ‘touchdowns’ just would not come about or exist, and cricket is no different. Put simply, it is the ability for ‘fancy footwork’ which gives them this capacity – the capacity to outstep, out manoeuvre and out-speed their opponent and ultimately succeed in scoring a goal, a basket or a touchdown.

It all comes down to small versus medium versus big - the amount and length of our stride that is! Athletes in these sports are constantly asked to out-step, dodge and weave their opponent if they are to even reach the opposition’s territory mark, and given the pressures to perform under pressure, are required to use this ‘fancy footwork’ to do so – admittedly more so in the aforementioned sports than say cricket, but the implications are vast and far-fetching in cricket too. It is blatantly obvious and slammed in viewers faces in the major sports we just mentioned but it is considered a critical precursor and defining skill in batting also, it’s just we don’t see it so plainly and clearly that’s all! The footwork is nimble and precise once and wherein a player in possession of the ball is seeking to elude and weave his opponent and step through opposition players to gain the opening. Once and if he is able to elude the opposition successfully and still has the ball, now suddenly he must gain yards or yardage and spree for the finish line or goal mark using substantially larger or bigger strides. But he wouldn’t have been in this position had he not stepped and weaved and used this fancy footwork in the first place and in the beginning or when the ball was in back or mid-field, right! So these guys, especially soccer players and rugby players, are essentially using a lot of footwork to first weave, step and manoeuvre their way past the opposition usually using small and precise foot movements and then larger foot movements to finally spree for goal so to speak, and both are a defining feature of how good they really are.

So now that we are aware of this phenomenon of footwork being the value creator or play-maker in the major sports and being defined as one of the if not the most valuable skill to have whilst contesting and winning the game, should we not consider it's application and the way it works in the act of batting? Of course we do and it would be silly to not do so!

Footwork is generally considered of infinite importance and value in the act of batting and simply can't be overlooked from a coaching angle of correct formative guidance, however, the good news is that in cricket the footwork is not so various nor does it involve numerous scenarios or factors, but rather is relatively easy to teach, understand and acquire – there is only a few different feet movements we must learn and master so in a sense we can say that it is easier than in other sports. So are we saying that cricket and batting is an easier sport than the major ones aforementioned? No! because in cricket and batting even despite foot-work being a key precursor and skill to have, it is not everything! In batting we must use hand-eye coordination in conjunction with foot-eye coordination and a mental presence and approach, so it makes sense to say that it equates to the fact that it is actually a harder sport? Well this is also a no, because as we just mentioned there are not multiple and numerous scenarios to master in regard footwork of batting, but rather just a few which we must be able to do with consummate ease, precision and speed. So what we can possibly say is that the same demand of big versus small versus medium still exists and defines a major part of what batting is about and succeeding and scoring runs, but it is of a different type or style – usually in batting we are trying to determine where and when we should plant our foot, so as you read in beginning of book it is more a static type of feet movement or demand on our feet movements in cricket. It is only sometimes that we are required to initiate a dance down the pitch or charge the bowler but this again is more a quality of the mind and our estimation and reaction to where in the z-box the ball lies and an exact estimation or projection of the final positioning of the ball as it journeys through the air and toward our body/bat – not so heavily dependent on 'fancy footwork' but more so 'fancy mind-work' and picking the length early.

Every good batsman has that ability to both be nimble and precise as well as using bigger strides to create a scoring opportunity off a not so bad ball, and uses this phenomenon of foot-work not only in attack but in defence also. Skilled and experienced footwork, which as we said is significantly dependent upon our seeing the ball early and where in or around the z-box the ball will pitch, is the difference between you keeping your wicket but most importantly in you scoring at a higher rate in competitive cricket.

Remember earlier in the book we showed you the three different scenarios for playing a front foot defensive shot to a good ball, and how marginal differences in its exact length will dictate how you will play the ball – dictate whether you will take a tiny step forward, a big lunge forward or a medium sized step forward. That's one scenario of footwork being critical to our batting, a few more examples are as follows:

- **Driving the ball on the rise in the V along the ground** – take a big step forward as big as you can and hit through ball with elbow up and full body motion
- **Driving through mid-wicket or on-driving the ball** – take a small step forward as small as possible
- **Square cut off front foot** – take a big step forward and back your hand-eye co-ordination to play the ball away from the body
- **Square drive** – take a medium step forward and be balanced or anchored on both feet as opposed to balanced on only front or back foot and glide bat through ball with slightly open face.
- **Pull/hook shot** – take a small to medium step back OR take a big step back and across. If the ball is not that short and you still want to play pull shot, take only a small step back and let body/hands do the work. If the ball is quite short and you want to get under it and hit for six then take medium to big step back.
- **Back-foot punch** - take a medium to big step back and across.
- **Late cut** - take a small step back and across and let ball glide off the face of bat and close to body
- **Charging the spinner** – medium to large step/lunge forward, depending on exactly how full the ball is and exactly where in the z-box the ball is anticipated to bounce(forward or backward of Y-point).

Tendulkar and Aravinda De Silva are the best exponents of such fine and distinguished footwork within cricket – the ability to know when to go forward and back and by how much, and knowing when and by how much to charge the spinner to convert it into a half volley or 6 hitting opportunity.

Take these 8 examples as oath and imbibe them into your mind. Study the differences in your step and how big or small it should be and try notice the differences between shots – ones which are vastly different versus ones which are only marginally different, and appreciate the difference on paper first before practicing them in real life. For example notice the difference between the cut off front foot and the late cut – the difference in footwork that is, and study the demands on footwork of each shot on paper first and compare them on paper and engrain it in your memory or computer as we said in earlier chapters.

So good footwork can go a long way in our tasks as batsmen and our task of keeping our wicket and scoring faster also, and is just as important in our chances of winning in competitive match situations and just as critical as it is in other major sports we spoke about earlier. In an advanced stage of one-day batting when the pressure is on to score runs at a required rate and the bowling is a lot more threatening too, footwork and seeing the ball early at or before z-point are the major weapons we have to counter-act this, and so its inclusion in your cricketing education and formative training cannot be stressed enough. If you were not able to grasp what we are talking about properly then ask your coach about some tips and maybe a one-to-one demo – of the differences in big versus small versus medium steps in batting footwork that is!

So it is fair to say that the difference between the tail and the specialist batsmen or the very good and not so good batsmen, is primarily centred around footwork and also the batsman's ability to read the length early and estimate exactly where in the z-box the ball will land and how far away from the y-point the ball is projected to land, and that fine footwork is a goal every batter should aspire towards. This combined with hand-eye coordination and becoming a master at picking the length, as we spoke of in earlier chapters, are the very stuff which batting is made of and the cornerstone and mantra behind training to be a great player. Yes, if we can get our feet moving correctly and precisely then that's 80% of the battle won, the remaining is just a matter of playing late and with soft hands and concentrating on our visionary process and executing the final and last stages of batting – actually hitting the ball, keeping our elbow up and following through by leaning into and through the ball with timing.

In consistency with our opinion that the batter has the advantage in competitive cricket, we must get our footwork functioning at an elite level and degree of preciseness if we are to score faster – which is the ultimate goal of batters in one-day cricket and what draws the crowds. What we need to do is use our footwork and mastery thereof to get ourselves in position early and early enough to play 'good cricketing shots' and not have to resort to playing baseball or risky cow-shot slogs to maintain the required run rates – not only that the tail can also do this but we more often than not are able to actually score faster by consistently playing good and orthodox cricketing shots, the good majority of which we have elaborated on a few paragraphs earlier. Front or back foot? small step or big step? This once again centres around our visionary process and how we judge the ball's length in relation to the z-points and z-boxes we discussed in regard both spin and pace bowling, and particularly the y-point which gives us a starting point as to whether to go back or forward.

"Mastery over footwork separates the goods from the greats, especially in one-day cricket."

.......Nikhil Jain

Don't feel scared or worried if you don't immediately estimate where the z-box or y-point lies on the pitch for any given bowler. Yes, It will also be different for each bowler, but you will soon gather to know where the bowler's good length zone or z-box is and you will do this intuitively – you wont need to mark it on the pitch your eyes will automatically estimate and remember it and you will be well on your way to ***taking a yard if given an inch*** and batting like the greats.

Being tall or taller does not really offer any major advantages nor disadvantages whilst conducting footwork in batting, however, it is generally theorised that being on the shorter side does offer certain advantages in playing certain shots, so height is generally NOT considered a precursor for good batting, but personal mastery over using different footwork for different cricketing shots which IS!

Chapter Thirteen

Batting Under Pressure: Nerves Of Steel

There will be times when you are under pressure as a batting unit, either by virtue of being able to set a good target whilst batting first on a good pitch or chasing down a big target or a moderate target after the fall of several top order wickets. The batting tasks ahead of you and your team may not always fall within standard parameters, but rather, may demand of you a certain ability as a team to think on your feet and change your game plan as well as even your whole outlook on the game, and even the entire way you bat and your rudimentary technique. We want to help you bat better under pressure situations and not let your team down for lack of out cricket or mental cricketing acumen – remember the game is won in the field, once your bowlers and fielders have done the job consider the game as 80% in the bag and over, as like we explained earlier bowling is the harder part to cricket and batters have the advantage. So what does this mean, well it means that you guys as batsmen don't want to let your bowlers down and allow the hard toil and hard work of your fielding innings go to waste, and you owe it to them to chase down the runs in any cost and formally secure the victory.[39] Once the bowling and fielding unit have done the job according to what is a good score on that pitch, the hard work is complete and the rest according to the laws of mathematical possibility and probability is only a formality - chasing a moderate score with batsmen all the way down to number 8 or 9, as many teams can!

---

[39] Unless of course the skill differences in the two batting units is that drastically different, otherwise this theory applies – batters owe it to the bowlers to win and secure the game by getting the runs.

Similarly, if we are setting a target, we want our batsmen to sneak in a few extra runs just in case and give our fielding and bowling unit a little more to defend – just scoring what is a good score on the pitch may not be enough, you need a few extra runs to comfort your bowlers.

So let's get cracking and teach you how to bat under pressure and talk about the things we must do differently and the adjustments we need to make in high pressure situations when your team's batting unit is really being put under the pump and tested through the fall of early wickets or having to chase a huge score. What do we do? What do we do differently? How do we do it?

Well the number one and first thing we have to get used to doing is to not panic and lose our minds and feel overwhelmed by the required scoring rate. Remember those two words, mathematical possibility and mathematical probability we mentioned earlier? These are the two chimes in the church we are trying to ring and if we can do that then we win the game, simple. We are not here to panic and be flustered or overwhelmed by the pressure and seeming enormity of the task ahead of us, but rather, we are here to wield and flail the willow given to us and take this opportunity given to us, in the most mathematical and scientific manner possible, and one which oozes of good shot-selection and skill as well as a calculative game plan and strategy, and the ability of our individual batters to execute it. Just before we go further, you may be wondering well who decides the game plan and strategy for the batters to follow? Well it can't always be the captain and sometimes the captain is neither the smartest man for the job nor the best one to develop and change game plans as the game changes and make necessary calculated decisions for the team's interests – it has to be the coach usually, but it is important you as a batter to know this chapter well and the theories involved for education's sake as you may not always have a scientific and calculative coach leading from the front. Our job as players is to conduct our batting and bowling well and increase our physical playing potential and cricketing skills, this is hard enough in itself and is actually the hard part. Our job isn't nor should be to develop game plans, make calculated decisions for the team nor harness the team's horses – that is the captain's and coaches job, but no matter how and where we fit into the team's strategy to win and score runs under pressure, it is important we all have the skills of batting under pressure and know what is required of us from a technique standpoint.

Who is the greatest batter ever? Bradman, Lara, Tendulkar, Waugh, Aravinda, Kohli, Warner? Who can we say resumes this status? There were many who came close to Tendulkar's records and even had higher scores and perhaps even better statistics in some aspects of batting, but none had that tremendous ability to bat well under extreme pressure and under big game conditions. We will find countless little gems and cameos from Tendulkar in a career whose signature trademark was to score runs under pressure, bat according to the requirement of the team and score runs when the team needed them. How many times has this man won the game or saved the team from defeat off his own back – he was simply the most capable batter ever under pressure situations, that's what made him so great. It was as if there were no task in batting or no scoring rate required which could bother or scare this man, he was simply able to do anything with the bat, and that too under extreme pressure and could do anything mathematically possible for the sake of the team and India's victory. He was simply the best because of the never say can't, never say die, and never be overwhelmed attitude toward batting. This plus the fact he was and was even commended as being so by Bradman, the most technically correct and powerful stroke-maker ever to play the game. So what separates the other greats from Tendulkar? Simply, Tendulkar had a tremendous innate ability to play well and bat well under pressure and was equipped with all the skills, physical and mental to get runs under pressure and not be scared by the seemingly enormous task ahead, while the others crumbled under pressure and had no game plan Tendulkar stood wide awake like a soldier in helping India's chances of victory.

What good is the talent if you don't have the mental cricketing acumen nor the ability to withstand and come out on top under pressure? Nothing! That's why you are reading this chapter, so that you don't let yourself down and fail to do justice to your talent as a result of being mentally weak or misinformed. Remember we said cricket becomes very mental at the top, and it is usually mental aspects of our game which separates us from our competition, not athletic ability or our ability to play a cover drive according to textbook, or our ability to score a century off 100 balls. We are trying to outplay our opposition, and we will do anything and everything and what it takes to do so – scoring a century off 105 balls may not be what we need to outplay our opposition on a 330 pitchand against a team who bats down to number 9, agree? When you have a team which bats down to number 9, scoring a 80 or 90 off 120 balls not only may not be of any assistance in winning the game, but rather, could prove to be a liability or jeopardy to the team's winning interests – we must assess the reality of what is required of us correctly and mathematically and learn to raise our tempo, and ultimately "bat under pressure". We must do this on a team basis as well as an individual basis – so if we chasing 350 and bat down to 9 and have good batters till 9, we may not need a slow 50 or even 100 at the top, but rather an innings which keeps up with required run rate pressures.

Cricket is a tough sport, tougher than it looks, and requires not only game plans and strategy along with technique and skill, but our ability to execute game plans under pressure. Unless it is a Test match and you have all day, as batsmen in one-day cricket, we must learn to bat under pressure – there is no time for hand-to-mouth batting in high level one-day cricket. We must determine our plan and execute our plan, both on a team level and individual level, we must have the mental cricketing acumen to determine first what is required of us, and then we must have the skills under pressure to actually execute our plan and etch closer towards victory. A talented batsman without the proper mental acumen and ability to perform under pressure is not likely to help you win and is as good as nothing. As we will opine in the Captaincy section of the book, we are better off picking a less talented batter but one who has the fight to stick around and do what is required for the team's interests in winning, and not only personal accolades, than to pick someone who is reputed but useless under pressure.

The thing we need to know is that batting hand-to-mouth is the biggest no-no and the very thing we are trying to avoid in our one-day cricket batsman-ship. Having the approach of just playing each ball on it's merit as in a Test match, is simply not good enough, we need to be able to change our technique and approach to batting, sometimes ramping up our defensive shots and sometimes ramping up our attacking shots, and sometimes our ability to simply rotate the strike also. We want to at least make an attempt and try to have a game plan and use the necessary resources and talent we have on the team to successfully execute our game plan and achieve mathematically possible and probable victory for ourselves. All that is required is an approach and game plan for our 50 overs and how we are going to use them. Even the greatest batsman in the world may be caught guilty of playing hand-to-mouth and lose his wicket just at the crucial time when the team needed him – anyone can be caught out and found wanting for batting hand-to-mouth. Sometimes yes the ball is a good ball but getting out was really not needed and could have been prevented had you followed your game plan. For example, your opener gets a caught behind when you really expected him to score a fifty and the team absolutely needed it – well this is where he had to get his back lift dead straight in defense, and cut out the risky shots early on. This is where he had to guard against getting out early with a game plan and one which says do not at any cost get out to a good ball on the stumps and make the bowler bowl to you, whilst scoring slowly and steadily – simply knowing your game plan and what your role is for the team can make all the difference to your individual game, and you succeeding as an individual. Here is where you needed to tighten up in defense and not worry so much about scoring quickly, and for want of this, you failed in having the required mental cricketing acumen and were caught out batting hand-to-mouth. It sounds strict but it's really not, it is simply adhering by a game plan which has been formulated and calculated as playing your cards right as a team and helping each card be a winning card and not a potential 'dud' – this is what is required of you batsmen in one-day games, not just the ability to simply play each ball on merit like a Test batter, but to etch closer and closer to victory for the team by keeping your top order wickets early and scoring at the required rate.

Another example is a gun batsman goes in, the gun batsman of your team and the one you rest hopes in of making the most contribution toward victory, takes guard at middle only to find the bowler is left-arm over the wicket and that the major threat here is the late inswinger on a length and getting out LBW. He is not played in and not warm, he gets out to an in swinger LBW, when all he had to do was take guard at leg or middle and leg to keep the pads out of the way for this particular ball – again for a want of mental cricketing acumen and good out-cricket, we are found to be batting hand-to-mouth. It is not being strict it is just simple coaching strategy and being aware of how mental aspects of cricket are so important at the top level. In an ideal world a batsman would know this but in reality we expect our coaches to hand down and teach this vital mental aspect of the game. Just like this, you may find so many examples of gun batsmen getting out in big match situations and letting their team down, simply for a want in not being caught out batting-hand-to-mouth and being slightly more informed and astute.

Just say you are playing in a real important match and the pressure is really on to chase down the runs and for the top order to do well, how do we give ourselves the best chance of doing so? Well we as top order batsmen must change our approach and even technique to do so. We need our top order to play in the V early, revert to a dead straight back lift early on to guard against the rattle ball, and generally cut out the risky shots and make the bowler bowl to you, at least for the first 3-5 overs of the innings. Your aim early on should be to not get out, build a partnership and punish the loose ball – that's all! The pressure is on for you guys to start and mold the innings and prevent collapse whereby all the pressure is on our middle order – basically we are trying to deploy and delegate the pressure of winning the game by following a game plan which outlines what and when is required of each batter. Just as in batting in general, we must pick our ball to hit and be tight in our shot selection so as not to get a miscue and get caught.[40]

When things aren't going well and we have a collapse at the top order and now suddenly our team and our middle order is under pressure to chase down the runs, we need to basically have a game plan as to how we are going to play our cards and how we are going to use our resources and our wickets for victory. It is easier said than done I know, once the bowling team get their noses in front and start building all the momentum in their favor, it is not easy to claw our way back into the game and change the momentum of the game, yet it is perfectly possible. All we have to do is build a partnership which secures the bulk of the runs and gives our big hitters toward the end a realistic target and task to deal with. It is now where you simply need to concentrate a bit harder and try pick up singles and twos and keep rotating the strike, as well as cutting out the risky shots. Make the bowler bowl to you by being immaculate and prudent in your shot-selection and only aim to hit or play a big shot to the loose ball. By doing this we are increasing our chances of not getting out and building that partnership which we desperately need, also try pick up singles early once the collapse happens – this helps in shifting and slowly swerving the momentum of the game back in your favor, and if you can get just 4 runs

---

[40] WC2019 India vs NZ semifinal: Rohit Sharma was being entrusted to get the team runs and momentum in the beginning, in knowledge of this pressure and expectation, he did not adjust his technique to be more straight in bat swing, and was caught playing a hand-to-mouth shot where the backlift came from 2nd slip and then again turned outward the other way.

an over through singles, the middle order have a good chance of getting the rest.

When batting under pressure and the team really needs you, there are a few things to remember. Firstly make sure you get busy picking up singles and trying to build a partnership, but most importantly we have to remember to pick the ball to hit. We don't want to try hit a boundary off the wrong ball and get out just when the team needs us, rather, we want to pick the ball to hit carefully and hit hard and long and with all our heart – this is no time for half-hearted shots, you either hit big or leave the ball go or defend. We don't want to be caught out as a hand-to-mouth batsman who is neither defending nor attacking, but we want to be clinical in our shot-selection and really know what we are doing with each ball. But remember that you are there to steady the ship, you don't need to play big shots just yet, that's the middle order and later order's job – your job is to be clinical in the way you keep the required run rate under check and pick up the ones and twos and putt along at 4 runs an over. For example if you are 5/125 chasing 230 and the required run rate is around 7.5 an over, you as a batsman don't need to be getting the full 7.5 runs an over, you merely have to keep the run rate required under check lets say scoring in between 4.5 and 7.5 so 6 runs an over. The remaining run rate required will be negotiated and scored by your big hitting batsmen who are due in next. The important thing to remember here is to not leave it to late, keep the runs ticking over and set your big hitters and your final few recognized batsmen up for the acceleration towards the end and one which is realistic and possible.

What if we need a huge total to win and the pitch is a 350 pitch or we are chasing 350 for victory? Well here also we need to be judicious in the way we play our cards and structure our batting order and the instructions we give to each batsman. Generally, here we need a century from someone and for the team to play around one or two core batsmen who can stay there and get a big score, that's usually the only way bigger scores are generated – with one or two centurions that is. Generally, when playing on a belter of a pitch and when we need a big score, the tactic should be to cut out certain shots early on and at the beginning of the innings yet still keep scoring at a high rate. So play good cricketing shots and try score quickly in the beginning through good orthodox cricketing shots, and then use your middle order or latter order to play the big shots, cow shots or baseball style shots toward the end of the 50 overs. The important thing to remember here is that we can't restrict ourselves to just cricketing shots for the duration of the 50 overs, we must sooner or later 'start playing baseball' if we want a huge score – so don't leave it to late, you must start accelerating through playing big shots as early as you as a team feel confident doing so – when you have enough runs on the board to guard against a possible collapse that is.

Batting under pressure may require a few adjustments to your fundamentals also and require you to make small changes in technique to assist in being more clinical in defense especially if you are a key batter. Like we spoke about, bring your bat down dead straight, try to have soft hands whilst playing all your defensive strokes and be prepared for the good ball as opposed to being on the look-out for the scoring opportunities.

But the biggest change we need to make is to our back-lift as mentioned in previous chapters, and moreover, the tightness in defence. Remember by tightening our defense we are also forgoing or giving up the capacity for cowshots and other big bottom-hand and horizontal bat shots, and this is exactly what we want – we want to score steadily and without risk and without giving our wicket away. A simple holding and keeping our bat close to the body is all that's required here, also playing straight and being prepared to play every ball with soft hands, especially the rattle ball. Bring your hands up a tiny bit higher when you take stance and keep them close to the body(maintain your grip on bat as usual however) – you really want to tighten up in defense, even if you forgo some run scoring opportunities![41]. Making the bowler bowl to you, is what we are trying to do here – as you learnt in previous chapters.

Whilst batting under pressure to score quickly and bump up the run rate, there are certain things which we can and should focus on as batsmen. Some of the things we need to focus on and remember are as follows:

- Play on the rise
- Try to loft the ball over the in-field
- Start focusing on the gaps in the field and where we can pick up runs
- Start using the feet more rigorously
- Start trying to give yourself room by either getting inside or outside the line of the ball
- Be more aggressive in regard punishing loose lines and lengths
- Bring your back-lift to around 3rd or 4th slip so you can really wind up as well as hit across the line and hit the ball square of the wicket powerfully.

---

[41] Watch Aravinda Desilva's stance carefully – notice how he holds the bat higher and closer to the body compared to other batters.

When we are under pressure to get the runs and the required rate is getting high, this is where we can and have to start batting as if we were batting on cement or synthetic, and start really backing our eye and visionary process to score off of semi-bad balls – this is our only way as it is now do or die and there are only limited overs in the match. We best to have tried and failed than to never have tried at all and this is no time for playing textbook Test-match cricket, but time for us to launch our final assault or final throw of the dice so to speak. We can do this by both playing cricketing shots as well as 'playing baseball', or both. Playing 'baseball' is best achieved by a pronounced round or un-straight backlift which comes from 3rd or 4th slip and facilitates the swatting of the ball hard and long, playing across the line on the onside and trying to hit over the infield[42].

We must use our feet, use the lofted shot, drive on the rise and begin to start looking for subtle and marginal looseness in regard line and length of the bowling. Once we determine where the gaps are we must start using the crease and our footwork to execute shots and find the gaps – sometimes this means getting inside the ball or outside the ball and inside out, and sometimes it means dancing down the track, but we must use our footwork as a weapon to launch our final assault and find runs from somewhere even if the field and bowling is becoming difficult. Now is the time to bat to our full runs scoring potential and speed through both cricketing shots and the slog shots. So a simple adjustment in our approach and shot selection is all that is required here, one which adds more lofted shots, driving on the rise and use of footwork and the crease. Simply by using our feet to

---

[42] Contrast this to playing in the V and playing with a straight back-lift whilst trying to play 'cricketing shots'.

get inside of or outside of the line of the ball, can give us a very risk free way of playing more scoring shots and that too cricketing shots – it is not necessary to only play slogs and cow shots, we can lift our scoring rate by just playing normal cricket also by just using our feet a little more aggressively. Important to be in 100% attack mode and change our vision to look out for the loose ball only and forget about the length or good ball. Bat as though you are batting on cement or synthetic, and don't worry about checking your shot or allowing for the deviating ball so much – now is the time you must bat as though you are a master of chapters 5 and 6 on seeing the ball and anticipating its length, position and pace, and really start batting in cement cricket mode or net practice mode. One crucial element which helps us get boundaries whilst under pressure to score fast is bringing our normal stance and back-lift to around the slips as opposed to being straight and giving ourselves room outside leg-stump by planting our front foot as far toward leg-stump as possible.

So hopefully you have a better idea now about the things we need to do and be aware of whilst encountering difficult situations, and what exactly is required of us as batsmen when the going gets tough and we are under pressure. Remember the two words mathematical possibility and mathematical probability – there is no need to panic, we are here to give the best effort humanly possible and guard against being a hand-to-mouth batsman who has no plan and no courage to execute his plan.

...........When the going gets tough, the tough get going!

Chapter Fourteen

Practice To Be Great And Not Just Good

"Your beliefs become your thoughts, Your thoughts become your actions, Your actions become your habits, Your habits become your values, Your values become your destiny."

...Gandhi

What does this famous quote mean to us as cricketers? You play according to how you have practiced, how you practice is how you play & batting is 70 % mental and in the mind. The remaining 30% is translating that mental process into physical execution via hand eye coordination and footwork.

There are many things we need to talk about in this chapter as there are many things we need to think about, remember and do right whilst practicing and during our practice routine if we are to develop our skills and prepare for pressure match situations. The biggest thing we need to practice is our visionary process and adjustment thereof, our technique and back lift and adjustment thereof and what we call our propensity to score faster threshold.

Here is a list of the things which come to mind when we think of a great batsman and the hallmarks or cornerstones of the batsman who do the 'little things' right and are classed in the categories of the very best and greatest:

- Good temperament to build an innings and not panic

- Shot selection – defend or attack whole heartedly
- Agility to adjust technique
- Agility to adjust visionary process
- Ability to take a yard if given an inch in regard line and length[43]
- Ability to use the pace of the ball to play glances, late cuts and deft touch shots
- Good use of footwork
- Calculative mind – playing for teams requirement
- Learning from your mistakes fast
- Leaving the ball go technique
- Strong bottom hand play – ability to play baseball
- Ability to defend good length ball
- Not being caught out playing hand to mouth and flirting at the ball
- Ability to square drive and front foot cut
- Ability to play one-day cricket even in a test match, aka Virender Sehwag
- Cutting/pulling short of a length ball also flicking it through midwicket, aka Tendulkar
- Driving on the up or on the rise

How we practice is how we play so we must take our practice sessions seriously and have a set routine and plan in mind as to what we are doing and how we are going to do it. Batting is one of those athletic tasks which very much relies on 'muscle memory', so for you batsmen the pressure is really on even during practice, for you to get the most out of your 30

---

[43]This particular trait is what made Tendulkar the man that he is, and the greatest most prolific run scorer of our era.

minutes or so you get in the net to hone your strength, develop your weakness and find your form or touch.

Batting does not come easy, and does not just click into stride or into top gear come match day, but rather, requires strict and prudent preparation and pre-match practice on our behalf as serious athletes. Without strict practice you will never be the great player you are dreaming of becoming – it will take judicious practice and hard work and may be harder than you actually think so be aware of this and get used to working hard during practice.

Somewhere along the line an elite batter and one who can perform well in live match conditions and one who is that good, has partaken in what we would call hard practice, and there is no other way or shortcut as they say in successfully reaching and attaining this level of batsman ship in competitive level cricket! As we will discuss in the next book about being a chooser and not a beggar, we must have practiced playing 3-5 different shots to the same delivery and ball and must have practiced this well before match day or real life games. This takes tremendous effort and practice on behalf of you guys as batsman but there is no way out of this and no shortcut, the only way you are going to raise your skill levels and tempo in one-day cricket is through prudent and strict preparation not to mention laborious effort in the nets. The fact is that despite looking easy to the naked eye, batting is harder than it looks and does not come without hard work and laborious effort in the nets. We must practice hard and be laborious in regard the conscious effort and energy involved in successfully engraining the basics and our stroke selection process into our sub-conscious mind – this is the only way to reach elite batter standards!

Without diligent practice and honing your skills you will never be the elite batsman you are dreaming of becoming. Essentially batting is all about muscle memory and comes down to the way we have practiced and how hard we have practiced![44] We must be able to play 4 to 5 different shots to the same ball and practiced this and engrained it during our net sessions, but this will all be dealt with and discussed in depth in the next book on batting coming out soon.

We may not be able to and it may not be practicable to play shots on match day and in match conditions which we can play in practice and training conditions, but that does not mean we do not practice them and emphasize them during our practice sessions. What we are doing here is essentially called increasing our propensity to score faster threshold, that is, training and disciplining ourselves and stretching our minds and shot selection to score faster and take risks and improvise shots, such that when we meet with a match situation we have a good practice and 'feel' for playing and scoring at speed and simply playing steadily which is all that is required of us on match day suddenly becomes so much easier, and if required to, we CAN click into 2nd or 3rd gear a lot easier as we have practiced this in previous net sessions. However, simply playing in 1st or second gear becomes so much easier and risk free and comes so much easier, as we have done a good effort of practicing our 2nd and 3rd gear in our practice sessions – that's the idea behind this method of training for one day cricket. We could just practice playing each ball on merit as we would in a game but then what new is that teaching us and our muscle memory and sub

[44] We quote Tendulkar as an example of the prudent, strict and hard practice necessary in reaching elite standards – he practiced a good 8 hours a day for years before possessing the perfect one-day technique under pressure of live conditions!

conscious mind, that's something we can do anyway without any major practice.[45]

The next thing we need to practice in the nets which is important for our preparation for big match day, is our visionary process and back lift and adjustment thereof. We need to practice both for the beginning of our innings when we are not warm and the threat of the length ball is at its peak, as well as practice for free flowing stroke play once and once wherein we are warm and played in during the second half of our inning. How do we do this? Well the bowlers also need their practice and majority of the balls you will receive will be good balls and ones in the troublesome spots, so getting quality practice for your defensive technique and the beginning of your innings is the easy part. For practicing your free flowing stroke play whilst leaving your peripheral vision open for the defensive shot, you may need to get someone to chuck the balls at you for this – out of ten let three or so be on a length and 7 be loose. Whereas when we were practicing for the beginning of our innings where our primary vision was focused on the defensive shot, the ratio is flipped from 7 on a length and 3 loose – this is about on average the number of loose balls you get from a bowler in the nets during serious practice.

Give an inch and he'll take a yard. What does this saying mean? This means that the batsman is working within small and fine tolerances, has his eye in, is well played in and is punishing anything even slightly

---

[45]Mark Waugh of Australia, one of the great batsmen of one-day cricket, use to have only a 10 minute practice session if any at all, as his movements and technique were so well engrained into the muscle memory and sub conscious mind and he had a good mental picture of how to 'take a yard if given an inch' – Batting is 70% in the mind!

loose in regard line or length. That the ball may be only marginally short or pitched up and the batsman is in such good form that he is hitting attacking shots to even semi bad balls. For example the ball is not that wide and he is still cutting, the ball is not that full and he is still driving, the ball is not that short and he is still cutting and pulling, and so on. This is something the best of batsmen are able to do when in top gear and you should aspire to do too. Make it a part of your practice routine to not only practice your vision but this particular aspect also. Some of the best exponents of this were Sehwag, Waugh, Tendulkar and Aravinda. This is a rather advanced stage of batting but make sure you incorporate it into your routine somewhere down the line as we are training to be great and not just good remember, and to be picked for our state and country.

All good batsmen have the agility to both force the pace as well as use the pace. What does this mean? This basically amounts to playing baseball and hitting long and hard as well using deft touch and using the pace of the ball to simply deflect the ball behind the wicket. Practice this during nets, especially your glances and late cuts. Practice playing cuts and late cuts to balls which are not that wide of offstump or not that short and test yourself during practice – remember in match and on turf pitch we may have to cut the shot out but that does not mean we don't play it during practice in case we need it in pressure of match. Also practice your deft touch shots aka Ranatunga, where you let the ball come on to the bat and let it deflect and go through slips for four.

Bottom hand play is just as important, we must practice cutting, pulling, driving on the rise and playing across the line during practice with full ferocity if we want to be in the league of the best and score at a faster rate and be a great limited overs player. Practice taking a yard if given an inch in regard to bottom hand shots in particular, and practice timing and executing them well and off the middle with your head down. Concentrate on your footwork and getting in position early enough and early enough to create a big shot opportunity out of a ball which is not that bad – remember by now you are picking the length like an expert almost like Sehwag or Tendulkar, now is the time to start hitting the ball.

It is ok to make mistakes and get out but it is NOT ok to get out in the same way again and again! Make a note of how you got out and what you did wrong and correct it during your next net session. Remember we stated that what's in between the ears is the greatest asset a batsman can have - do not be tardy and let it go, you must seek help and correct your technical error asap. This is one of the traits of great batsmen and great athletes overall – their ability to learn from their mistakes, and cricket is such a technical game and there is so much to learn and so much that can go wrong, so it is only natural for us to make mistakes but it is not ok to keep making mistakes, that's all we are saying!

It can't be stressed enough that we take our net session seriously especially as an opportunity to practice our shot-selection. That is our ability to pick our ball and either defend or attack and do so with all our might and whole heartedly, and not be caught out flirting or fishing for the ball. Remember we stated that the trick to doing this is deciding your shot early and getting in position early, which in turn depends on picking the length early which in turn depends on our visionary process. So what does this mean? We must really train and practice our visionary process and our defensive technique hard during practice sessions according to the outlined advice spoken about in the book, and we must develop confidence via our practice sessions in our ability to do so and do so to the best of our ability and under pressure of match conditions.

We appreciate that cricket is a tough sport and that it is easier said than done and that it can look stupid on TV when a batsman plays a silly shot or fails in his shot-selection and is caught playing hand-to-mouth, but remember that you have now read the batting section of this definitive manual and the definitive chapter on picking the length, so you are now in the box seat in regard developing your shot selection properly and accurately – it will just take some concerted effort in the nets, you know the science behind it now! Yes, whilst batting on turf this sometimes becomes difficult, to display perfect shot selection that is, but this is no excuse and we should have the necessary adjustments in technique to counter act this.[46]

Just remember to either defend or attack whole heartedly and with all your might, and try make your decision as to which you will do as early as possible – this is the key skill we are trying to drill into you and your batting habits. Follow the guidelines to footwork we have outlined in previous chapters to give yourself the best chance against the moving ball, and remember to be judicious about which balls you decide to play at – you must leave the ball at times when it is too good and moving or deviating late.

---

[46] Watch the ball harder, play the ball late and watch the ball all the way onto the bat with head down – these are some of the things we must do whilst playing on turf as opposed to synthetic.

Great batsman are great innings builders and not so great batsmen are not so good innings builders. This quality is more or less temperament or concentration related and again to do with what's in between our ears. Our ability to not panic and keep our wits and maintain a calculative mind under pressure are cornerstones of a good innings builder, and the very things we need to be thinking about in matches. It may be hard at first, but try not to panic and think only in terms of mathematical possibility and what is humanly possible and what is not and giving your best effort. A calculative mind in regard understanding the opposition's game plans and field positions, etc. is crucial if we are to come out on top and build an innings as batsmen – whilst practicing try batting to your standard 6/3 fields which fielding teams place whereby 6 men are on offside and only 3 on onside and bowler is bowling outside offstump, and the only hope of runs is through onside – this is where you must practice in nets flicking the ball from outside off and through midwicket and sometimes getting inside the line and playing 'inside-out'..

The leaving the ball go technique is important as we must guard our self against the good ball and not getting a caught behind. The general principle here is to leave the ball go or drop the hands if and once if the ball deviates outwards, and sometimes also inwards. Like we mentioned before, try get right behind the ball with your body directly and perpendicularly behind the ball and just drop your hands if the ball moves or deviates late.

Footwork is important for us as batsmen as it allows us to best position ourselves to better hit the ball and hit the ball harder and longer and with more timing. The best shots are played only when our feet are in a good position. Sometimes this is as easy as moving forward or back and sometimes we must use our feet and dance down the pitch. This is not recommended generally unless of course to a spinner, but if you are to resort to this tactic of changing the length of the ball and making a good ball into a bad one, then we offer one tip: wait for the ball to have been released from the bowler's hand before you make your movement down the pitch, as the bowler can change his length and line and leave you vulnerable to a stumping or a bowled. This is something which can be practiced in the nets as there is no threat of match conditions and match pressures – try to practice the timing of your advance down the pitch and the exact moment when you jump down and advance down the track.

Driving on the up or on the rise is one of the great skills a batsman can have, even if a ball is not that full a great batsman is still able to hit through and drive the ball with timing, power and all the way along the ground as if it were a half volley. Whilst practicing this shot in nets, use a curved bat and practice getting head down and over the ball and elbow up and using elbow as power generator. Focus on being able to play the ball along the ground.

Defending the length ball and a sound defensive technique requires of us not only a certain visionary process and adjustment in backlift, as we opined in earlier chapters, but an adjustment in our hand position and the way we take our stance. Because we really want to tighten up, make the bowler bowl to us and only play balls close to our body, we want to really bring our hands up a bit higher and a bit closer to our bodies while we are taking stance and waiting for delivery (we are talking about our arms and hands being a bit higher once taking stance – NOT actually holding the bat differently!). This effectively allows us to cut out the shots which are away from the body and helps us to concentrate on only those balls which are accurate and directed at our stumps and at our bodies – in cricket we call this ***making the bowler bowl to you.***

One of the attacking things which batsmen do when in attacking frame of mind and when in form is to play the short ball or relatively short ball off the front foot. The cornerstone of playing these shots is being in form, having your eye in and reading or picking the length well and early. If practicing for a crucial one-day match, try practicing these shots and work on your ability to see the ball well and confidently enough to play short balls off the front foot. Once again it is an advanced shot and centres around your seeing the ball like Viv Richards or Virender Sehwag as the relevant previous chapter was titled – the two V's, yes, is the starting point for developing these strokes.

So just remember to practice and prepare well and according to a set protocol whilst preparing for matches. Use the guides from this chapter as a pointer as to what you need to do, but more importantly see what your weaknesses are and start plugging them in the net. But don't forget to practice your visionary process and defending the good ball early in your innings and practice this well in the nets before match day to give confidence on real live match day that you CAN keep your wicket and stay at the crease no matter how good the bowling is.

Chapter Fifteen

Converting Talent & Skill Into Runs On The Board!

"What good is the talent if it can't perform under pressure – nothing!"

.......Nikhil Jain

Remember this quote from earlier chapters where we talked about just how important mental toughness and mental facets of batting become as we rise the ranks, and that players are so well prepared and the game becomes very much centered around the mental acumen which a player can bring to the game or to the table so to speak. Well in this chapter we are going to explain to you how you can be a more mentally astute and shrewd athlete and convert your talent and skills into the performance and runs which your talent deserves on that particular day.

Batting is a very difficult and sometimes complex and tedious task and there are so many things we need to do right and so many things we need to be aware of and account for if we are to actually perform on the day and get a useful score for ourselves and the team. Often, in the real world of cricket and especially in countries like India, preparatory processes and being mentally shrewd, prepared and tough are ignored or overlooked and sheer talent and reputation is given the utmost priority or made the object of obsession. This type of attitude and pre-occupation with reputation and 'big name' status is dangerous and as you now know that batting has so many variables and inputs and so many things that can go wrong, and that we really need to be mentally in charge and in control of our innings, our game plan and how we will best execute our game plan.

As batsmen, there are so many things known as 'outcricket' or mental cricketing acumen, as we talked about before, that need to be accounted for and taken into consideration – that is things other than our skill and batting technique and our physical capacities with the bat in our hand and also adjustments to our physical movements and rudimentary technique according to the situation. For example, the pitch and how the pitch will behave; the age of the ball and how much deviation the bowler may expect to get; the cloud cover and how the ball might behave; being aware of the other teams game plan and field positions; the required run rate for victory; the importance of your innings and what the team needs from you; whether its Test match or limited overs cricket – these are all factors and variables which affect and make a huge impact to you batsmen and your hopes of coming out on top under pressure and playing a match winning innings, and we are foolish to just walk into a big match simply thinking that: "I know how to play". Rather we need to be mentally astute and allow the mental aspect of batting to consume the majority of our energies, if we are to succeed against quality bowlers and live match conditions. Not to detract from anyone or any individual player's skills and talent, but this alone just simply might not be good enough to perform well and win the game on the day – we must be mentally prepared and shrewd about our approach and technique.

How do we do this? We are about to mold and convert you into a perfectly orthodox and astute batsman within the space of one chapter - and one who has the mental presence and toughness to assess the situation and get runs for the team regardless of the situation or conditions. Regardless of what level of cricket you are playing even up to first class cricket, the theory which we are putting forward applies and should not be ignored or overlooked – remember how we said many a talented player has fallen away for want of mental cricketing acumen and mental toughness?

But first let's give you the wrap of what we are talking about in this chapter and why you are even bothering to read it. Well the simple fact of batting is, given it's complexities and demands on the body and mind as well as the fact that in cricket conditions and situations are always changing, that in high level cricket where the bowling is reasonably good if not great, we as batsmen cannot play and win this game without a justifiable and detailed strategy and plan and the courage to execute this plan. Yes, that's right, we are claiming that no matter how good the batsman is and how much status and reputation he has, that on the day he may be caught out playing hand-to-mouth and fail without being mentally prepared, shrewd and alert in regards mental aspects of the game. Whether it is Kohli, Warner, Chris Gayle, Steve Waugh or any other great player with great skills, there is only a 50% chance that they will succeed on the day without having prepared mentally and without having a plan and strategy in mind and a plan and strategy of how best to execute it and exactly how they are going to play the bowling. We are advocating and as has been justified throughout the book thus far, that talent and skill is not a precursor to success in high level cricket but rather mental toughness and temperament – a pretty big claim to make that on the day, an unprepared Kohli or Warner should not be picked in the team in front of a Jonty Rhodes or a batter with heart, patience and courage and one who is prepared, and that after all we play the game to win on the day not just to have our name counted.

Even the most talented and skilled of batsman can be caught out playing hand-to-mouth, that is simply playing each ball on merit and not according to the situations and conditions at the time. We must inject the 'overall picture' and 'overall requirement' variable into our approach to our innings – that is what we are getting at, and not just be living for the next ball and that's it!

Like we said in earlier chapters, we as batsmen must adapt and change our technique and visionary process sometimes and be aware of certain mental things which need to be done right if we are to actually convert talent into performance and runs on a consistent basis and especially in big match occasions.

Both India and Australia bowed out of the semi-finals quite emphatically after their respective batting units let them down, despite being a strong team on paper. What does this tell us? Well like we said, without a game plan and plan of how we are going to play the bowling and what is required of us, that at a higher level of cricket a batsman only has a 50% probability of succeeding, and that our theory has overflowing and dramatic implications to us as batsmen and serious athletes and that this particular skill or aspect to batting cannot be ignored. We are foolish to walk into a game with our head held high on the basis of talent or reputation as cricket is a demanding sport and having a 50% chance of success is just not good enough. We need to substantially increase and guarantee our chances of success through prudent preparation and strategy or game plan and strictly following this determined plan.

So take the variables and factors which have dramatic implications to you guys as batsman as the primary focus of your energies whilst batting and don't be caught out hand-to-mouth batter who has no plan and no courage to execute his plan. Like we said your technique and physical skills by this time should be engrained and locked into your muscle memory and should not consume all of your effort and energy whilst batting.

We are all serious cricketers and these variables need not be discussed in detail, just that in context of these variables, an astute and mentally shrewd approach to our batting is a must if we are to call ourselves top-order batsmen, and that we are foolish to enter a game without a plan and foolish to let the game just happen without being mentally present and alert regards the changing face and conditions of the game at the time. We acknowledge this applies mostly to 50 overs cricket but don't be complacent even in a test match – you must be mentally prepared and present and be able to adapt your technique and action as well as mindset to the game if you are to reach an elite cricketer status – a status even certain first-class cricketers may not be able to claim!

Do not be ashamed to embrace the fact that batting is a highly mental task and mindset, approach and mental toughness can make all the difference in whether we get runs in live match conditions or not! Even the greatest and most skilled of batters can on the day do injustice to their skill level for want of having a good mental picture of what is required of them and having an overall or 'birdseye view' or plan as to exactly how they are going to think, move and behave according to the situation and the bowling.

You will see some practical examples of what exactly we are talking about in the end of the book in the 'why india lost the semi final' chapter coming up.

Chapter Sixteen

Vector Forces and Shot-Selection: Is That all Cricket Is?

The answer is YES that is all cricket is! Since you have now read and understood the previous chapters about the physics, mathematics and computational logic demands within a game of cricket, we feel it is now a good time to put forward and prove our theory that:

"cricket is just a game based around vector forces and shot-selection - nothing more!"

Yes, it sounds too simple to be true but it is in fact and indeed this simple! The very fundamental and crux upon which the game of cricket is based upon and centers around are simply vector forces and shot-selection, and the act of performing and executing good cricket is invariably dependent upon the knowledge, understanding and application of this little concept from the sciences and its practical implications to people on a cricket field physically contending the sport.

The inevitable conclusion thus derived and formed is that cricket is not an Art but a Science and it is an act which can be not only explained, justified and understood via theory from the strict sciences namely physics and mathematics, but an act which can be improved and perfected with the help of mastery over the specific science and theories applicable per say. In consistency with this premise and the surrounding explanatory writings postulated so far within the book, we now seek to illustrate and prove how exactly the understanding of vectors can impact YOU as a cricketer and student of the game and why it is a must you should consider mastery over the subject as pivotal toward your personal development and growing from just an average cricketer into an elite one or a great one. Yes, with the help of vectors we show you not only how to understand the game and what is happening around us, but how to use this little secret or fundamental of the game to improve your confidence and performance as a cricketer and help you benefit from this understanding - as a cricketer and not just a reader or a scientist. Every man on the field including batsman, bowler, wicketkeeper, captain, fielder and even coach is directly affected by the understanding of vector forces and how to read them, and its implications to us as cricketers and how we perform and act on a cricket field are resoundingly far and wide, and simply just cannot be ignored by any cricketing enthusiast or student of the game.

Implications of vector forces to batsmen:

Well so far we have only touched upon the vector forces and diagrams for the longitudinal plane, that is path and deviation of the ball up ways and down ways or vertically and in the longitudinal plane if we see from the eyes of a batsman, and predicting the levels of bounce and speed of the ball upon reaching the bat. This is only half of the knowledge complete, we will now discuss and illustrate vector forces in the horizontal or lateral plane and show you how to pick the balls side way movement and accommodate this in your technique and ultimately answer the bowler's proposition securely and confidently through confident footwork and picking the swing or movement generated early or by z-point. The problem here is that we don't have any law or guide to rely upon such as

Snell's law or vector analysis, and because sideways movement is usually generated by adopting a certain grip and using a specialized bowling action on behalf of the bowler and is often subject to uncontrollable factors, and we can't see this as the ball comes out of the hand, we are forced almost to rely on guesswork or a best guess. But don't worry, we are going to show you how to contend with the moving ball anyway, either inwards or outwards in-swingers or out-swingers. The laws of physics in regard swing bowling and why the ball deviates or swings has been often taught and discussed in the cricketing fraternity, but we as batsmen don't care about the why and the exact scientific reason the ball is affected by air resistance and ultimately generates swing - we care about the how it will swing and by how much and when it will swing and by how much. But the fact remains that no-one in the game even the greatest can actually judge this or calculate this as the ball once bowled may take one of several different paths, but the good news is that we have a strategy up our sleeves to give us a chance of still picking the ball's vector early and getting our feet in position early just like the greats facing the quickest bowlers in the world. In regard spin bowling, we know the spinner has some basic tricks up his sleeve in the form of the straight one, the stock spinner and the dusra or googly which goes the other way to the stock ball, and we know that this is primarily due to and a result of a certain action and wrist positioning, so this one is a little easier to contend with for you batsmen as we can watch the ball hard for subtleties in action.

But before we go ahead let's look at the implications to batsmen based upon our current understanding of vectors. Of vectors in the vertical or longitudinal plane as opposed to the horizontal or lateral plane that is.

Well the fact is that when you become good at picking the length and reading vector forces behind the ball and reading them early AND the ball is not swinging too much, we suddenly become able to bully the bowling. We can play the short ball off of front foot and we can play the fuller ball off back foot. We can play square drives and late cuts with ease and commit to our stroke and hit hard and long. This is how the best in the business think and play too – once upon getting played in and picking the length early they suddenly start playing un-orthodox and improvised shots and hitting the ball harder and longer. Upon reading vector forces well and allowing for Snell's law of incidence equals reflection, batsmen are able to do all sorts of wonderful things like drive on the rise, hit across the line, loft the ball over fielders, engineer footwork and foot positioning to hit the ball through hard to find gaps and so on. The advantages especially in the first fifteen overs of batsmen picking the length early are 10 fold – we can pierce hard to find gaps and loft the ball over the infield being the main ones, which we wouldn't have the confidence of doing if we didn't get into position by the Z-Point as previously illustrated.

Ok, so how do we negotiate the moving ball in the lateral direction, that is the horizontal plane as seen from the batsman's eyes or simply put the swinging ball, and how do we use understanding of vectors to benefit us? Again we define a Z-point to work off and aim to get feet in position by the time the ball reaches Z-point. Often in competitive cricket bowlers can generate as much as 1.5 to 2 feet in sideways movement, that's just for pace bowlers spinners sometimes even 2 to 3 feet – that's a big deviation to contend with without early foot positioning. Let's take an out-swinger to begin off with as we journey you through the strategy used to play swing and that too vicious swing by extremely quick and accurate pacers – which the cricketing ranks of all countries is full of as all it takes to get a ball to swing is correct grip and a shiny side and rough side. The ones to watch out for and concentrate especially harder on are the pacers with swing, control AND accuracy – this is the scenario we are going to elaborate on now as in top level cricket you are going to encounter top level pacers with control and accuracy. Inspect the following diagram:

Diagram XVIII:

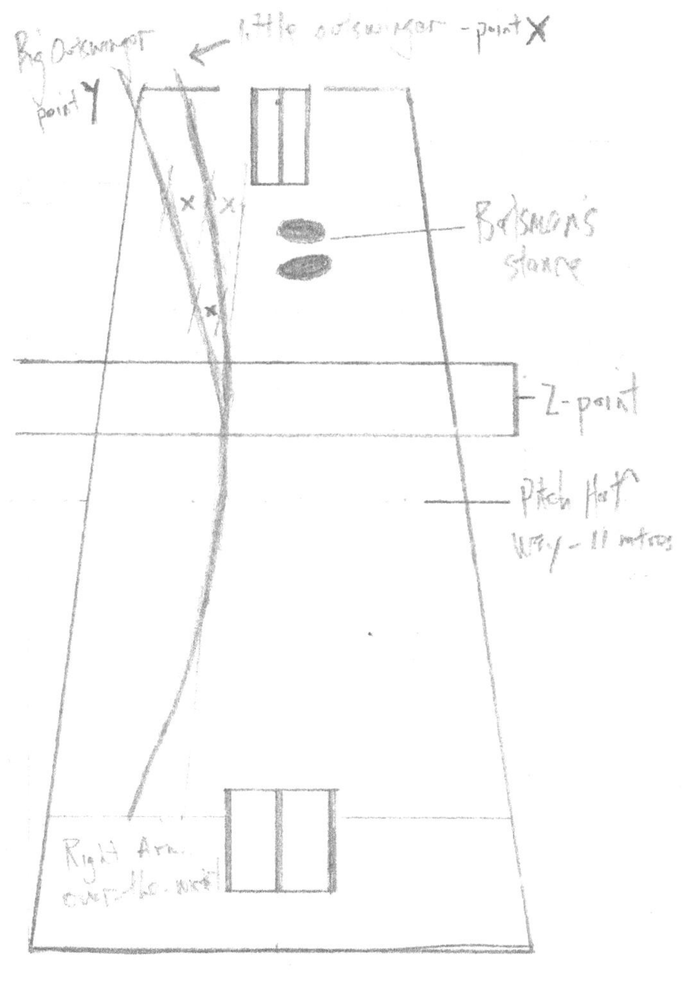

Note there are 3 possible paths the ball might take – straight one, little out-swinger and big out-swinger. Note that the Z-point in this diagram is a little further than mid-pitch or half way or 11 yards. This is the time the z-point as we call it, that we want to be in position for the ball and in position early enough to play a proper committed stroke without wrongly positioning our foot and creating trouble for ourselves. We want foot-eye coordination to happen and dictate where we are going to plant our foot and then we want hand eye coordination to play the ball as it swings and moves away like a banana and we want ideally our hands and arms to do most of the work and the feet to be just nimble and quick and make the small initial movement. So take this as almost set in stone and a key fundamental of batting:

"Foot-eye coordination is a precursor for good shot selection and playing the viciously swinging ball. Hand-eye coordination comes second along with playing with soft hands and playing late"

Back to our diagram. We want to be directly behind the ball and not playing away from our body, or at least in the beginning of our innings and must plant our foot in the correct position by z-point and no later. Where do we put it? By z-point you should be able to see the ball curving and swinging upon watching the ball hard as we suggested is critical in batting, and should see signs of an out-swinger or an in-swinger or a straight one. By this point you should be able to come up with a projection of where the ball might be upon reaching you and the bat based on a 'best' and 'worst' case scenario – so there will be two projections one at point X and one at point Y for our little and big out-swinger.[47] What we have to do is estimate both point X and point Y from what we have seen up until Z-point, and put our foot in the exact middle of these two points where the small 'x' is drawn, This way we are able to play the out-swinger closer to our bodies in the event that it happens and this is what we anticipate, and comfortably even leave the ball go if it swings big. By doing this we are maximizing our chances of being behind the ball and if we are not we just let the ball go outside off and through to the keeper. So there are 3 possible scenarios and 3 possible foot positions as is shown with the small 'x' in the diagram. There are 2 for if we playing off back foot and just one for if playing off front foot. For the forward defense or front foot shot, we plant our foot in the middle of the little out swinger and bigger out swinger as we don't really know how much the ball will swing we must settle for a half way point and if the ball continues to move further outward we just leave the ball alone but if we get the small in swinger we can still play the ball close to our pad by getting inside the line. For well directed out swingers which force us onto back foot, we have two options to get behind the ball, one is to go back and across a little bit and the other to go back and across a little further. However, it is not a danger if we just looking to defend we can just go back and across a little and leave the ball if it swings big or bigger than we thought. It is only if we availing big shot scoring opportunities that we watch for the bigger swinger and do this such that our bat is closer to our body when playing an attacking shot to the big out swinger – the backfoot punch..

---

[47] Note it is not common or usual for the ball to deviate beyond this amount – about 1.5 to 2 feet for pacers and 2-3 feet for spinners. That's why we are asking you to make this 'projection' before committing your footwork!

<u>So just remember this:</u>

- If ball is on a length we must go forward and plant our foot directly behind the straighter one, and if you see the ball swing place your foot in the mathematical or geometric center between where you anticipate the ball to be for a little outswinger and a big outswinger. If the ball swings big just leave the ball go.
- If the ball is short of a length go back with your right foot and place your foot in the geometric middle of the straighter one and the little outswinger and play defensive shot – there is no room to glide the bat through the line we are forced to just defend
- If the ball is short of a length go back and across and place your foot in the geometric center of a little outswinger and a big outswinger and play punch off back foot – we want to try get close to the ball and play the backfoot punch while the ball is close to our body; OR, just go back and across a little only and defend and if it swing big just drop the hands and let it go

"This is how the greats do it too when they are new to the crease or the ball is swinging very erratically at pace – being nimble and precise with your footwork is key!"

So you as batsmen must be thinking in terms of mathematical and geometric units and rely on visualization of these various points and center points and where exactly they might be on the pitch. We are not allowed to mark the pitch we have to just visualize where it is on the pitch and remember it. Once we are a little played in and have observed the pattern and capability of the bowler in terms of how much swing he is getting and can estimate the exact amount, we can then start using a different footwork method – one which allows you to get directly behind the ball and hit longer and harder, but until then we must shield ourselves by planting our feet at a center point estimate between the projected best and worst positions that the ball will be at by the time it reaches our bat.

Just to re-iterate our theory and why we advocate this approach to shot-selection and feet positioning based on what you see up and until z-point, and why it is important please inspect the following diagram:

Diagram XVIIII:

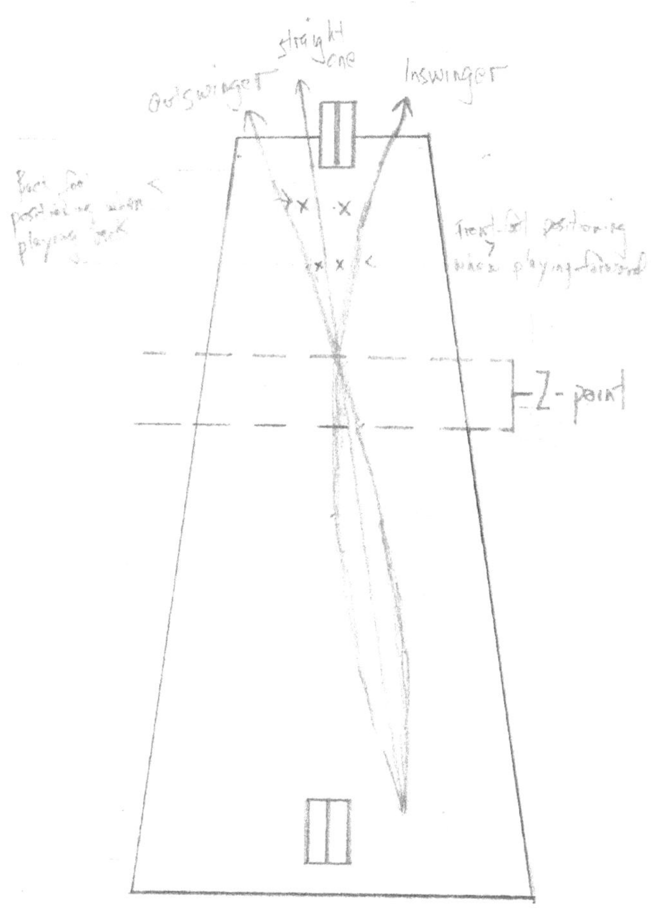

See the difference between the path of in swinger and out swinger? it is a big difference almost up to and around 4-5 feet in length, and requires completely different foot positioning to play properly. If we didn't observe the behavior of the ball up until z-point and watch the ball's initial path hard we would get our footwork completely jumbled up and get out[48]. We must observe the ball at z-point and determine and decide whether it is going straight, moving in or moving out to have any chance against bowlers who are that quick and get the ball to swing in varying amounts(ie. small inswinger Vs big inswinger). That, and the ability to pick and observe the action of the bowler and detect early just from the action itself whether it will move in or out.[49] Notice the differences in foot positioning – it is quite a significant distance between the 'x' or foot position suggested for playing an in swinger as opposed to outswinger or playing an inswinger off front foot and outswinger off back foot!

It's actually pretty straight forward don't let the drawing scare you, we are basically preparing ourselves for either an out swinger or in swinger and the big out swinger vs the little out swinger and playing the percentages and 50-50 probability of a 'biggie' vs a 'smallie' as the bowling is so quick and we must make a decision and react fast in regard feet and body positioning to not get LBWs and bowled or caught behinds. This calculation is not that hard as we will immediately upon being at the crease a little longer start judging the 2 distances – the ball positioning of the

---

[48] This is the scenario faced by Virat Kohli in WC semi final: a quick one well directed and swinging in, but how was he to know which way it will swing and where to plant his foot?

[49] Fast bowlers are taught in coaching sessions to generate swing in both directions. The difference in action and movement of the hips, shoulders and arms contribute to this ability to swing the ball further and later than it would have if a standard action was deployed by the bowler.

biggie versus smallie and innie versus outtie. This will happen intuitively without you knowing as you will soon start reading the bowler's pattern and the stretch or limit of his sideways or lateral ways movement and what he is capable in regard generating this movement. We can inevitably even draw it out on the pitch and make marks for where we might plant our foot depending on the path of the ball, but even just a mental picture or visualization is ok. This is exactly how the greats and best in the business play the swinging ball at pace also – it is actually simple stuff but just so you know the method and mental process of playing swinging deliveries and ones which swing in varying amounts. Of course when the ball is not swinging life is so much easier suddenly as all we left to do is estimate and judge the path as is consistent with Snell's law and Euclid's idea of vector forces.

Note, we are merely trying to explain to you a theory, don't take the size, proportion and geometric scales of the diagram as accurate or perfect.

If you are a batsman get some guidance in person about this topic, and ask the fast bowling coach to show you how a bowler changes his action to generate either inswing or outswing – this is extremely important when you are playing pacers of that quality, accuracy and speed and can't be stressed enough. Make sure you have a one-to-one with the fast bowling coach.

The implications of vector forces to bowlers:

Every time a bowler bowls a ball they must assume that its exact vector force has been summed up and judged by the batsman by the z-point. This is the only way to force you to disguise your variations, encourage a fast zippy action and use combinations and pin-point accuracy to successfully setup and deceive the batsman. In the ideal world of elite cricket no bowler is able to get a batsman out in one ball, it takes several and many deliveries to setup the batsman for the wicket taking ball. As the batsmen are so well prepared and trained and alert to vector forces involved in judging and playing the bowling and have such good defensive techniques, it has to be earned and worked for – the wicket taking ball that is. It may take you 4 deliveries or it may take you 40.

For pacers you should generate speed along with accuracy and use your in-swinger, out-swinger and straighter one intelligently. For spinners it can't be stressed enough that a quick, zippy and fluent action are keys along with variation and disguise. All this speak of the science behind seeing the ball and picking the length as is discussed in academies and within this book also is stacked in the batter's favour and as anyway the batsman has the advantage in cricket as we opined leads us to believe that "oh, it's too hard!". But it is not! It is hard but not too hard – you are essentially picking one of the hardest things to do in modern sport anyhow, the act of bowling in a game of competitive cricket, so don't be discouraged.

The implications of vector forces to wicket keepers:

A wicket keeper's view down the pitch is similar to that of the batsman and your job is similar to that of a batsman in that you must be reading the ball's length and judging it's final path once it bounces, including and accounting for any longitudinal or lateral ways movement which may happen. The difficult aspect of keeping is when you are keeping to the spinners. It is here where you need to really be reading his flatter ones, his loopier ones and variations in amount of turn being generated and keeping your hand positions either high or low. When you see the top spinner or loopier one you must immediately get your hands nice and high. When you see the flatter one or faster one you must position your hands low and be prepared to bring them higher after the z-point of the ball in case there is an edge.

Based on the sideways movement being generated by the bowler and the way you see a particular ball shaping up, you must be prepared to either take off from the left foot towards the right for leg spinner or be balanced on both feet if the ball goes straight or comes in like an offspinner. But the main thing for you keepers is to know when to lift your hands up high for the one which bounces a bit more and keep them low when the ball is expected to skid through or stay low.

When keeping to the pacers just remember to read the ball up until z-point to determine and accurately guess whether the ball will move inwards or outwards and be ready to bounce off either your left or right foot to move in the other direction.

So position of the hands and which foot to bounce off from is the key for you keepers. Reading the spinner's loopy one or bouncy one is important too.

The implications of vector forces to fielders:

Some of the best fielders in the world were Jonty Rhodes, Mark Waugh, Ricky Ponting, Azharuddin, Yuvraj Singh and now Ravindra Jadeja. The most crucial fielding positions in cricket usually are point, cover and square leg. It is within these positions that fielders are keenly watching the ball beyond and after z-point and also watching the feet work and back-lift of the batsman to get an idea of which way the batter might hit the ball – it could be either to his right or to his left or along the ground or in the air. The fielder is watching for the vector force generated when the batsman glides his bat and hands through the ball and is eagerly awaiting to anticipate going either left off his right foot or right off his left foot. Depending on if the ball was pitched up or pitched short a fielder may know when to begin a lunge in the air before or just after the ball deflects off the bat or similarly when to prepare to collect the moving ball off the ground and throw at the stumps. The best fielders are the ones who are looking out for and anticipating these vector forces both out the bowler's hand and off the pitch as well as the vector force generated when the ball hits the bat or bat hits the ball.

For example, if the fielder is at point and sees the batsman get behind the ball and not play away from his body, then he can conclude the ball will be hit through covers or ***forward of point*** – and can begin bouncing off his left foot to move rightwards. If he sees the ball pitched a little short he can conclude the ball may not be hit along the ground and prepare to lunge skyward for a catch. If he sees the ball pitched up than he can conclude a drive along the ground is probable and begin bouncing off his left foot as soon as possible to stop the ball at forward of point area.

These are some common examples of the implications of vector forces to fielders on a cricket field, and the way in which they save runs, get catches and complete runouts.

Implications of vector forces to captains:

Just as a wicket keeper must understand what the bowler is trying to achieve and be able to pick or read the bowler, the captain also must have a similar relationship with the bowler. At a minimum the captain must understand the bowler's variations and what the bowler is endeavoring to bowl versus what the bowler is actually bowling, and set the field accordingly. The captain needs to have an idea of what the bowler's wicket taking ball might be and give him an appropriate field with fielders in catching positions. So if the out-swinger is the one he is trying to get the batsman to play at or entice the batsman to play at then captain has to give more fielders in slip positions. If against spinner for example and he is trying to invite or entice the lofted shot give fielders in close in catching positions and out-deep positions also.

As a captain you should support your bowler by having faith that he will produce the 'good one' or the wicket taking ball and place an attacking field with catchers where the bowler needs them and is aiming to get the mishit or miscue.

Implications of vector forces to coaches:

The coach understands or should understand his team the best. He should have an understanding of each player and their strengths and weaknesses and in particular, their current comprehension and ability in the very fundamental and crux of the sport – vector forces. The coach ideally is the go-between man or interface between a player's expected and desired performance and his actual performance. It is the coach who understands the most of a player's game sometimes even more than the player himself and it is the coach who is responsible and in charge of getting the most out of the team he has and the students who appear before him. To do this the coach must be the one to analyse and review his players' technique and provide feedback when something goes wrong both via observation in nets and in live games. It should be the coaches responsibility to educate and inform his troops and team members about the game and the tricky nuances of the sport and exactly what is required to perform better and better and particularly at representative levels. So exactly what is required of us to perform and perform at the top level? Well we have pretty much talked about everything you need to know via the discussions put forth within the book thus far, but the fact remains that we as athletes cannot perform at any sort of peak efficiency or representative or elite level without being adequately guided and coached whilst we are practicing and practicing for high pressure matches – we as humans and contenders of a relatively difficult sport, need to be monitored and advised along the way by captains and coaches in order to 'pull it off' on match day and do your talent justice and there is no shame in accepting this, the fact that we all need a good coach supervising our game.

The fact that the coaches role suddenly becomes so critical means that for the coaches out there you must get your head around vector forces and how they apply to batsmen especially but bowlers too, and successfully convey this to your student or team member and be able to deliver a demo of this one-to-one.[50] To the batsmen you must convey the nuances in regard vectors which bowlers use and for bowlers you must convey the tricks and nuances batsmen use against bowlers. This makes for an all-

---

[50] Z-points used in fast bowling as well as spin bowling are a key towards coaching batting and coaching elite batters to play better and better

round education and understanding of the game for all parties and in the end only raises the standard of your own cricket as a team but the community wide standard as well as the international standard and produces great cricketers, ones who can come out on top regardless. We as elite cricketers and aspiring elite cricketers are not afraid of this knowledge and secret of the sport being spilled or told to everyone, it is a one for all and all for one situation and a win-win situation for global cricket, but most importantly it is the coaches way of guiding and marshaling his men in a competitive team versus team battle and a battle which sometimes is contested between enemies, foes or maybe in front of a bigger wider audience and the stakes of winning or losing are somewhat high – both financial and personal. The coach must look after his team in regard providing a proper education of the theory and fundamental techniques and methods pertaining to the sport – if the coach doesn't then who will??

You must observe if your student is seeing the ball in time at or before the z-point that is and that his foot-eye coordination and hand-eye coordination is in sync with what he is seeing, and help him if his visionary process and fundamental technique is not optimal as per the theories and guidance presented in previous chapters. Particularly, you must teach your students how to adjust their technique and how to approach their batting as depicted in Gantt charts of chapter 11, and especially how best to prepare for the bowler's 'clever tactics'.[51]

---

[51] Virat Kohli on WC semi final match day should have been told and warned by the coach and the onlooker of the bowler trying to send a nippy inswinger into the pads and getting out LBW.

A simple it is time to straighten your backlift or its time to rotate your backlift to 4th slip or the bowler is swinging it both ways be judicious about footwork and watching the ball hard until z-point or its time to build a partnership and sacrifice boundaries, is all that is needed on a coaches behalf – anything to give a batter some starting point as to approaching the bowling and the situation.

You must work with the bowler, in high level cricket that is where batsmen are better equipped and prepared to dominate the bowling, in regard to what may be a correct formula and a wicket taking formula if that's what is required and also a containment formula if that's what the game required at the time.

Just as we stated earlier about how the batsman has the advantage and bowlers may struggle to get a batsman out if it were not for limited overs cricket and run rate pressures which put pressure on them, a similar argument in regard bowling can also be deduced and that is that whilst the bowler may struggle to deceive, defeat and remove a batsman from the crease, he may still bowl accurately and restrict the scoring rate in any circumstance if so required, and that a coach should teach his bowlers strategies toward doing this – bowl accurately that is and contain or restrict the batsman in a limited overs format of the game. Not only do you help identify a bowler's strengths and exactly how to use strengths to take wickets during practice but you show them and make them aware of how best to contain and restrict the scoring rate in pressure one-day match situations too. If a bowler bowls well and with all his heart and full acceptance of the fact that batsmen almost always successfully read vector forces and read the ball out the hand, then there is no reason why a bowler with the right attitude and faith cannot bowl well and do the job in one-day formats of the game and etch his team closer to victory – it is only natural and a part of the skills which specialist bowlers have or are expected to have and the coach should encourage and foster this particular skill in practice sessions also along with the potential to take wickets and remove well trained batsmen from the crease.

Chapter Seventeen

Introduction To Spin Bowling

Not only are vector forces important in batting, as we have now discussed, but they are of significance and benefit in the act of bowling and especially spin bowling also.

Spin bowling is essentially about getting the right trajectory or flight in layman's speak as well as getting the ball to grip and turn off the pitch at the same time. These are the first two skills a spin bowler should be endeavoring to attain before anything else. So, if we ever had the luxury of a computer or robot which could do what we ask it to do it would be based around getting turn and purchase and at the same time holding a certain and desired trajectory along its journey down the pitch – note that both these factors can be varied with each other so there are already 6-8 combinations/permutations, and we have not even talked about the other aspects of spin bowling yet. We may want a flatter one with big turn or a loopy one with small turn or a loopy one with no turn, and so on. Other things we want to vary are the pace on the ball and also the angle of delivery from the crease and also grip to create a certain shape or drift on the ball. So now that we know what we have to do and what it is that we want to happen, lets talk about how we as a human can best make it happen. We are not robots and pre-programmable computers but the good news is there is nothing a human can't do and there is nothing which is impossible as a spinner if you practice and you are good enough, which we would like to happen and which cant happen. In fact unlike maybe batsman-ship and fast bowling, a spin bowler has potential and margin to actually perform better than a pre-programmable robot if we were living in a fantasy world, so there is a lot to learn.

Lets define the 5 different types of spin bowling and the 5 different types of spinners first, as you are going to have to decide which style and which method you wish to pursue – it is not just as easy as saying I am a spin bowler or that I want to be a spin bowler. These are defined as follows:

1. **Off-spin bowling ---sideon (Murali)**
2. **Off-spin bowling ---fronton (bhajji)**
3. **Leg-spin bowling ---slow (Warne)**
4. **Leg-spin bowling ---medium pace (Kumble)**
5. **Off-spin bowling ----containment or 'chorr bowler' (Jadeja/sehwag)**
6. **Left-arm chinaman – same theory involved as 3 and 4 (Michael Bevan/Kuldeep Yadav)**

All styles of spin bowling require a degree of artistry and guile as both flight, pace, angle of delivery, spin ratios, drift, bounce and amount of turn can be varied and must be optimized or decided upon by the bowler before delivery as to exactly which ball and which characteristics he desires in his next delivery; however, if you are a 'chorr' spin bowler as many allrounders and part time bowlers are, then your job is quite easily mastered. We have allowed for a separate chapter on each style of spin bowling so that we can adequately go through all the skills, finer points and combinations/permutations with the aspiring specialist spinner except for 'chorr' bowling, as this is quite straight forward.

The main skills of a good spinner are:

1. Control over and variation in flight
2. Being able to fizz, grip and turn the ball visciously
3. Being able to bowl variations
4. Certain grip – leading to drift in the air
5. Accuracy
6. Variation in side-spin/top-spin ratio

Lets talk about some of these basics of spin bowling so we can later get to the nuances and finer points in the next chapters and the points which all you aspiring spinners are itching to know and need to know to actually improve your bowling.

Firstly, take the four names mentioned above as the Gods of spin bowling as each is a fine exponent of his particular style of bowling – remember there are only really 4 styles of spin bowling which theoretically exist in cricket and which a person can aim for. So effectively, whatever you are doing with the ball and whatever your style is, it has been done before, it has been done before with super efficiency and effectiveness and your style will fall into one of the four broad categories of spin bowling aforementioned. Note that the majority of spin bowlers come from categories two and three, however one and four have produced some of the highest wicket takers ever to play the game also.

It is the potential for deception and guile and artistry as well as the many combinations/permutations possible, which makes spin bowling a uniquely human task and one who's quality cannot be replicated by a machine, robot or computer - and it is no wonder that the three best exponents of three of the four styles of spin bowling are also the most successful cricketers and wicket takers in the history of the game. So your work is cut out for you, there is a lot to learn, a lot to master and a long journey ahead of you aspiring spinners but just remember when learning and mastering spin bowling to not go to quickly, don't give up and don't get frustrated when it doesn't come out right and expect perfection from yourself too soon.[52] Striking that rhythm is not so easy in fact is probably harder than in fast bowling, so don't get frustrated when you are not striking that perfect rhythm immediately – there are so many combinations and permutations in spin bowling and each component of your action must be perfected individually before we expect full rhythm and the perfect ball!

"Take it step by step, one at a time, don't try to bowl the dream ball, the perfect ball or your desired delivery straight up or expect yourself to – first practice accuracy and only accuracy, then practice the ball turning the way you want it to turn and coming out the hand well, then practice control over flight, etc, etc. Practice and master each skill individually first and then combine to create the perfect ball – remember what we said there are so many combinations and permutations for spinners and we must master one skill before we move on to the next and lay a good foundation for ourselves and better and better deliveries to be bowled ahead"

....Nikhil Jain(Australia state level leggie)

---

[52]Practicing and mastering spin bowling is amongst the hardest things to do in cricket, it requires of us much dedication to get the basics right and lay the foundation if we are to expect perfection from ourselves down the track

Now for the big question and the question on all of our minds by now, and why we are reading the book!

So what does it take, what does it take to be a good spinner or if you are already a good spinner and reading this book in the hope of becoming a great spinner, what does it really take and what is the process and method to get there?

Don't despair or wait too much longer, by reading the next few chapters of this book on spin bowling, we will teach and show you all the answers in the coaching manual and well beyond. I am not only skilled and experienced in all 5 varieties of spin bowling, but have been coached at a senior state level from a country where cricket is almost as big as in India and has the best and most rigorous coaching regiments and resources in the world, and I am prepared to share my gains with you - I will teach you everything I know so hang in there. I have been coached from a country which produced not only Shane Warne but numerous others like Stuart McGill, Tim May, Greg Mathews, Peter Taylor and now Nathan Lyon – what I have been taught by my state level coach is exactly the same as what these guys have been taught.[53]

Further, I have the experience to explain to you and coach you in the method involved to bowl like the great sub–continental spinners too – Kumble and Murali, as I also used to bowl this way in nets and during personal practice sessions.[54] These two styles are two out of three of the

---

[54] Whilst playing competitive cricket and in matches as a youngster I only focused on slow leg-spin and front on off-spin as only so much can be handled or juggled

greatest bowlers and wicket takers of all time(the other being Shane Warne – slow leg-spinner) so obviously there must be some if not a lot of you aspiring spinners out there who are molding yourself in their footsteps or in their style – I know I did as a youngster and did it with great zeal, enthusiasm and success, and you can too if you just follow the simple advice I am about to give you.

As aforementioned in the chapter in our main skills of spin bowlers list, the one named variation of sidespin/topspin ratio is probably the most important and the one we need to talk about first. When we impart spin on the ball and send the ball down the pitch and set it along its path of trajectory, there are two components of spin being put on the ball – as we spoke about in previous chapter on vectors. Whenever we deliver a spin ball this is also a vector force in the making depending on what the bowler decides – it is usually a combination of sidespin along with over-spin or topspin but in varying ratios. A straighter one is 100% topspin with no sidespin and goes straight on and bounces due to the overspin on the ball; a huge spinner which grips and turns viciously may have 80% sidespin and only 20% overspin thus making the ball grip and turn sideways upon pitching – then we have all of our subtelties and variations in between these figures. As spinners we must put top-spin on all of our deliveries as this is what creates the flight, dip and bounce – even if we did as a spinner create a vector with sidespin only and no over-spin, the ball would not have any flight or any bounce and would be rendered virtually useless or a dead ball or 'Gimme'. It is the top-spin and the amount of top-spin we put on the ball as spinners that is the key to our success and creating a

---

in a match, however I did find slow leg-spin to be more attacking that's why I didn't use Kumble or Murali style in games.

decent delivery and one which will force the batsman to play at our proposition. Without the top-spin there would be no forward force on the ball and that is the entire objective for us as bowlers – that is to deliver a ball with enough forward force on it to make a batsman confused, deceived, mistaken or enticed into playing the wrong stroke to the wrong ball.

Now what I've just told you here is the very cornerstone or mantra of spin bowling – get used to it and just accept it but by all means understand it by thinking it over and viewing diagrams etc. In fact it is this skill which separates the good from the great and it is this skill which allows us to create unplayable and magnificent deliveries.[55]Without our topspin component we can't get the ball to follow a steady line, get decent flight and dip and ultimately create that 'dart-like' accuracy which we see in the good spinners – young Yuzvendra Chahal especially. We can't get a good flight or loop without over-spin on the ball, we can't get a dart like accuracy without over-spin on the ball and we can't get a good bounce without over-spin on the ball – being a spinner is not just about imparting sidespin on the ball, that is only the half of it or not even half the skill of spin bowling, the key is that we must get the ball coming out our hand well with the right ratio of both.

Now to the run-up. Imagine a fast bowler trying to bowl fast with no run-up! It would just not happen, and the same goes for spin bowling, we could

---

[55]See an improved Shane Warne after copping a beating from Ravi Shastri against India in 91/92, and observe his 'Gatting Ball' in the Ashes series – it is the sheer amount of topspin put on the ball along with substantial sidespin which created the trajectory, drift and late dip. Note his lack of forward force on the ball against India compared to the new Warne against England and his Gatting ball.

just not impart enough and the proper forward force on the ball in the form of topspin if we did not have a smooth, rhythmical and forward moving run-up.

The run-up is an equally important part of our delivery stride and action for us spinners as it is our run up which creates the forward force on the ball, which then creates topspin, which then creates flight loop and late dip. Your run-up and approach to the crease as a bowler should be proportionate to the pace and energy needed at point of arm coming down, so for a spinner it is less energy than a pacer so our run up also has to be slower. We want our upper body to have just enough momentum at the point of delivery to allow for our arm to pull down at optimum or required speed. So basically we don't want too much and we don't want too little, just the right amount.

The biomechanics of spin bowling or the components of the entire process are defined as follows:

- Run-up/approach to crease
- Follow through
- Pivot on front foot
- Ball coming out hand/fingers
- Wrist position for variations
- Round-arm vs straight-arm
- Position of elbow upon approach

The makings of a good spin bowler revolve around three main things:

- Accuracy
- Variations
- Flight, loop & trajectory
- Guile and intelligently 'setting up the batsman'

Practice method and routine 1: for spinners:

A. Practice ball coming out of hand and wrist positions for all your variations – along a short, maybe 10-17 yard length pitch;
B. Then, practice your length with all vairiations over a full length 22 yard pitch;
C. Then, once you have struck a length whilst bowling variations and ball is coming out well practice line also, making it line, length and variation all in good control – the ideal ball
D. Once length &line is in control and stable, only then practice subtle variations in length and line and flight – known as guile or deception or setting batsmen up

Practice method and routine 2: for spinners:

A. First practice length without your full tweak of spin on the ball, just bowling little flatter and faster ones;
B. Then, practice length and line;
C. Once length and line is stabilized;

D. Then practice length and line with the full tweak of hand and variations and flight, loop and trajectory

These are basically the only practice routines possible for spinners, both are systematically setting you up step by step to be in complete control, 'have the ball on a string', and bowl the type of balls we want to as spinners – that is one with the perfect trajectory, revolutions and accuracy, and one which is desired in match situations. This may not come easy. It requires systematic practice and patience, as we mentioned earlier, spin bowlers have the hardest time striking that beautiful rhythm that we love to bowl with where everything is going smoothly and perfectly, so stick to a practice routine and be a winner by partaking in 'smart practice' as opposed to hard practice.

If through the course of your practice routines you find another routine which works for you, then by all means use that – we are ultimately gearing up for consistently being able to bowl our stock ball well and our dream ball, it doesn't matter how we get there!

TIP FOR WHEN YOU CAN'T STRIKE THAT PERFECT LENGTH AND THE BALL FEELS BIG IN YOUR HAND:

Sometimes the ball feels so big in your hand and you just can't seem to strike that length. The ball is just lobbing up and you are bowling too many full tosses, don't worry this is transient and will disappear. Just use this simple technique of using a bigger ball about 9cm in diameter, there are plenty of places you can get one but make sure it is made of rubber or plastic. Practice your stock ball and imparting sidespin on the ball at full tweak whilst maintaining your length and aiming for that perfect length. Use this process and technique of practicing with a bigger ball until the ball no longer feels big in your hand, when you do this for a while say four or five overs and then come back to bowling with a normal sized cricket ball your control over length should immediately improve. Sometimes your fingers and hands just aren't working as if they were in full rhythm and you must slowly get them used to controlling your trajectory with that size of ball – a normal cricket ball that is. Get your fingers and hands used to a bigger ball first and then revert back to the normal cricket ball – trust me, your control over flight will improve via this training technique!

"To be a top level spinner, the ball must feel right in your hand and you must have full control over the revs you are putting on the ball and the trajectory you are attempting to create"

...Nikhil Jain

Just remember to **stretch your groin** before assuming any bowling responsibilities, especially in match situations where the pressure is on and we can often strain our groin whilst trying to change direction whilst running or moving. You don't want to injure yourself and put a burden on the team by being sidelined and injured. This is as much for yourself as it is for your team's sake too – just stretch your groin at a minimum quickly before bowling and batting in match conditions.

Chapter Eighteen

Offspin: Bowl Like Murali

Like we have stated in last chapter, Muralitharan is one such exponent of a type of spin bowling classified as side-on spinner or side-on off-spinner as opposed to front-on spinner or front-on off-spinner. This type of off-spin bowling is the hardest and cannot be done by just anyone – in fact there are very few people either professional or amateur who can actually perform or have even attempted to perform this high energy style of off-spin bowling. It is very effective and difficult to play if one can do it properly, however like we just said it is difficult and is not attempted by many people around the world, myself perhaps being one of only a handful to even try, but I'm sure you can learn your basics from this book to get started!

The problem whilst facing this style of bowling is that we come in from an angle and are literally side-on at moment of delivery and moment of ball releasing from hand. This means we get the full strength of not only pivot from our body and front foot but because of being side-on upon moment of delivery and then pulling arm down vertically, we are able to put tremendous amounts of side-spin as well as top-spin at the same time on the ball – hence extracting tremendous sideways movement and bounce off the pitch too accompanied with a great looping trajectory and late dip. You try playing that if you are a batsman - no wonder this guy was the greatest bowler and the leading wicket taker in the world. This style of bowling is perhaps not so easily taught via written communication like some of the others, and may require a full demo or one-to-one training if you are interested in or show promise in side-on offspin bowling.

Side-on off-spin is simply when our bodies and our chest is mostly or fully side-on to the batsman upon delivery, as opposed to being straight on or facing the batsman.[56]This style of bowling is a high energy task and is a combination of being side-on as well as extreme and sudden wrist movement also whilst releasing the ball and imparting tremendous amounts of revolutions on the ball. As the bowler of this style approaches the crease from a marked and visible angle he builds up kinetic energy going in the lateral, sideways or perpendicular to the pitch, and when he releases the ball and pulls the arm over straight in order to bowl the ball straight and straight down the pitch, all that sideways kinetic energy generated from the run-up is transferred onto the ball in the form of sideways spin, and the ball consequently turns more than usual. What is usual? Well usual is the usual off-spinner which 99% of offspinners are and that is a front-on offspinner and one who approaches the crease relatively straight during his run-up.

This style of off-spin is considered superior to the 'usual' style as more spin can be imparted due to the side-on action and quick snappy release, however is not easy to perform and is not very common. We can however, strike a balance somewhere in between where we are partly side-on and partly front on like so many off-spinners have done successfully. Some who have attempted to reap the benefits of a side-on action and attempted

---

[56]To contrast the two, look at Harbhajan Singh in IPL vs Muralitharan in regular test match play – already Harbhajan was a front-on bowler but due to IPL conditions and perhaps age, became even more front on.

to be at least partly if not fully side-on at the moment of delivery or release are: Carl Hooper, Rajesh Chauhan, Venkat Raju and of course Bishen Singh Bedi. These guys were not entirely side-on but were side-on enough to reap some of the benefits of side-on offspin bowling – had they been completely side-on they may even have been as successful as 'Murali'!

Generally the biggest plus-point or hallmark of this bowling is bowling the big turning offbreak followed by either the big bouncing straighter one or the dusra. Because of the angled approach to the crease and the side-on body upon release, the bowler is better able to disguise his variations and suddenly with the combination of offie-offie- topspinner or offie-offie-dusra this bowler becomes very difficult to not only play but even pick out of the hand. This style is more about defeating the batsman outright with sheer spin, turn and bounce as opposed to subtle variations in flight and spin or combinations/permutations, as spin bowlers are often demanded to rely upon in their bowling.

Like I said, this style of bowling is a little difficult to teach via written word only and requires some one-to-one coaching, but we will try anyway. But remember, this method is superior as our variations are harder to read and more effective, especially the dusra due to the deception of our action which suggests that a big spinning 'offie' is coming.

It sounds silly but the way to master this style of bowling is to first start out approaching the crease as per normal but then as we get to delivery point we want to practice chucking the ball and getting big spin and high revs on the ball[57]. Once we have perfected our biomechanics we slowly start training ourselves to straighten the arm whilst still maintaining the tremendously high revs imparted on the ball. So come in from an angle say 35-45 degrees from the line of the pitch, sometimes even more, and aim to run in to the crease slowly and steadily yet smoothly – the key here is we have to lift our knees a little higher as we run in to create the rhythm and the deception of either pushing the ball through or holding the ball back. The way we run in and move our knees absolutely assists us in doing this and prepares us for the vicious spin we are about to impart on the ball. Another important thing is to try keep our arms and our overall arm rotation as short as possible as opposed to stretching out – this is what the chucking helps us to do, to shorten our arm length and give the ball a greater flick.[58]The next thing is the pivot on the front left foot. This is as usual and as per regular off-spin bowling only we want to make it a little quicker and shorter – remember we are trying to get a big flick with a short arm, the quicker shorter pivot plays a part in this also.

Use your Dusra as often as you like but just try not to overuse the topspinner as already in this style of bowling we are putting greater overspin than usual, and the batsman may start getting used to your rhythm and start playing you better if you overuse the topspinner.

---

[57] It has been scientifically proven that chucking or bending the arm whilst performing side-on off-spin can yield greater revs and more turn. However note Murali was officially cleared and was not a chucker but may have used chucking as a practice and training method.

[58] Pat Symcox of South Africa used to really stretch his arms right out and try get his whole body and leverage onto the ball – this is just what we DON'T want to do, we want a short and powerful nippy arm motion upon release

Like all spinners, you have a very good chance of picking up wickets in this style of bowling in one-day matches or limited over matches where the batsman is looking to score and play big shots and we as a good spinner are adept in 'tossing the ball up' or giving extra loop/flight to the ball. We can often get caught behinds and stumpings from this style of bowling as our loop is superior due to the extra top-spin imparted from this method of off-spin bowling.

If you are having problems with your accuracy whilst practice or in match situation, just remember the simple rule – faster and flatter. Go faster and flatter for a few balls then slowly work toward adding the loop and flight to the ball which we as spinners ultimately and ideally desire. Even during your practice sessions practice slower – higher Vs flatter – faster as you may be required to come in on the death or at the end of the innings to merely contain and choke the runs. This is a good skill for any spinner to have anyway – being able to interchange your trajectory between slower-higher and faster-flatter, and is one of the necessary skills of spin bowling in limited overs cricket, so you should anyway be incorporating it into your practice routine. A good spinner should be able to perform the role of 'chorr' bowler when and if he needs to – make sure you also devote some time to practicing your faster-flatter trajectories and being accurate and at the stumps, many times as we have so often seen, even these bowlers can pick up big wickets and be somewhat successful and make great contributions to the game. [59]

---

[59]Aka Yuvraj Singh, Sehwag, Tendulkar and many more from various other teams.

The size of your hands may well play a contributory role in how much revolutions you can put on the ball, but this is something we cannot control so don't worry about it too much. But if you do have average to slightly smaller than average sized hands you are one of the lucky ones who have the best chance of imparting maximum amounts of spin on the ball just like Murali, and have every chance of being a great spinner.[60]

Remember to warm up in the recommended way for spinners which is to loosen up with two or three medium pacers, and then bowl an over or so just getting your accuracy right, after which bowl three or four each of your stock variation balls . Once you are a bit more comfortable with the ball coming out the hand relatively accurately then you can start practicing flight and variations and combining to bowl the ideal ball or ideal combination – do not just expect of yourself this straight up, it takes a bit of loosening and warming up.

Now for the key part and the pivot to your success in actually bowling like Murali or not - in the mould of a side-on 'offie' or merely a front-on 'offie', remember we opined earlier that this style is a superior brand of off-spin bowling as we get more revs on the ball both sidespin and overspin.

Only attempt 'chorr' bowling or front-on off-spin bowling if you are for some unfortunate circumstance physical or mental, unable to grasp, comprehend or perform this particular style of bowling – a style of bowling which has taken the most international wickets of any other bowler ever to have played the game, 'Murali'. We don't plan to fail, we plan to succeed,

---

[60]The best spinners had small to medium sized hands whereas the taller and bigger spinners like Pat Symcox or Kumble did not impart so much spin on the ball.

don't we also want to be the best bowler and especially, the best off-spinner ever to have played the game? – of course we do, if we can't we will die trying as the saying goes, we will at least follow and attempt the fundamentals and key-points associated with this style of delivery.

When we run in our approach to the wicket, which we have mentioned earlier has to be angled and around 45 degrees, we want to put all of our forward force upon delivery on to our front left foot and completely stop there – yes, that's right, we want all the forward force of our run up to come to a halt at our front foot and our delivery foot, our left foot. We want to have a quick, short and sharp pivot on our front foot. We want all our forward force of the run-up to be transferred through our pivot and through our hands and fingers. We do NOT want our body to move forward from this point onward – we want all this forward force from our run-up to be translated and transferred through our wrists and fingers, and unlike a front-on offspinner who's delivery stride and run-up contributes toward the forward force of the ball – we want to do the opposite, we want to halt our forward run-up force and sharply pivot on our front foot, henceforth putting all of or forward force through our left foot and our hands and fingers who will pull down viciously on the ball, and impart the side-spin/off-spin on the ball.

Upon left front foot pivot do NOT go through with your run-up – let your run-up completely cease upon front foot pivot and let all forces be transferred through your hands and your fingers in the form of wrist motion, sidespin and over-spin – that's right, it is your hands and fingers that we want to do all the work, not our run-up or forward delivery-stride as in pace bowling or fast legspin bowling or even front on offspin bowling.

Maintain your usual grip for off-spinners upon delivery, and determine the position of wrist cocking upon delivery as per what is comfortable and reaps maximum spin, upon practice and experimentation.

Remember, you are aiming to be the greatest, the greatest bowler ever and the greatest off-spinner ever, it may take practice – follow the basics I have outlined to you and best of luck!

Chapter Ninteen

Offspin: Bowl Like Bhajji

This style of bowling is known as a more front-on action or style to off-spin, and despite still involving a pivot on the front foot, the pivot here is not as great or important as in side-on off-spin bowling. Here we are sacrificing the tremendous amounts of turn we spoke of in side-on offspin, and we don't get great amounts of sideways movement or turn and our deliveries especially the top-spinner do not bounce as much.

Given this, we do not generally defeat the batsman for sheer spin or sheer bounce, rather, we use accuracy and subtle variation in particularly line along with guile and disguise to get wickets and bowl well. Due to the front on action and the fact that we can't get a better and more powerful rotation on our hip and front foot in the form of the pivot, we generally don't get as much bounce, however, we are still quite capable of putting topspin on the ball and generating decent flight and loop, just not as much. The same principle applies where we are trying to make the batsman commit to his stroke, and are therefore pushing the ball through a bit faster. This bowling has a dart like quality and as we mentioned relies heavily on maintaining a good line and bowling variations thereof. We are still bowling all our variations, the 'toppie', the 'dusra', the stock offbreak and the 'arm ball', and in full flight and vigor are posing danger to the batsman in the form of our accuracy and enough turn or purchase to find the edge or sneak through the batsman's defences.

This is a very exciting style of bowling, as Bhajji himself has shown throughout his career, and is just as attacking and wicket taking option as any, however does rely or depend on it's bowler being very accurate and guileful in regard to varying his line, length and use of the crease. Here is a list of all the deliveries bowled by front-on offspinners:

- Off-break
- Top-spinner
- Dusra
- Arm ball
- Little off-break
- Big off-break
- Carom ball

As we are not getting side-on and completely or partially wrapping ourselves and our body around the ball, but rather are letting our hands and fingers do all the work in imparting the sidespin and over-spin; this style of bowling suddenly becomes all the more effective, as we become harder to read and pick and size up the bowler's rhythm from run-up all the way to delivery stride and release.

As we are front on and are allowing our hands and fingers only to do all the work as far as putting revs on the ball, our straighter one suddenly becomes lethal and if bowled well, these bowlers are a huge candidate for LBWs and bowled with their combination of off-breaks and then the straighter one. Also the dusra is very effective too when it is bowled after a few relatively well directed straighter ones. But by far, it is our straighter one which is very well directed in regard line which is the hallmark of this style of bowling, and especially the one which is very accurate.

When we perform this bowling, we are not stopping at our front foot like Warne and Murali like bowling, but rather are following through with our body and feet as if we were a fast bowler. By decreasing our pivot on the front foot, we are essentially making it very hard for the batsman to pick the amount of sidespin and overspin we are putting on the ball – that's why it is such a successful style, as Bhajji has shown with his numerous match winning performances for India.

We can often argue that too much spin, too much turn and too much flight, dip and bounce as in Murali style off-spin, are not good anyway, and that this style of bowling is a better option in deceiving the batsman, and it is true to some extent. By reducing our turn, flight, dip and bounce we are better able to set-up the batsman using subtle and highly calibrated variations in line and length to deceive and defeat the batsman – look at the way Bhajji bowls, it certainly does not look as if this style of bowling, front-on offspin that is, is one which is merely limited and less dangerous!

Remember it is our dart like line and accuracy which is the key here to front-on off-spin, and that we want our hands and fingers to do all the work and not our body or our pivot. Our well directed straighter one which does not loop as much also is key.

Continue to use your dusra and vary your flight and particularly the slower and higher principle, which we talked about is a very important skill in spin bowling and just as important in this style also.

It takes immense practice to master this style as we are working within very narrow parameters and our ability to calibrate our bowling particularly in regard to line and length is of critical value and importance in being successful.[61]

It is a very challenging yet exciting form of bowling as it is so hard to pick and read and has enthralled cricket fans the world over ever since 'bhajji' came on to the scene. With it's match-winning audacity and well calibrated direction in regard line, it operates within such narrow parameters for its success, and that's what drew us to 'Bhajji' in the way we did whilst he was still playing international cricket.

The run-up is relatively faster in this style as we are primarily aiming for that dart like line and accuracy and only secondary to this are we adding on the flight and loop. We want all of our momentum to be carried forward at delivery stride and release and let our fingers further put additional forward force on the ball in the form of over-spin.

Practice routine: front-on offbreak bowling:

- Practice bowling line and pitching the ball on middle, middle and off, and then off and outside off by a fraction
- Then practice line and length
- Then practice adding the flight and loop in

---

[61]Harbhajan Singh of India, the perfect exponent of front-on off-spin, had to practice for hours each day before he was able to bowl with that perfectly calibrated line and length which we mentioned is the hallmark of this style.

- At all stages, test yourself in regard being able to vary your line by small and marginal amounts – this is the key to you being good at this style of bowling.

As we mentioned before, Murali style bowling is bowled with a short arm, however, this particular style is the opposite. It is better and beneficial to our dart like accuracy that we stretch out our bowling arm and try to bowl with a long arm as much as possible. It is our long arm action which helps create and compound our dart like forward force on the ball, which we opined that makes this style so lethal and exciting as a wicket taking option.

As in any spin bowling, it is important that you have done enough practice so that the ball feels right in your hand and does not feel too big. This style operates within narrow parameters and minimal room for error, so this particular idea, of the ball feeling right in your hand that is, is very crucial – if you are struggling in regard this, do the exercise mentioned at the end of the intro to spin bowling chapter.

Chapter Twenty

Legspin: Bowl Like Warne

This is legspin bowling in its most classical and text-book form. Or as we say the traditional and 'normal' way of performing legspin, and the way almost 80% of legspinners usually bowl or attempt to bowl. There have been many fine exponents of this style of bowling both in the past and in today's era – Rashid Khan, Chahal, Imran Tahir and Clarrie Grimmett, Richie Benaud and Chandrashekhar of yesteryear, but across all time frames and across all continents, it is Shane Warne of Australia who was by far the best exponent of this style.

Here is a comprehensive list of all the variations which are possible in slow leg-spin, however note that, even whilst performing this style we must try to zip the ball through and bowl on the faster side – as we mentioned in introduction to spin bowling chapter:

- Stock leg-break
- Googly
- Top spinner
- Slider
- Flipper
- Zooter

The only two hard ones here are the flipper and the slider, of which even myself can only bowl one of the two – I cannot bowl and do not know how

to bowl a flipper, for this you may need to consult a reputable spin bowling coach, I can however fill you in on the remaining five deliveries.
The objective of this type of leg-spin bowling, which we mentioned is the true and traditional approach, is basically to walk in slow and explode during the action and release phase of our run-up, thus creating almost like an illusion for the batsman. We want to bowl all of our deliveries on the faster side and really zip and fizz the ball through spinning the ball as hard as we can. This style is a really attacking style of bowling and requires the bowler to put or try to put tremendous work and revs on the ball, and truly is a great wicket-taking option in good attacking cricket. By zipping, fizzing and pushing the ball through with maximum revs on the ball and at the same time maintaining a decent pace, which we mentioned for spinners should generally be on the faster side, what we are doing here is really putting pressure on the batsman to commit to his stroke and make scoring runs a risky task – that is why this style is considered a great wicket taking bowler and an attacking brand of bowling throughout the cricket fraternity.

So the first thing is our run-up. Like we said by running in slow or by simply walking in and then following this with a sudden jolt, jerk and explosive release of the ball; we are in effect creating an optical illusion for the batsman who thinks based on our run-up that the ball will be on the slower side, however once bowled by the bowler who explodes at the end of the run-up and fizzes it through with pace AND turn, the batsman is really put under pressure in regard to consistently picking and getting used to the rhythm the bowler is generating. Due to the explosiveness at the end the batsman generally struggles to successfully pick the vector force behind the ball and moreover, due to the pace, struggles to be able to play the ball late or 'check his shot' – the batsman is made by the bowler to decide and commit to his shot early which then opens up a host of avenues for taking wickets.

This combined with the fact that the bowler has so many additional tricks up his sleeve like variations which turn differently, varying the flight, varying the pace and being able to vary the bounce also; makes for a very torrid time for the batsman if the leggie of this style is bowling well and striking a good rhythm.

It becomes very easy and possible for this type of 'leggie' to dominate and put tremendous pressure on the batsman, and that is why it is one of the leading wicket takers of Test cricket – Shane Warne of Australia with 708 wickets, after Murali.

So what made Shane Warne so good? Well like we mentioned previously, the crux of spin bowling is being able to bowl a delivery which has substantial amounts of top-spin coupled with substantial amounts of side-spin – and that is the reason why he was so good, his fundamental grasp and skill in doing this gave him the perfect platform and base from which to launch his other 'missiles' or other tricks which he had up his sleeve. Remember we said that it is this ability in a spinner which creates that dart like accuracy in regard line, creates a decent forward force and pace on the ball and most importantly creates that beautiful flight which dips late. So being an exponent of this style and one-day also bowling like Warne may not be that hard for all you aspiring youngsters out there, you just have to master your basics and get the fundamental skill of spin bowling right - getting the ball to come out the hand right with over-spin and sidespin both, the rest is simply about being taught the minor modifications we make in our action and applying our variations or 'tricks' in the form of variation in pace, direction, speed and bounce.

When taking the journey through learning and mastering spin bowling your biggest asset is the amount of work or revs you can put on the ball and that too with a decent pace and the ability to either push the ball through or 'hold it back', and this is what made Shane Warne so good and so mesmerizing to batsman.

So our stock ball is walk in slow and release the ball fast and have as much revs and pace we can absolutely put on the ball, but what about if we want to bowl a loopy one or more flighted delivery to get a stumping or entice the drive, what do we do then? All we have to do is walk in a little faster and drop the gear on our release making it slightly slower and bowling the ball slightly higher and slower. This is the best way to disguise our flighted one and the way Shane Warne used to do it also.

Both Murali and Warne made use of this technique of an 'explosiveness' upon release, and preceded by a relatively slow approach or run-up to the crease, and both used the technique aforementioned for their 'loopy one'.

Now that you know that this style of spin bowling relies heavily on your fundamentals of spin bowling being correct and well developed, that is spinning the ball hard with over-spin and sidespin, we can assume that the rest is not so difficult – that is you too can soon be bowling in the mold of Warne and Murali in a short space of time. How do we do this and how do we do it like the greatest, Shane Warne that is, and what minor changes to our current bowling style do we need to make? Well these are mere nuances in comparison with mastering the fundamental skill of spin bowling, so don't worry we will talk about it and guide you about this also. But first let's look at an important and revered moment in the entire history of leg-spin bowling, and that is the bowling of the 'Gatting Ball'. What made this so special and what made this ball so good?

'The Gatting Ball':

- Good pace on ball, was bowled with fizz, zip and pace
- Tremendous sidespin on the ball
- Tremendous over-spin or topspin on the ball giving it that dart like accuracy AND that beautiful late dip and drop
- Due to the age and shine of the ball and the grip adopted by Warne – the ball generated late drift
- Pinpoint accuracy on or near leg-stump
- Ball had the perfect leg-spinner's trajectory – above and to the side of the batsman's eyeline.

This ball was considered and still is considered the ball of the century – and that too by a leg-spinner or slow bowler. This ball is considered the perfect stock ball for a leg-spinner – fast and with tremendous revs on the ball. This ball shook the entire cricketing fraternity into seeing legspin bowling differently. No longer was it slow, boring and predictable and a mere war of attrition, but could be used as an attacking and wicket taking option and one which was riveting to watch too. Legspin bowling has not looked back ever since the feat of this great man, and you should not either. There are plenty of opportunities within this style of bowling for you to dominate and defeat the batsman in style and be an excitement to watch just like any pacer or fast bowler. We need more quality 'leggies' in international cricket – maybe you can be the next.

When trying to be good at this style we need to make good use of our variations and good use of the crease, as this is what allows us to get on top of the batsman and ultimately set him up for the wicket taking ball. This is the most attacking style of bowling which exists as the bowler is able to extract variation and movement both sideways and up and down, and coupled with cleverness and guile, becomes a handful to negotiate.

So the scene is set, you now know the hallmarks of this style of bowling and what makes it so effective, now you just have to practice your fundamentals well and practice getting into 'your stride'. You must practice a smooth and economical run-up and one which is slightly slower and practice this explosiveness upon release, however note we DO want to generate some momentum from our run-up here also, just not that much or as much as say a pace bowler, and we want to deceive the batsman with our sudden explosiveness upon release.

Practice fizzing, ripping and tweaking the ball as hard you can and then start getting down to your length and your accuracy. As far as accuracy is concerned, practice your length first and once and if you have practiced your tweaking and the ball coming out of your hand with maximum revs, then incorporate practicing the length AND line.

When you are bowling well and your stock leg-break is turning a lot, begin working the 'angles' and 'lines'. Start off coming in from relatively close to the stumps and really try to dart it into middle and off. Then come wider of the crease and try dart it into middle and leg in hope of getting an edge or miscue. Try bowling a few well directed stock leg-breaks which keep the batsman honest, and then try bowling a loopy one at around middle or middle and leg. Try also after you have bowled a few that zip through with not so much turn but well directed, and then bowl a slider slightly to the right or toward leg-stump slightly, OR you can follow these well directed zippy ones with a slower higher loopy one to try get the batsman driving at the ball after you kept him honest and scoreless. Try vary the angle of your arm to roundarm Vs straight arm and everything in between.

Ok, so lets define what these variations which we possess as 'Warne like' bowlers, and define exactly what they are and a few tips in bowling them well.

Stock leg-break:

Generally bowled with a somewhat round-arm but not completely and has 60% sidespin and 40% overspin imparted upon release. The angle of the arm can be varied to completely round arm and also to 85% sidespin and 15% topspin, but this is only sometimes as this creates a flatter ball which doesn't bounce as much. The objective here is to rip the ball with maximum turn, but we can still bowl a 'little leggie' if the situation demands or we are in that stage of setting the batsman up.

Topspinner:

Is almost always bowled with a straight arm action and its objective is to only put over-spin and not sidespin on the ball so the ball dips and bounces and goes on straight without turning. This is not that hard and requires a certain change in wrist position whereby the wrist and back of the hand are facing toward the batsman as opposed to your back of hand facing toward the right for a leg-break.

Googly:

Similar wrist position for top-spinner only further so that the back of hand is facing toward the batsman but slightly further to the right side. Googly and top-spinner have similar actions and are basically identical in execution, only googly requires you to further cock your wrist to the maximum such that your back of hand is facing down the pitch and to the right as much as humanly possible. This ball generally has a high component of topspin on it and turns the other way as well as bouncing a little more due to the over-spin.

Slider:

Just as in you were bowling a stock leg-break with vicious amounts of spin on the ball, only here we use our spinning finger which is the third finger to not get over and around the ball whilst releasing, but just push forward and follow through forward with the third finger pushing straight and down on the ball as opposed to over and around the ball to create legspin. This ball pitches as a leggie but then goes straight on instead of turning.

Flipper:

This ball comes out the back of the hand with a click of the fingers and comes out with a flatter trajectory and skids and keeps low upon bouncing. It also comes out faster whilst maintaining the slow steady run-up of a stock delivery, hence why it is so hard to pick and play and is a wicket taking ball usually bowled after you have set him up.

Zooter:

This is not a very commonly bowled delivery as it is merely being made to spin with backward revs on the ball instead of forward revs as in our other deliveries. This ball just hits the pitch and 'holds-up' as it has backward spin on it. Bowled out of the front of the hand.

So if there were three stages to spin bowling then the first two of simply learning the variations and perfecting your accuracy would make you 67% of a Shane Warne in a matter of weeks. The other 33% being the application of guile and artistry and applying certain mental acumen in setting up and dismissing the batsman through playing a false shot or beating their defence, being the likes of an expert. So it is not that hard, if you practice what is shown in this chapter you are almost Shane Warne already – so don't give up and believe it is too hard, it is not. It is only the professional and clinical approach and mental acumen which may not come easy and may require greater amounts of effort and concerted practice to attain.

And as we said in the beginning bowling the variations is not that hard but for the slider and the flipper.

"Just remember to make the ball fizz, zip and tweak as your first lesson in slow leg-spin bowling"

..............Nikhil Jain

As we mentioned in our chapter on bowl like Murali about the pivot on the front foot, and how we must stop our forward stride completely at our front foot and let all the energy and forward force be translated and transferred through our pivot and hips, we must use the exact same method in slow leg-spin bowling also. This, coupled with the fact that we are trying to bring the ball at and above and to the side of the batsman's eye-line, are the two single most important factors in your success at slow leg-spin bowling! Our stock ball is a big ripping leg-break pitching around middle and off, however our wicket-taking ball is the one which pitches middle or middle and leg, comes in at above and to the side of the batsman's eye-line and turns and dips viciously.

If we can get our pivot right and become adept at bowling the flighted one which floats and dips above and to the side of the batsman's eye-line, we are well on our way to mastering this style of bowling.

<u>Diagram XVII:</u>

Chapter Twenty One

Legspin: Bowl Like Kumble

Ok so you've decided you don't want to be a slow legspinner but want to be a medium pace leggie, in the mold of Anil Kumble. Well the basics remain the same – use your variations, spin the ball hard and try to have a few set combos to gradually set up the batsman.

This style of bowling, in order for it to be done properly, relies heavily on subtle and accurate variations in line and especially line. Length is also important just as in any style of bowling, but it is your line and subtle variations thereof, which will help and aid you in getting wickets and being a successful exponent of this type of bowling. The whole back bone of this particular method where we come in faster and off a longer run up is to basically generate more flight and dip through the greater amounts of topspin and over-spin being put on the ball. By coming in off a longer run and having greater momentum at the time of release and delivery, we are giving ourselves the best chance to not only bowl the ball a little faster, but like we mentioned in previous chapters about the over-spin ratio, we are essentially giving ourselves a lot more to work with in regard to bowling the ball with lesser or more top-spin,and if done properly not only greater amounts but tremendous amounts of topspin being imparted on the ball. We are using variations in our pace, dip and drift as opposed to lateral or sideways movement to successfully defeat the batsman, and it is now more than ever that our ability to bowl subtle and slight differences in our line which comes into play to get bowled and LBWs.

Due to the run-up and momentum at the time of release, we are better able to disguise our topspinner from our stock leggie, and moreover are better able to bowl a huge topspinner or one with significantly greater amounts of overspin than our stock leggie, and ultimately make the batsman's life difficult and our bowling hard to play overall. In fact, we are able to impart so much topspin on the ball through our medium pace run up to the crease that it has been known for bowlers to get the ball to lift up to batsman's head height and effectively be considered a bouncer or a no ball – myself being one such amateur exponent to do so. So why does not Kumble bowl a big bouncing toppie in matches? Well, in spin bowling and in batting too for that matter, our height does play a big role in the way we perform and the options open to us – you will see the great majority of international and great spinners were of short to medium height only. It is this lesser height which allows us to generate a certain flight and trajectory on the ball and get the ball to dip and drop late which perhaps a taller bowler may not be able to do. To help better understand and prove this lets take it to the extreme – what if a spin bowler was ten feet tall and the pitch was only 20 metres long, how do you picture this ten foot tall guy of getting any loop or flight on the ball?. He would definitely generate more pace and steep bounce but not that flight and loop which we are looking for in spin bowling and that trajectory which makes facing spin-bowling so difficult. So unfortunately, that added height of the bowler does not necessarily give an advantage in spin bowling, in fact the shorter the bowler is the better. Lets take say five and a half feet tall or 5'6" as being the optimal or ideal – the very same height of Murali, the greatest spinner ever.

Ok, so that's one facet and one advantage of this style of bowling but combine that with that added pace and bowler's ability to consistently get the ball to fizz and zip through – suddenly the batsman is under pressure to commit to his stroke early and our subtle variations as spinners become all the more deadly. I mean Kumble is not the leading wicket taker of India for no reason, and is not the only man ever to take 10 wickets in an innings for no reason – this style of bowling must be a very effective style of bowling. What makes it so effective, well that has been explained in the points aforementioned, your job now is to start perfecting your run-up, action and delivery stride as well as getting the ball coming out the hand as desired, but do not forget also to practice your huge spinning top-spinner which bounces.

Think of yourself as not a spinner but a medium pacer who can get the ball to bounce or lift sharply, and not so much as a spinner or slow spin bowler desiring huge amounts of tweak and turn. Unlike slower forms of spin bowling where the ratio of spin is 70% sidespin and 30% overspin, this style of bowling is the opposite, we aim to put 30% sidespin and 70% overspin and put the batsman under pressure with the extra pace and nagging pinpoint line. As we have more momentum, kinetic energy or forward force at the point of release, we give ourselves a good chance of transferring this forward energy through our hands and wrists and ultimately imparting more revolutions on the ball – just like a side-on off spinner, but here we are physically able to impart especially more topspin on the ball as opposed to sidespin. Like we said before, a good spinner is in-replicable and cannot be stopped or kerbed, even though on paper you might be thinking well that means you will be easier to play – that is not the case, this guy was not easy to play and had all the guile and tricks of any spinner in the world. This style of bowling is not what we would usually brand as ‘limited’ – this guy was one of the leading wicket takers of all time, all due to his mastery of the fundamentals and variations and subtle guile commonly known and used in spin bowling as per say. Even if the batsman starts reading you, it is the accuracy, zip and variation in pace combined with the big top spinner which makes it so hard to actually play – there was nothing as a spinner Kumble could not do and did not know, including variations and subtlety combined with guile, the potential you as a human have whilst attempting spin bowling which a robot cannot be programmed to do. He was truly an exceptional bowler with great skills and variety, despite what the media opined about him not spinning the ball and lacking variety.

Be careful with this style to not run in too fast and not too slow but more importantly perfect your run-up so as to be on the slightly slower side if anything, but just not on the faster side – it is the smooth, steady and correctly paced and not too fast run-up, which aids us in converting our forward motion in to the right pace and spin on the ball, especially the big top-spinner. As you practice you will find out and discover which deliveries require a faster or a slower run-up. Usually we bowl the big toppie with a faster run in to the crease, and our bigger legspinner or sideways turning ball with a slower run-up.

This style of bowling can be very effective and successful as the subtle and pinpoint variations especially in regard to line, can cause all sorts of problems for the batsman, and given we are bowling at quite a pace, we are able to thereby force the batsman to commit to his stroke early and open up more wicket taking possibilities.

There is no particular benefit of a pivot and rotation of the hips here, in medium pace leg-spin that is, and unlike side-on offspin and slow leg-spin, where we transfer all our run-up energy through the pivot of the front foot and hip rotation; here, we are putting all our run-up energy through our hands and fingers in the form of tremendous over-spin and some sidespin like revs on the ball.

Tremendous amounts of over-spin coupled with pinpoint accuracy in regard your line, are the hallmarks of mastering this style of bowling, and by coming in off a longer run-up, we are giving ourselves the best possible chance of putting greater amounts of top-spin on the ball.

Chapter Twenty Two

Captaincy: Managing Your Men Vs Harnessing Your Horses

The captain is only as good as his players and their potential, or as is often said an army can only be as strong as its regiment – this is true and must be accepted, but good leadership, planning & strategy go a long way and can make all the difference in how well your troops perform on the day. As well as charisma and tactile leadership, these are the qualities and traits along with good fielding, which add up to form what is known as 'out-cricket'.

What is out-cricket? Let's define out-cricket as any part of the game or our performance on a cricket field which does not demand of us any especially great amount of skill and/or exertion to successfully perform – so for example catching the ball, running between the wickets, making the right decision upon winning the toss, these are all examples of out-cricket. That is, little things and nuances of the game which we don't ordinarily focus on during practice but however DO add up to make a difference how big or small, on the match day performance of the team. So if you are a captain this chapter is highly relevant and mandatory for your reading and knowledge, as it is in your hands to maximize the performance and results from the batting and bowling talent you have, for the benefit of the team and the team's advantage.

There are so many things you guys as captains have to be weary of and account for but the most important thing when captaining and leading your men is to keep it simple and don't panic – let the game take it's natural course, however by all means try anything and everything tactically possible, and try to show a positive body language to your team on the field no matter how hard the situation seems. Obviously if the game is done and dusted and there is merely a 0.01% chance of winning then it is natural and only human to show a defeated body language, but until there is a chance you must remain positive as this is what lifts your troops and bowlers to remain relaxed and in control.

The first thing you must do is size up the pitch and then upon winning the toss make the right decision as to bowl or bat depending on how the pitch IS and WILL play – that is now and as the game progresses. Also see what your team's strengths are defending a target or chasing a target and decide what your team may be more comfortable with. Make a quick estimate in your mind before the toss about how much the pitch is worth, that is what is a good score or an average usual score on that pitch and just decide from there whether you would rather chase or defend.

Captaining in limited overs cricket is a lot harder as there are so many possibilities and only so many overs and so much time, but just try to stay cool. Try use the first 15 overs as a base or a benchmark whether you are chasing or defending. It is the start and the end which matter the most and most often decide who wins so it is important you as a captain make a quick calculation as to your desired run rate whilst setting a target as well as defending the target, for example we must restrict them to under 80 in first 15 overs to defend the total of 260.

A reliable pinch hitter or all-rounder to go in early and knock the ball around is a captain's dream but even if you don't have someone, you may want to send a pinch hitter early when you think it is a big scoring pitch, or even just give one of your openers 'the license' to go for it.

Now for the hard part, you must juggle your bowlers – whom to bowl and when and how many overs and from what end? This is not as hard as it seems. Just remember to bring your spinner on from the right end depending on the breeze so that to assist in getting drift in the opposite way he is turning it and so he is not bowling into the breeze, if there is any breeze that is. A good 'chorr' bowler or all-rounder is also a captain's dream in one-day cricket – someone who can bowl the remaining ten overs after you have finished your allowed quota of 40 from your 4 specialist bowlers, and someone who can bowl well and accurately stump to stump and just choke the runs. Often in one-day cricket your ability to some extent merely in keeping the run-rate down and choke the runs can prove critical to the matches outcome. Try bringing your part timer, your chorr bowler that is, on from one end while the other end is bowled by your wicket taking bowler. As we said it is the beginning and the end of the match, both from a batting and bowling perspective, which more often than not decides the outcome of the game. So what does this mean for us as captains? It means we must do our best to maximize and optimize our outcomes, especially during the early and latter stages of the innings and do our best to harness the resources we have on hand in the form of batting and bowling talent available to us. Knowing who the pitch is assisting also is a handy bit of information to have on board as a captain, as it is from here you can decide who you want your 'chorr' bowler to be – a spinner or a medium pacer. The shorter the version of the game is, for example

Test match cricket vs twenty-twenty cricket, the more chances and openings your spinners will have – use them as an attacking option and particularly try to have a good leggie on your team as this is one of the most attacking and wicket-taking styles of bowling in cricket. By all means pick a good 'offie' if you have one available but a leggie is always more of a chance to take wickets as it is the subtle variations in flight, pace and the googly and top-spinner which can pose a handful for a batsman who is already under pressure to score at a certain run-rate and is in 'one-day batting mode'.

So try have a good spinner if not two in your squad as these are wicket taking bowlers for the reasons mentioned in previous chapters regarding the variation in flight, loop and dip, which are possible to good spinners, and try work with your spinners and have a good relationship with them. Try to keep conferencing with your leggie and keep supporting and encouraging him as on their day they are capable of even going through the entire team – as Anil Kumble has successfully proven against Pakistan, a team who is already relatively adept at playing slow bowling. [62] Depending on how good your spinners are, try use your slow bowler or your spinner toward the beginning as opposed to the end of the innings as it is at the beginning that the impact of taking wickets is at it's most. If you bring him on at the end the most that can happen is a dot ball off a wicket taking ball, and it is toward the end that we want to merely bowl stump to stump and keep the overall target down. Try save your last overs for your more accurate and line-and-length bowlers and use your attacking

---

[62]Kumble's tremendous performance against Pakistan is a tribute to the fact that good 'leggies' are an asset to the captain and the team's ability to bowl out the opposition as opposed to just restricting the scoring rate

and wicket taking options early on so that you can take wickets and ultimately shape the target or restrict the target in your favour.
Even if your wicket taking or specialist bowleris taking a few beatings or conceding a few boundaries you as a captain must stay calm and support them to keep trying for that wicket. Keep telling your leggie or your pacer that he is an attacking bowler with a good strike rate, and that the wicket taking ball is just around the corner and to keep working hard on his accuracy and stock balls – that you may get beat a few times but that you bowl a wicket taking ball every 20 balls and that the good ball is just a whisker away, hang in there. Of course if you feel he is conceding too many runs, is out of form or is not looking like taking a wicket then take him off and bring your 'chorr' bowler on. It is a good tactic to bowl your 'chorr' bowler from one end to 'keep it tight' while your specialist bowler from the other end aims for wickets. If you can successfully contain the batsman and the scoring rate from one end through your 'chorr' bowler, than this puts pressure on the batsman to score from the other end and gives a small advantage to that bowler, either your leggie or pacer. Good leggies are at their best when one end is being contained and kept tight as the subtleties come in to greater effect and wicket taking potentials are at their peak.

However, by all means use your specialist from both ends if they are not conceding too many runs and it is wickets which you are striving for at that point in the game.

The batting lineup and the batting order are another very important part of your captaincy and one which can prove critical in the match's outcome. The general rule of thumb, as in any coaching manual, is to use your fast scoring batsman at the opening positions and toward the end, and use your technically sound, steady and best batsman in the middle or in the middle order.

The objective of your opening batsman is not only to score runs but to beat the shine off the ball so the middle order batsman have less of a task in playing the swinging ball, and can use their technique to score slightly faster and with less risk and aim for a century. It is a good idea for one of your openers to play a sheet anchor role while the other goes for runs at the required run-rate, and keep scoring steadily and at the same time occupy the crease and beat the shine off the ball. Remember, it is the good ball and the one in that hard to play zone which troubles any batsman, and it is this protection we are trying to afford to our best batsmen in the middle order by making one batsman beat the shine off the ball. However, note that this is not absolutely necessary, you may have a batsman who can occupy the crease AND score at a faster rate also; or, you may have a pinch hitter who can serve the same role of beating the shine off the ball and score relatively freely – it all depends on the talent you have on the team and how you want to play your cards. [63]

Put your best fielders in the crucial positions or wherever you feel there may be a chance for a catch or the chance of stopping the boundaries – this is usually point or cover but may be anywhere depending on the batsman's scoring pattern and strokeplay – just determine where the batsman is going to get most of his runs and place your best fielder there. Try give your

---

[63]Kaluwitharana of Sri Lamka in 1996 against a strong Australian batting line-up and fast scoring one, was used as a pinch hitter to successfully execute this particular tactic – he was able to beat the shine off the ball, occupy the crease whilst also scoring at above the required run-rate, and thereby making life for the talented middle order batsmen easier

bowlers a break from the pressure of bowling by placing them in slips or fine-leg or somewhere the ball is not being hit. Just remember to support your spinner, as they are a wicket taking option, with a good attacking field with catchers and don't put your worst catchers or fielders in catching positions while your spinner is toiling hard to get the miscue or catch in the outfield or slips.

These are just some of the common points which captains should be aware of whilst leading their men on the field – hopefully you have a base understanding by now of what it takes to harness your horses Vs simply managing your men. For more finer points regarding captaincy and field placings, I recommend finding further reading in the form of another book, as the scope of this book is mainly centered on batting and spin-bowling skills, however we are going to show you how good captaincy can make all the difference in winning 50 over cricket in the next chapter.

Remember, use the little things and 'outcricket' to harness the skills and talents of your resources and players to achieve the best outcome on match day and real-match situations – talent is 70% of your quality as a team but so is the remaining 30% which is in the captain's hands and how he 'harnesses his horses' for the advantage of the team and the team's results![64]

Another finer tactic of the game which most captains employ, and you should be too, is bringing on your bowler which has a good history or upper hand against a certain batsmen, and moreover bringing him on at the

---

[64]The quality of your fielding is also part of this 30% which the captain has part control over.

right time. We want to put as much pressure on the batsman as possible through the use of a few good maiden or low-scoring overs, and then bring him on. This tactic has been used for a long time – you too should use this in good captaincy![65]

---

[65]For example, Warne Vs Cullinan or Harbhajan vs Ponting – the mere psychological trauma of being repeatedly dismissed by the same bowler makes the next dismissal all the more probable and difficult to evade for the batsman.

Chapter Twenty Three

Captaincy: Winning 50 Over Cricket

Limited overs cricket is heavily dependent on strategy, out cricket and team selection. It is our ability to assess the ever changing situation of the game at the time and having the judgement to use the right player at the right time, which can often mean the difference between victory and defeat. Yes, that's right, simply the ability of the captain and coach to harness his horses as opposed to simply managing or marshalling his men can make all the difference and can mean the difference between winning and losing, in one-day cricket. Playing your cards and determining your strategy and batting/bowling order according to a set and predetermined protocol before the game is all well and fine but what if the team has a collapse at the top of the batting order, or you are only defending a very meagre and moderate target and you didn't get enough runs on the board, or you are suddenly faced with chasing a huge target for victory? Who is going to alter your strategy at that moment and point in time and according to the changing situation and demands of the game at that point in time? It is the captain of course, it is the captain who understands his team and their individual strengths and weaknesses better than anyone else. It is the captain who is accountable for his team's winning or losing and it is the captain who has the authority to make changes to the team's strategic protocol and changes thereof. As a captain you must be aware of the importance of your role in being flexible in regard your strategy and batting/bowling orders, and have the judgement and courage to change these during the course of a limited overs game, depending on how your troops are performing at the time.

When defending a target which is not so great or only mediocre, we really want to get off to a good start in the first 15 overs which we said before often decides the outcome of the game. What can we do to give ourselves a fighting chance of bowling well here? Well there is a tactic where you try choke the runs in the first 5-10 overs by just bowling line and length, keep the scoring down to an absolute minimum and don't care about wickets; then after you have put pressure on the batting team by restricting them to a meagre scoring rate then bring on your wicket taking bowlers around 10th over mark. This is one such tactic used by the lesser teams of the 80s and 90s such as NewZealand and SriLanka, and has proven to be a good little approach to captaincy in the past – you too can use this tactic in one-day formats when the pressure to defend a small target is on. The main thing we should remember here is to put the new batsman under pressure and really strive to get as many dot balls as you can and use field placings to try restrict the scoring rate – that is bowl to your field and count each dot ball and set of dot balls as a small victory and continue to keep the scoring rate down with dot balls. For example, have a 6/3 offside field and ask your bowler to bowl on the offside only. Try give a single to the recognized and in form batsman and keep him off strike.

There are two scenarios here really for you captains to exercise sound and good judgement in regard to and they are: [1] the batting team has wickets in hand but may not be keeping up with the required scoring rate as per say(but not doing bad either); OR [2] the batting team doesn't have wickets in hand but are keeping up with the required scoring rate. In both instances we are playing limited over cricket and containing the scoring rate through dot balls is crucial, however, if it is scenario 1 which is happening then we should tell our bowlers and fielders to aim and strive for that wicket at the same time as striving to keep the run rate down. If it is scenario 2, then wickets are not so important but dot balls are, and we merely count a wicket as in a sense merely a dot ball and keep striving for dot balls and keeping it tight – we instruct our bowler to keep it tight and our fielders to be on their toes! This is how one-day cricket matches are won from tight situations and fine lines – not by letting the nerves get to you but exercising sound judgement and captaincy and instructing your troops as to exactly what you want out of them!

As a captain of a cricket team, we are generally looking for and hoping for the team to do well, not just one individual nor are we counting our successes on a personal milestone basis. As a captain it is important for you to encourage your batters to form partnerships and always view your batsmen and their innings in context of the team's objectives. It is a perfectly normal and healthy part of cricket for one batsman to be scoring faster than the other, and one to be either better 'played-in' or even just more talented, but your objective is always to see how the two batsmen perform as a duo and as a partnership under live match conditions, even if one is contributing more than the other. Find out which batsmen in your team bat better and with whom and what may be a good partnership forming opportunity. Also if possible, make use of the Lefthand – Righthand combinations while structuring your batting order, especially for the opening partnership.

The same may apply to your bowlers, there may be certain combinations whereby each bowler lifts his game in the presence of the other, it is here where you must try bowl them in tandem with each other as sort of a tactic and a way of harnessing each's performing capacities in a match situation for the benefit of the team.

Especially in one-day cricket and limited overs formats of the game, it can't be stressed enough that your batting order be structured and planned accordingly to the situation, and that you do not waste or jeopardize your horses and your team's full run scoring capacity but for a mere error in captaincy, planning and strategy. This means you and the coach have to have plans for different scenarios and be able to modify and adapt your plan according to the situation of the match at the time, and not simply abide by a predetermined protocol or strategy. As a captain and coach it is not good enough to just set the batting order and sit back with our arms crossed in expectation and hope, when cricket is a game which can change in the space of one over and one ball, and requires of us a certain degree of presence to know and realize what the reality of the situation is and what the reality of what is required for victory is. Captains and coaches are urged to not only go off skill and talent but to pick at least one or two batters in the side who exhibit fight and courage and who revel and can persevere in pressure situations. What good is the talent if it doesn't come off on the day or doesn't know how to handle pressure or adversity? A batter may be good on his own terms in his own conditions or when he feels comfortable and free of pressure, but what about when the struggles and difficult or pressure situations present themselves upon the team and the team's hopes of victory? You need to have a fighter on your team, someone who can keep the runs ticking over with singles and twos and not get out and build a partnership. Someone who values his wicket to no end and can fight and build an innings under pressure and stop the opposition from walking all over your team once they get their noses up and get a few early wickets. Jonty Rhodes of South Africa was in the team for this very reason, his mere presence in the field was enough to save them from the jaws of defeat, but then he was this cool, calm, fighting and very busy batsman who could do anything for the team's benefit. Despite not being the most talented or skilled of batsman on the domestic circuit, his inclusion in the team was a huge plus for South Africa – he was Mr dependable and had nerves of steel under pressure. Again not the most talented batsman but nerves of steel and the fight and will to hang in there for the team's sake.

When chasing a target and a few early wickets fall and the opposition is dominating, it is all so easy for the required run rate to start creeping up and up above 6 an over. It is important here to send your fighter batsman in and build a partnership whilst scoring around 4 runs an over without risk. It is not time to panic there is plenty of overs left in the match it just depends how you utilize your batting order and how good your partnerships are. It is important here to not be complacent and leave it too late, you must start addressing the run rate required as early as you can by getting singles and simply pushing the ball around without risk, and give your big hitters a realistic task and target toward the end of the run chase.

Just remember when facing a batting collapse to not panic. We are not here to worry and panic but we are here to play the game according to mathematical and scientific principles and vicissitudes. No matter how hard the task seems do not panic, our job as a team is to harness the best possible outcomes and score from our top-order batsmen. You have batsmen till number 8, it is nothing to panic about but rather now more than ever, simply a test of your calculative, mathematical and scientific approach to the game and a test of the strategy you have calculated for yourself and your team. No matter how hard the situation there is always a way out and a mathematical answer – your job is to simply calculate this answer and convey this plan effectively and purposefully to your horses, who will be the ones to execute the plan for a victorious outcome.

So for you captains out there, even if you are 4 for 0, do not panic you still have many batsmen to come it is just a matter of how you use them and harness their potential. Use the next one to two wickets to build a partnership and then use your later order batters to accelerate towards the end. Remember, the game is won or lost by virtue of the performance of our bowlers and fielders – the batting part of it is just as important but the hard work has already been done by your bowlers, and the batting where you are chasing a target should not be seen as such an enormous task, as batsmen anyway have an advantage in a game of cricket. The bowlers and fielders have worked hard to reduce the target for you batsmen, and so it is important you as a batting lineup appreciate this and remember to pay them back with a victory, even if there are some hiccups and you have a collapse.

If you bowl and field well and restrict the opposition to a meagre target, that's 80% of the job done and the batting is merely a simple task of using and planning your top eight to chase down the runs according to the calculation and strategy required. Cricket is a bowler's game and the hard work is carried out by the bowling and fielding unit, that is why it is important for you as a captain to make it clear that you expect the batsmen to do the job as it is 100% mathematically possible and requires merely the correct planning and discipline in regard the required approach taken to chase down the runs.

So for you captain's under pressure to select the right team, structure the right batting and bowling orders, and ultimately win the game for your school, state or country, the words of advice cannot be reiterated enough that in a one-day game of cricket your job is critical and contributes 30-40% of your team's playing potential on match day – that's almost 50%!.

Try generally, whilst chasing a small total as well as whilst chasing a bigger total, to use a pinch hitter – someone who you can send in at the top of the order whose wicket is not so valuable or prized to the opposition, and someone who can go out and try knock some quick runs on the board and shift the tempo of the game your way. If it works it works if it doesn't than the most you have lost is a tail-end batsman's wicket. Theoretically speaking, in one-day cricket it is better to use our lesser valued and tail-end wickets early and at the top of the order and save our better players and hitters for the end of the game, and especially when you are facing a collapse this tactic MUST be used. Let's cite India Vs NZ semi final WC2019 as an example. India made the mistake of not using a pinch hitter when experiencing a collapse and moreover failed to save their best and big hitting wickets for the end. They instead sent Jadeja in the end when they should have sent him early and earlier than Pant and Dhoni. Dhoni and Pant should have been saved for the end when they were to accelerate the scoring and ebb closer to the target, and their lesser or less valued wickets/batsmen should have been sent earlier to either pinch hit or build a partnership. They failed to do this, they failed to structure their batting order according to the situation at the time, and they failed to win the game by just a very narrow margin all but for a lack in mental cricketing acumen and team strategy when they had all the batsmen and reserves of talent at their disposal even despite being 3/5. From a position of even 3 for 5, India had the team and the reserve of talent to easily win the game and in the end lost by a mere 18 runs when they should have in fact easily won with 18 balls to spare, and why? All for a lack of correct one-day strategy on captain's and coach's behalf – they simply did not plan and structure their chase after being 3 for 5, and simply set their match protocol and strategy before the match and sat back and watched with arms crossed. India had the firepower and horses, they were just not harnessed for the benefit of the team through correct captaincy and strategy, here they were watching poor Chahal a tail end batsman to score the last 20 runs off 10 balls, when in fact they should have sent him in early in hope he might knock a few runs and boundaries around. A mere lack of small mental cricketing acumen cost India a chance to make a world cup final when they had played so well throughout the group stages of the tournament and easily looked like the one to take home the trophy. A similar thing happened with Australia, they just did not have the discipline and match nerves in regard their batting to score a decent total for themselves after losing early wickets, when they could easily have salvaged a good score of 250 plus had they stuck to a game plan with heart and discipline. They were left defending a small target against a strong England batting lineup – the game was lost by that point, the point where the batsmen failed to get their heads down and work towards a realistic and planned total of 250+.

So 50 over cricket demands of us a constantly changing and evolving strategy and one which is right and on the money according to the situation at that very moment in time. Unlike Test cricket where games are won through sheer batting and bowling talent on the side, one-day cricket requires a thorough game plan and several backup plans and potential modifications to your ideal or pre decided game plan. You as a captain must get good at assessing the situation of the game and using your horses(players) to maximum benefit for the team's best possible outcome, and not let your team lose for a mere lacking in mental acumen or strategy or being flexible in regard your tactics and approach to winning the game. We said talent is 70% of the game won and captaincy is 30%, well, in one-day cricket it may even be up to and as high as 50%[66]. That's right, simple mental cricketing acumen and our calculative approach to the game and our ability to adapt our tactics and orders can impact the outcome of the game by as much as this much.

Obviously when we are defending a meagre total and the other team bats deep, our only hope of victory is early wickets. You must give your bowlers the encouragement and the license to go all out and attack the batsmen with their best wicket taking deliveries without worrying about anything else.

Follow the tips I have outlined and suggested in the previous two chapters as a guide to improving your team's performance under pressure, but by all means explore and learn deeper and finer points you must know for captaincy through the reading of more books and 'talking cricket' with the coach.

---

[66]This figure goes up to 50% as fielding is also very important in one-day cricket. All these components of this 50% comprising of 'harnessing your horse', is known formally as OUTCRICKET!

Good luck, and remember, don't let the team down for a mere lack of harnessing your horses – have the ability to change your game plan according to the situation of the game in front of you and take your job as the one responsible for victory or defeat a little more seriously! Don't be afraid to think outside the box and use your cricketing brain even when you are not physically on the field yourself, and directly contributing toward the game's outcome. Conference and talk cricket strategy with your coach before, during and after the game – you must sharpen your insight into how best to harness your horses, and this is the best way to learn and perfect this skill, talking cricket.

Chapter Twenty Four

Can Physical Fitness Improve Our Performance???

Like we discussed in the beginning of the book, cricket is one of those sports which is a bit different and centers around the batter and bowler and the battle between the two, and that cricket does not require of us that standard of stamina as in football, rugby, etc., but is rather more based upon skill and mental alertness.

So on the whole cricket does not demand of us such high stamina and fitness levels as in the other sports however it does often involve a fitness component if we are fast bowlers and perhaps fielders who field in certain positions around point and covers. Fast bowlers require certain aspects of fitness and strength to both bowl their best and bowl their best for longer periods without getting tired. A bowler may be accurate and quick when he is fresh but then this might wane once and if he is bowled for longer spells. Suddenly your strike fast bowler may become a potential liability on the team if he were not to have the fitness credentials being a fast bowler demands. So what are these fitness credentials exactly? Fitness credentials which are so important for our fast bowlers especially in Test Match cricket where we need to work hard for the breakthrough?.

Well it all comes down to explosive strength Vs endurance strength! Explosive strength draws upon certain fibers in the body called twitch muscle or fast twitch muscle whereas endurance strength draws upon certain fibers called slow twitch muscle.

It is the fast twitch muscle which gives the bowler that pace and zippiness and speed at which he can bowl whilst he is fresh, but what if he didn't have enough slow twitch muscle strength? Well he would tire and not be able to reproduce the same pace or zippiness once he had already bowled 10-30 overs, that's what.

There have been many examples in Indian cricket of bowlers having great pace and talent and zip too however just not being able to keep it up once they were asked to bowl more and more overs – this is due to the conditioning or lack thereof of the person's slow-twitch muscle fibers or endurance based strength.

So it can't be stressed enough for you coaches and captains out there, you must encourage your fast bowlers to develop upper body strength and conditioning via regular gym exercise and not allow your strike bowlers who are often assets to your hopes of victory to be caught lacking in correct fitness. The correct fitness is to develop both fast twitch and slow muscle fibers in parallel through a dedicated gym routine.

Certain fielding positions demand of us the ability to dive and stretch out our arms and bodies. Jonty Rhodes was a true run saver in the field, and someone who used his physical fitness and flexibility and agility to make notable contributions to the team's chances of victory. Mohammad Azharuddin was another who used to field at point and covers and save a lot of runs for the team.

So yes physical fitness CAN and WILL help your team to perform better, it's just that it is especially more important for your fast bowlers and not so consequential to batters, spin bowlers and fielders/wicketkeepers – tasks which are more skill dependent and not so much stamina dependent, as we opined in the start of the book!

Chapter Twenty Five

Cricket: Beyond The Coaching Manual

We cannot teach you every finer point and the exact coaching you may require at any particular moment in time depending upon the status and level of your game, as this requires the monitoring of your technique in person, but here are some of the things to be aware of and a few points which you may want to seek coaching or guidance for after you have understood and applied the basics and finer points explained in this book, and before you go for senior trials or present before a selector. These are some of the things which senior selectors may look at once you have been selected in the squad or NCA or Academy of higher level teams.

Spin bowlers must make the assumption that every time we bowl a ball that its exact vector force and value has been judged and picked by the batsman – this is the only way to force you to disquise your variations and develop not only guile but the ability to set the batsman up using intelligent combinations and permutations and pin point accuracy.

The same goes for fast bowlers – you must learn to beat the batsman via getting the ball to deviate and deviate late ideally if you are to be successful in your cricketing journey. You must also have set combos to gradually setup the batsman at the same time, and be able to consistently move the ball through the air. This is no time for just bowling your fastest – you must extract movement in the air **AND** off the pitch.

For the batsman, well there are so many of you batsmen out there and there is so much desire and interest in attaining a batting position in school and state teams that it is crazy, particularly in India where the population is high and everyone wants to be a batsman – we must sometimes attempt even to put good balls away or at least score something off of them. Along with the length ball or the one well directed in regard to line, batsmen of today's era, when required to chase a big total, may be required to improvise enough to convert only semi loose balls into a loose ball and put these balls away also. This may be something your 20-20 selector or 50 over match selector may look for, but not necessarily. The ability to use your feet to convert a good ball into a bad one against the spinners and the ability to play both sides of the wicket against the pacers, and particularly your ability to use the wrists to play balls pitched on the offside and hit them through the leg side as well hitting balls pitched on the leg side and hitting them through the off side. Your ability to play lofted shots to successfully hit over the infield may also be eagerly watched.

For bowlers, well the simple fact that since the batsman has the advantage means that we must practice our accuracy very well and must be able to interchange between a wicket-taking bowler and merely a 'part-time' bowler and one which simply contains the runs and scoring rate, and be able to do this at will. Selectors may look at your ability to bowl stump to stump and be merely accurate also, as opposed to tossing it up with flight and looking for an opening for a wicket. If in a trial situation, first and foremost try to demonstrate your ability to toss it up and aim for a wicket but **DO** throw a few balls which 'zip through' and show your ability to restrict the scoring rate and the fact that you can do this, be a 'containment' bowler that is, and do it just as well as any other part-time spin bowler on the team. Just remember to maintain a steady pace, that is, maintain your pace on the faster side even if you are a slow bowler, as this is what creates difficulties for batsmen and makes them commit to their shot early – always try bowl your stock deliveries on the faster side as opposed to the slower side.[67] Only when we bowl our loopy one do we slow down our pace, and this is only after we have set him up for it also, and does require a subtle change in our run-up or approach also.[68] Show to selectors that you can bowl the slower-higher one as well as bowl the faster – flatter one. ie, the arm ball or flipper.

For batsmen, selectors will almost certainly and eagerly look at your offside play and particularly your ability to play the ball late from the offside and play the late cut, square drive and cover drive – these shots are considered one of the hallmarks of a better batsman. Remember to receive some coaching in regard playing the ball late through the offside – this pertains to the positioning of our elbows and bat as well as either playing with deft touch or playing through the ball. Your ability to not only transfer your weight and play decisively and clinically off the front foot and back foot will be tested, but particularly your ability to play relatively short balls off the front foot and be in attacking or aggressive mode. These shots comprise of the straight batted swat, the square cut off front foot and the drive on the up or on the rise. Knowing where your off stump is is considered one of the great skills to possess as a batsman and this almost surely will be eagerly watched by selectors – your ability to leave balls go

---

[67]The latest legspin sensation Rashid Khan from Afghanistan also bowls on the faster side whilst bowling his stock deliveries – it is only when he wants to toss it up a little extra that he reduces his pace!

[68]We basically do the opposite – walk in a bit faster than our usual run-up, and bowl the loopy one with a slower action upon release

as well as strike attacking shots off of only slightly loose balls in regard line or simply hitting through the off side. Your ability to pick the length and prey on marginal and small error in regards the length of the ball is one of the signs of a great batsman and is an aspect of batting which can make you a big name just like the stars and elite batters of international cricket. For example, the ball is relatively full and you can play late cut off back foot through gully area, or the ball is relatively short and you can play off front foot to drive on the rise, square cut off front foot or straight bat swat. The cover drive is the cornerstone of a good batsman and those batsmen who can cover drive well and drive at the ball confidently even when the ball is not that full or is relatively short and drive on the rise are almost always going to win the selectors favor – there is nothing more soothing and serene to watch in cricket than a well-executed technically sound cover drive!

Who said batting was easy, not us, we only said that it may be slightly easier than bowling, but nevertheless requires tremendous amounts of concentration, all that effort and tensile force going through the body and last but not least great demands on our temperament and judgement.

Remember what we said about not focusing on your strengths but plugging your weaknesses, well this is the time now, the time you are giving trial or presented before selectors that this will be tested and you want to be able to demonstrate your flexibility in regards your stroke selection process and 'one-day batting technique' – we don't just play our regular front and back foot shots but must use effort in our footwork to play the balls in between and convert back foot shots into front foot ones, and vice versa, especially the drive on the rise, the square cut off front foot and the late cut to a ball which is relatively full and playing it off the back foot. These aspects of batting skill and technique will almost surely be eagerly watched and tested by selectors during your trial process for 20-20 or 50 over cricket!

This is all sounding very deep and daunting I am sure but it is the potential for this ability that the selectors are looking for, it is not only dependent on your skill levels as a batsman but your temperament and your propensity to be willing to think outside of the box and improvise, something which takes a degree of concerted effort and labour. In a country like India a land full of batsmen, selectors may not be impressed by merely batsmen who strictly abide by and adhere by the textbook in its strictest sense and can only play straight and solid. We have to show signs of ingenuity and the sheer will to score runs from any situation in our batsman-ship – that is, the ability to improvise and not just follow the code we presented in chapter ten. The textbook approach is known and practiced by all – we must now show signs of individualism and a will to succeed against the bowling even if it is relatively accurate![69]

---

[69] This will be the topic of the next book – how to play one-day cricket that is, and bat like a professional and be able to find the gaps as well as play an array of different shots to the one ball – all critical factors in impressing one-day cricket selectors and rising the ranks and attaining an elite level of batsman ship. Make sure you read the next book which will teach lessons which last a lifetime!

Chapter Twenty Six

Career Advice For Serious Cricketers

So what do we do when we are a good cricketer aiming to lift our game and be a great one, or a serious cricketer trying to rise the ranks and play representative and higher-level cricket?

It is advised to always have a certain self-practice period before we go searching outside for match practice or coaching or present for trials. During this self-practice period, we must really test ourselves to the limit and ultimately determine and pinpoint the areas in our game which require attention or more work and areas in our game which can be identified as weaknesses. This can be done in the nets with a friend or against a bowling machine or if you are a bowler, even on your own(you can enroll in an academy and request coaching staff to watch you play and report to you upon weaknesses also, but we are trying to save you money – one of the very reasons this book was written). Challenge yourself and put yourself to the test, attempting to do the hardest things in cricket, really give yourself a good 'workout' on all aspects of the task you are preparing for either batting or bowling, and aim to be able to produce a list of all possible strengths and weaknesses in regard your game by the end.[70]

Once you have an idea of your strengths and weaknesses and have a list of possible weaknesses which you now must plug and improve upon quickly

---

[70] This mainly pertains to your visionary process and stroke selection process but also your physical technique in regards playing all the shots in the book.

and correctly, seek guidance in the form of joining an academy or getting one-to-one coaching. Present your identified weaknesses to the coach and seek detailed advice and guidance for only these particular issues in your game which may not be the greatest at this time. After you have made attempts to improve upon your weaknesses through seeking coaching and formal instruction, once again, either on your own or whilst being part of a group or academy, begin practicing your weaknesses religiously and clinically. Focus on the lessons you learnt from the coach in regard your weaknesses and pay attention to what he instructed that you were doing wrong and pay attention to the process involved to change this and do it right.

There is nothing like match practice but ideally we should plug our weaknesses and perfect and train our physical skills and technique first through dedicated self-practice, such that we can make full use of the available match practice to make an impression. However, this may not necessarily be the case, many people argue that match practice is a good opportunity to improve upon identified weaknesses so essentially there are two ways here. Our theory states that a match is accompanied with immense pressure to perform and a few bad or unlucky performances could even jeopardize your future in that team, and that it is better to have done your own practice in regard plugging your weaknesses before you present yourself outside, however we can always do this in tandem – plug our weaknesses privately and draw upon our strengths in match situations to make an impression and put our name forward.

Our ultimate aim through all this practice is quite simple, we want to get picked for our county or get picked in the state trials of your country, and we want to present for Board or county and state trials, get picked and get more match practice where we can then etch ourselves one step closer to the prize – playing higher-level representative cricket. Because of the amount of real-time match practice afforded to the county circuit of England, it is often considered a good idea to try play county cricket as a good exposure to high level cricket and a good opportunity to see where you stand in regard how good you really are. Further, it is a good chance to plug your weaknesses before presenting to a selector back in your home country and also a good chance to implement your practice routine in match situations. For example, a batsman who has decided to be a fast scoring opener through bottom hand play and improvisation, i.e.Sehwag. Or a bowler who has decided he wants to work on his ability to contain and choke the runs in one-day cricket and his ability to curb the scoring rate for the team. Playing the County circuit provides us with this as this type of cricket is of no consequence to society and you can use it to train yourself for higher level representative cricket either for your state or your country back home.

So it is always good to enroll in an academy or play county cricket as you do get opportunity for match practice, however your objective first and foremost is to actually build your game, raise your skill levels and successfully plug your weaknesses, before you go out and seek match practice or the opportunity to impress. It is these two avenues which we are working toward basically, we want to have prepared ourselves and practiced our game sufficient that we get picked in a trial or get picked to play county cricket, however, we advocate you not being in a hurry to bypass this practice stage and jump into giving trial or jump into trying to play the county circuit. First try seeking guidance through formal coaching or admission into cricket academies wherein you have an opportunity to build and perfect your game through hard work and practice, and then aim for giving a trial or expecting a good performance of yourself in match conditions. The reality is that we must perform in match conditions which are abound with the pressure of team objectives and the pressure to perform sooner or later, but we need to train ourselves a little first and train ourselves to play as a complete cricketer first and one who can be of use in any match situation which may present itself. As the saying goes, ***prepare yourself for the worst***, we must plug our weaknesses in case these are the exact skills required on match day. Real life matches are not easy to organize and require funding and are considered high-fly big events – you don't want to put yourself in match conditions and put a string of poor performances together as a result of not plugging your weaknesses, that's all that we are saying, and that too in front of all those who are watching.

Once you feel you have made a decent effort to plug and practice your weaknesses either through self-practice or through participation in a formal cricket academy, you are now ready to put yourself to the test and try give trial or try get admitted onto the county scene. Like we said there is nothing like match practice and now is the time to start trying to test your all-round game in match conditions and start seeking match practice in the form of formal matches which are watched by selectors. Especially focus on your stroke selection process and your ability to 'force the pace' and improvise and your ability to play multiple shots to the same ball – if you can show selectors evidence of your capacity to bat as if in 'one-day mode', then you are a very high chance of being picked in the squad or team!

Match practice and performing in matches is a great confidence booster and it is important you have had a bit of match practice howsoever trivial or from whatever grade or level of cricket, and be able to walk into a trial with the confidence knowing that you **CAN** and that you **CAN** in real life, and not only against the bowling machine or your friend in the net.

Ok so you have worked hard on your game and have been selected into NCA or into your state team or onto the County circuit and successfully improved your game sufficient enough to deserve this honor, congratulations - what now? Well like we said in batting chapters, it's about steel and not only talent or skill and now is the time you must show your commitment and dedication to the game not only your mastery over the fundamental skills of your trade. You must make a habit of developing and using the mental cricketing acumen which we mentioned is almost 50% of the game, and you must impress upon your captains, coaches and selectors of being able to successfully do so in conjunction with the skills you have attained and used to reach this far.

Try to display that you have a good understanding of the stroke-selection process and conditional logic involved in batting and the strategy and science involved in batting or bowling, and that you are well aware of the fact that you may be relied upon in game situation to execute this for the team's sake. You must impress upon selectors not only your fundamental skills in batting or bowling, but that you have the mental toughness to be considered ready for high pressure international games, which as we mentioned become highly dependent upon strategy, mental cricketing acumen and most importantly our visionary and stroke-selection process.

The best way to demonstrate this during trial is to play the relatively short ball off front foot and use the wrists to maneuver the ball through gaps.

For batsman, well you have been picked in trial by virtue of hard work you put into your self-practice, but now is time for real match conditions, and time to show your courage, resolve and 'steel' or mental toughness under match conditions –remember as we said about batting that there are so many batters with good skills, but it is now that you must distinguish yourself by actually performing under pressure. You must show to all watching your county, state or academy game that you can play well under any conditions, against any bowling and in any situation the game may be in when you come in to bat. You must show that you don't let the pressure of the situation to affect your stroke-play and your stroke-selection process and that you have the skills to play slow and steady as well as hit hard and accelerate the scoring. For example, opening the batting and batting against the new ball as opposed to batting toward the end against the old ball – both require a certain adjustment in technique which we have discussed at length already. The ability to play in the V against the new ball is something almost always eagerly looked at by selectors.

For bowlers, you need to show everyone that you have the ability to contain the batsman as well as the ability to chase wickets and defeat the batsman. Try to work on your accuracy in match conditions and pressure situations and your ability to bowl your wicket-taking and stock ball at will – as we say in cricket, 'have the ball on a string'. You must demonstrate you know how to get on top of the batsman through accurate lines and lengths and thereby your ability to choke the oppositions tempo and scoring rates. Your biggest skill being tested here, which may not be so fair, is your ability to merely bowl stump to stump and be accurate and effective in choking the runs. You may be a strike wicket-taking bowler but in county or academy situation, they may be looking firstly for this ability as it is this which may help them win a match. So your work is cut out for you if you are a bowler and if you want to make the bigtime – we must impress with our wicket taking potentials and at the same time with our containing potentials, in order to impress and rise the ranks. However, do note that as we mentioned earlier these county games are not of such great consequence to society neither locally nor internationally, so just use them primarily to practice what you need to at the time, that is focus on your weakness at the time and issues in your game which will benefit your race for a representative position in the long run – don't worry too much about the result of these games as they are meant for drawing crowds and providing a source of entertainment to local viewers and cricket fans only. But by all means if containment is your weakness as a bowler then practice this during your opportunity for match practice.

For you wicket keepers out there, just remember to concentrate that little bit harder when your main bowlers or strike bowlers are on and don't make the mistake of dropping a catch when the team really needed a wicket. There are so many wicket keeper batsmen in the ranks and your margin for error is very little – selectors, captains and coaches hate keepers who drop catches at crucial times, not to mention the poor bowler who toiled so hard for an opening.

Just remember it is a good idea to plug your weaknesses through self-practice before you present yourself in front of the big crowd – captains, coaches and selectors that is. However, by all means use any match practice possible to do this in tandem with impressing selectors, working on defined weaknesses **AND** making yourself known to be a good performer in matches that is, and furthering your chances of rising the ranks.

Worldcup 2019: Why India Lost The Semi-Final Against New Zealand

India bowled and fielded beautifully, everything was spot on from fielding to bowling orders to every aspect of captaincy – Kohli did an absolutely splendid job at marshaling his men and harnessing his horse. India could not have asked for more from their bowling unit and the out cricket, strategy and mental cricketing acumen used by their captain; and the batsmen really owed it to the bowlers, themselves and the fans to secure a victory, after having a modest target to chase down for victory and having done the hard job of restricting the total.

The batting was the problem and the ability of India's top order and middle order both, to perform under big match pressure and nerves. Unfortunately, the pressure was too much and India was well and truly shaken and rattled under pressure and under conditions which really tested their nerves and mettle, and conditions which really tested just how good they were and just how badly they wanted to win. Where did it go wrong and what should they have done better? Well the answer quite simply is strategy, mental toughness and mental cricketing acumen. This was just not good enough against a team which is well known to be extremely good and effective at using out-cricket and mental cricketing acumen to harness results in their favour, despite not having the reserves of talent like the other teams. In the face of this, India was supposed to prepare themselves in a certain way, train a certain way and think a certain way in response to the clinical and accurate onslaught which was about to happen at the hands of their opponent, a prior world cup finalist.

It seems and looks very bad on the face of it, India's loss that is, but many would agree that India was a better team, a more skilled team and one which had more depth and all round talent. So why did they lose and that too so emphatically? They were simply just not tough and disciplined enough in the mental aspects of the game and hard-nosed competitors like the ones we have seen to win previous World Cups like Australia and Sri Lanka, that's why.

The top-order collapse was a mere failure in mental cricketing acumen and mental toughness. At 3/5 India was in a position that they would never have thought, especially after their string of top-order successes, but a few wicket-taking balls is all it takes to turn a game of cricket on it's head, and we all know that, and what's more it has happened many a time in cricket history.[71]

1st wicket to fall: Rohit Sharma–guilty of committing a fundamental error of batting when not played in, and that is, not adjusting the backlift to be straight and bringing down bat with soft hands and opening/closing face if necessary. It sounds silly, but it is not so funny when your key batter and key to winning the game is caught behind for a mere lacking in adjusting his backlift early on. Simple batting error and lack of concentration and technical acumen early on from a key batter's behalf – not good enough!

---

[71] As we mentioned in previous chapters, even when a team is 4/0, there is no need to panic and you can still win as a batting team, especially only in a 50 over game.

2nd wicket to fall: KL Rahul – caught behind playing a rather meaningless shot, not attacking or defending. Could have just let the ball go if not choosing to strike hard at the ball – found guilty of hand-to-mouth batting. This was the time and occasion he really needed to concentrate hard at making the bowler bowl to him and cut out the risky shots – pretty simple stuff. From an opener and one who wants to be the man at the front for India, rather lax and irresponsible batting – again not good enough!

3rd wicket to fall: Kohli–LBW to an in swinger from a left arm over the wicket pacer. There is always a threat the ball will come in late and strike the pads, usually batsmen guard against this by taking a leg-stump or middle and leg guard, that's all Kohli had to do and would have still been there – again not good enough![72]

Jadeja and Dhoni do a good job at increasing the run rate and swinging the game back in India's favour, however, it is too late and the pressure towards the end and the seemingly enormous task, get to both and they both depart through unlucky circumstances.

Jadeja, being a relatively less valued wicket, should have been sent in earlier. India needed a partnership at 3/5 nothing more, they needed steady and risk free scoring at 4.5 runs an over and someone to just stay at the crease until the big hitters came in toward the end. In one-day cricket tactics you usually save your best and big hitters toward the end when you launch a final assault and accelerate the scoring rate, and use your so called

---

[72]This is a finer point of coaching which is usually conveyed by coach to player, it is not entirely reasonable to expect Kohli to have been aware of this little nuance of cricket, but should have been coached to know about it!

lesser wickets up front to merely build a partnership and score at a steady and average scoring rate. India used their two bighitters and key batsmen of the middle order, being Dhoni and Pant, in the beginning when they should have sent Jadeja, Pandya and Karthik in early to steady the ship and resurrect the innings. The key wickets of Pant and Dhoni plus the fact that they are a lefthand-righthand combination, should have been saved for the final 10 – 15 overs.

A simple failure in commonsense everyday one-day format cricketing and mental acumen and deployment of strategy. India had no such strategy in mind, let alone give themselves the chance to execute their strategy in pressure conditions, and simply just did not look like world cup champion material, and deserved to lose!

Any team which is caught playing hand-to-mouth cricket and is flustered by pressure and situations which may not be according to their own terms and conditions, the way India was, simply just do not deserve to win the world cup, and NZ despite a less talented team but superior mental cricketing acumen and mental toughness, fully deserved their win against a puzzled India under pressure. The bowling attack of NZ however, cannot be detracted from, it was still very formidable and good enough to give the big name Indian batsmen something to think about.

Perhaps this was a cry from Indian cricket for help and coaching in regard mental toughness and mental aspects of the game and perhaps a blessing in disguise. You can't just enter a big game hoping to win entirely on the back of supposed talent and big names, you have to be mentally tough and prepared for any situation. Indian cricket team authorities need to address this issue as was sorely exposed on big match day in world cup2019, and a day we saw the best side in the tournament bow out like sitting ducks all for the want of the basic mental toughness qualities and acumen relevant to the sport. India deserved losers against a spot on, clinical and mentally tough and prepared NZ. This side did not deserve to win the world cup for the reasons mentioned.

It is a well- known theory that the sides such as Australia, South Africa, England, and New Zealand are a lot more mentally tough than India, but why? Should not teams like India or Pakistan also consider mental toughness an important and worthwhile aspect of the sport as opposed to just spotting and preparing talent for selection? What about preparing that talent to actually win in pressure situations and make full use of their talent and not waste it for a lack of mental toughness – something which as we stated can improve a player's performance on a cricket field by up to 20 – 50%!

Hopefully this book goes a step in the right direction toward addressing this problem with Indian/Pakistani cricket and the coaching system at representative levels. It is not just about finding and selecting talent, but teaching and coaching them how to perform and win, especially under pressure and conditions which may not be so familiar or immediately comprehendible. We cannot as sportsmen, expect to just play and live according to our own terms and conditions and perform when we feel comfortable and safe, but rather, must prepare for contingencies and learn to perform under adverse or pressure situations – this is what makes us special and makes everyone to want our autograph!

Appendix

Explanation Of Scientific Principles

Scientific definition of vectors:

A vector is an object that has both a magnitude and a direction(in cricket terms – a speed AND an aim/direction/bouncing position). Geometrically, we can picture a vector as a directed line segment, whose length is the magnitude of the vector and with an arrow indicating the direction. The direction of the vector is from its tail to its head.

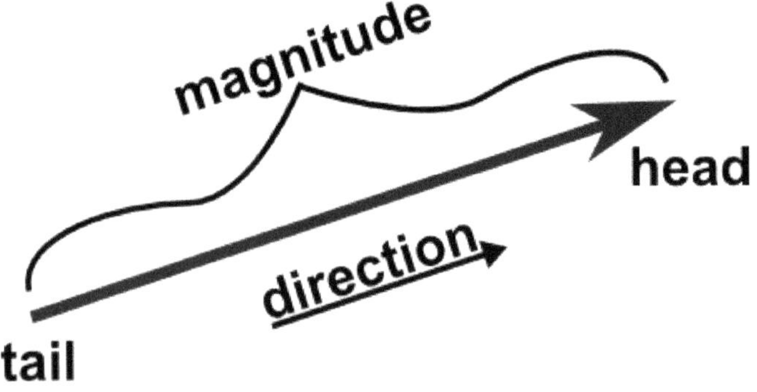

Two vectors are the same if they have the same magnitude and direction. This means that if we take a vector and translate it to a new position (without rotating it), then the vector we obtain at the end of this process is the same vector we had in the beginning.

Two examples of vectors are those that represent force and velocity. Both force and velocity are in a particular direction. The magnitude of the vector would indicate the strength of the force or the speed associated with the velocity.

In mathematics, physics, and engineering, a **Euclidean vector** (sometimes called a **geometric**[1] or **spatial vector**,[2] or—as here—simply a **vector**) is a geometric object that has magnitude (or length) and direction. Vectors can be added to other vectors according to vector algebra. A Euclidean vector is frequently represented by a line segment with a definite direction, or graphically as an arrow, connecting an *initial pointA* with a *terminal point B*,[3] and denoted by AB

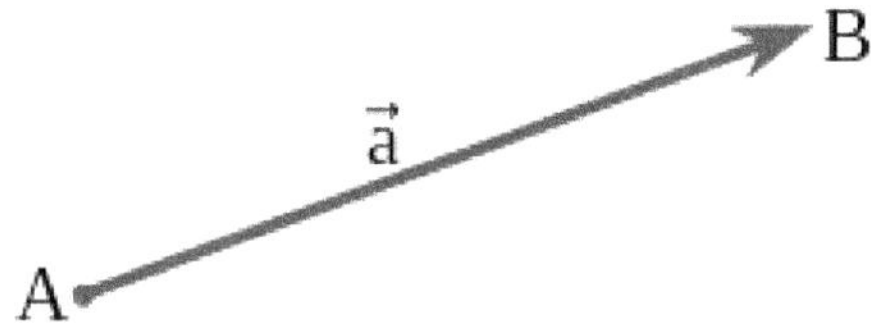

A vector is what is needed to "carry" the point *A* to the point *B*; the Latin word *vector* means "carrier".[4] It was first used by 18th century astronomers investigating planetary revolution around the Sun.[5] The magnitude of the vector is the distance between the two points and the direction refers to the direction of displacement from *A* to *B*.

Scientific definition of Law of reflection:

Ancient Greek mathematician Euclid described the law of reflection in about 300 BCE(however, it may have been discovered earlier than this by other countries, namely India). This states that light travels in straight lines and reflects from a smooth surface at the same angle at which it hit it. Light is reflected in the same way that a ball would bounce off of a frictionless surface, and so Euclid claimed that light travels in rays that are discrete, like atoms, not continuous, like waves.

Light is known to behave in a very predictable manner. If a ray of light could be observed approaching and reflecting off of a flat mirror, then the behavior of the light as it reflects would follow a predictable *law* known as the **law of reflection**. The diagram below illustrates the law of reflection.

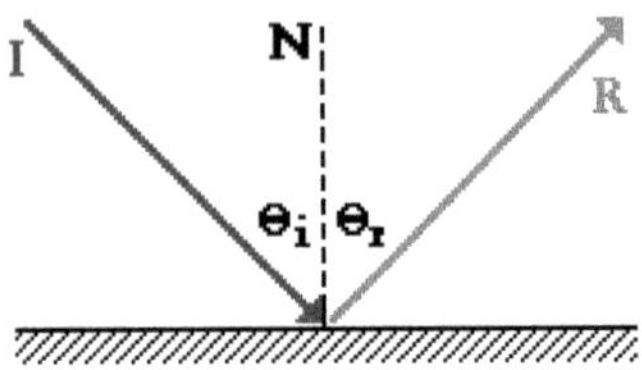

In the diagram, the ray of light approaching the mirror is known as the **incident ray** (labeled **I** in the diagram). The ray of light that leaves the mirror is known as the **reflected ray** (labeled **R** in the diagram). At the point of incidence where the ray strikes the mirror, a line can be drawn perpendicular to the surface of the mirror. This line is known as a **normal line** (labeled **N** in the diagram). The normal line divides the angle between the incident ray and the reflected ray into two equal angles. The angle between the incident ray and the normal is known as the **angle of incidence**. The angle between the reflected ray and the normal is known as the **angle of reflection**. (These two angles are labeled with the Greek letter "theta" accompanied by a subscript; read as "theta-i" for angle of incidence and "theta-r" for angle of reflection.) The law of reflection states that when a ray of light reflects off a surface, the angle of incidence is equal to the angle of reflection.

Computer programming& Computer code:

What Is Coding? Coding is the process of using a programming language to get acomputer to behave how you want it to. Every line of code tells the computer to dosomething, and a document full of lines of code is called a script. Each script is designed to carry out a job.

Put simply, a programming (or coding) language is a set of syntax rules that define how code should be written and formatted. Thousands of different programming languages make it possible for us to create computer software, apps and websites.

Computer programming is the process of designing and building an executable computer program for accomplishing a specific computingtask. Programming involves tasks such as: analysis, generating algorithms, profiling algorithms' accuracy and resource consumption, and the implementation of algorithms in a chosen programming language (commonly referred to as coding).

In programming languages, the expression which translates to an instruction is called a programming statement or just statement.There are a number of recognized basic programming constructs that can be classified as follows:

1) Sequences (First Floor)

2) Selection (Second Floor)

3) Repetition (Third Floor)

In this book and in the context of using computer code to develop batting technique, we are using programming constructs from the fields of 'selection statements', here is a little more description about them.

2. Selection

A selection statement provides for selection between alternatives, alternative as in available route options for instruction execution.

A program can take certain route depending on a situation and selection statements help in choosing between the routes.

For example,In a factory, if an employee is present then calculate the salary for 8 hours, otherwise do not calculate the salary, just put a big zero (no work no doe).

So depending on the state of the employee (whether present or not) you are asking the program to do one of two things - a) when employee is present calculate salary, b) when employee is absent put salary as 0 and the processor will choose between taking "path a" or" path b" but not both. So this is an example of Selection with a little bit of illustration below:

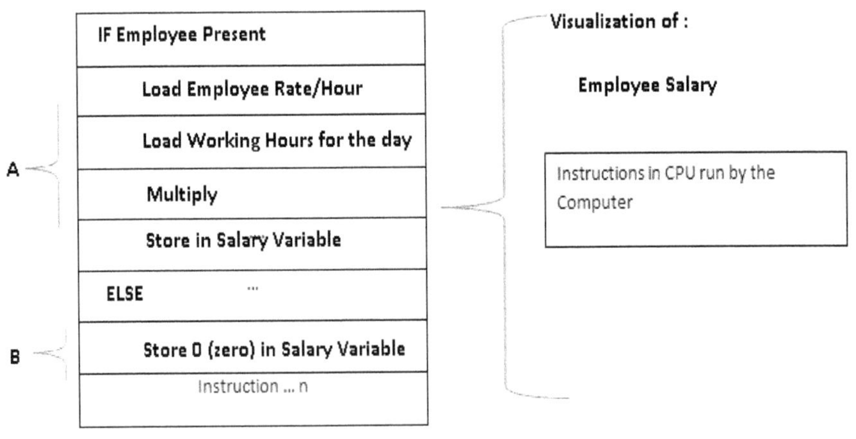

Selection - Either Choose Route A or Route B

Mathematics and Physics of parabolic and projectile motion:

Projectile motion is a form of **motion** experienced by an object or particle (a **projectile**) that is thrown near the Earth's surface and moves along a curved path under the action of gravity only

(in particular, the effects of air resistance are assumed to be negligible).

Projectile Motion - A Vector Perspective

The Vertical Motion of the ball

The acceleration due to gravity is causing the ball to

slow down as it goes up

no vertical motion at the top

Projectile Motion is a combination of the two motions

speed up as it comes down

g

y

x

Adding Vectors

The Horizontal Motion of the ball

There is no force in the x-direction so there is no acceleration

When you kick a soccer ball (or shoot an arrow, fire a missile or throw a stone) it arcs up into the air and comes down again ...

... following the path of a parabola!

(Except for how the air affects it.)

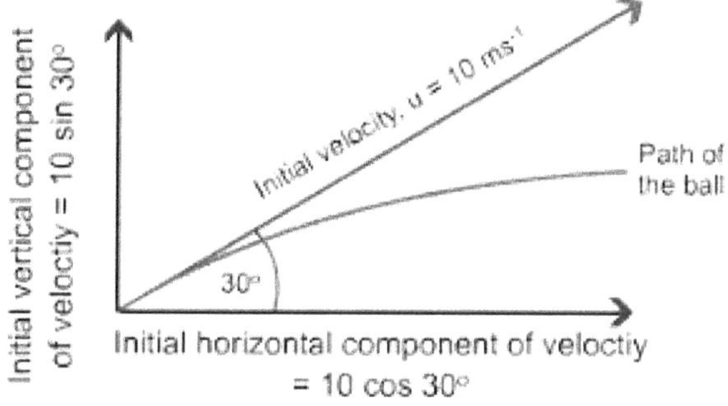

This horizontal component is what gives the ball the forward force, and is the important part of the vector for the batsman to try pick and estimate. Obviously as a batsman with a bat in your hand and not a calculator we can't think 10cos30, but we slowly become adept and skilled at instinctively picking the horizontal component in batsmen's math and the mathematical estimate of the naked eye. In spin bowling, the topspin imparted changes the final path of the ball such that it no longer obeys the law of projectile motion, but can be observed to deviate from common projectile motion in a quantifiable and predictable manner. This must be estimated by the batsman also in effectively estimating vector forces of spin bowling.

Glossary

'Chorr' bowling: when a bowler may not have the striking abilities of a specialist bowler, but rather, is bowling with the aim of containing the scoring rate

12thman: Usually implies, in cricket, the member of the team sitting out, but in context of this book, implies someone who is in their 12th standard formative years, and is undergoing the study of various science subjects and hopefully also interested in science of cricket as a 12th grade subject.

A-Length: That spot on the pitch where batsmen find hard to not only defend but to score freely from

Arm-chair sportsman: Someone who seems to know everything whilst sitting on a chair, but has no practical experience in playing the game firsthand and no formal playing experience to give advice.

Backyard bunny: Someone who has only played informal cricket like at home or in street and who has not played enough high-level competitive cricket to coach or teach

Batsman's talk: A jargon or informal speech used by batsmen to comment on the bowling or the pitch, which is not elaborate but requires interpretation and deduction on the listener's behalf

Bottom-hand player: someone who likes to hit through the ball with great power and use of the bottom hand as in baseball

Check his shot: When the batsman is afforded the luxury of being able to change his shot or adjust his shot in the face of late movement or a change in path of the ball

Computer code:

Cricketing Cap: putting your cricketing cap on and switching into cricket mode, thinking cricket and using your brain in context of a game of cricket. Usually relates to our smarts and intelligence whilst on a cricket field.

Dart-like-line: this is where the ball whilst in trajectory holds a completely straight andcurveless trajectory in regards line, and spins and turns after a dead straight line and trajectory.

Dip: when the ball is made, due to the topspin, to take a different path from a perfectly symmetrical parabola, but rather dip toward the end of its trajectory and hit the pitch at a higher angle of incidence – resulting in more bounce than usual.

Drive on-the-up:

Driving a ball which is short of a length or short of a half-volley

Game of length: Cricket is a game of length – bowlers are trying to get their length right and batsmen are trying to spot any inaccuracy in length to score runs

Gimme: A ball which is so obvious to see and pick and can be easily seen and despatched for a boundary., ie a full toss

Good eye: A batsman who is seeing the ball well and hitting the ball well. A batsman who is good at picking up the length.

Guileful: use and usage of smarts and mental expertise and mental acumen in regard disguise as well as setting the batsman up for a false stroke as opposed to a sheerly brilliant ball.

Have the ball on a string: When the bowler is bowling with extreme control and accuracy and the flight of the ball from hand and down the pitch is exactly as desired or perfect

Hold it back: When a spin bowler gives the impression he is about to bowl a normal delivery with the normal pace and force on the ball, but then at the last moment and during his delivery stride, he bowls it slightly slower than a stock a ball

Keeping low: When the bowl is keeping low upon pitching, usually means the pitch is playing low

Leggie: A legspinner or a stock legbreak ball bowled by a leg spinner

Length ball: That perfect ball which bowler bowls and which is dangerous for the batsman as it requires careful negotiation, and is hard to score off too

License to go for it: when a batsman is told to not worry about losing his wicket or getting out but instead to just try hit as many boundaries as he can and take the necessary risks to accelerate the scoring rate.

Light-footed: usually means when we stand on the toes of our feet during shots and have an ability to transfer weight on to our front or back foot or both within exact parameters and tolerances to successfully execute the stroke. Most important when playing the square drive.

Little leggie: one which does not turn as much as a stock legbreak but only turns a little bit – usually this ball has more top spin on it but not necessarily.

Lofted-shot: One which is picked up by the batsman and hit through the air and usually over the infield.

Loopy one: When a spin bowler bowls a ball which has more flight in the air and more loop as well as being slower and higher.

Make or break :A decision point where you can either go up or down but not both.

Make the bowler bowl to you: cutting out the risky shots and only playing at the ball if it is loose or if it is on the stumps

Make-do coach: Someone who claims to be providing quality coaching advice, but is actually just out to make money and deceive his students into thinking he understands the game well enough to coach you and launch you into playing better cricket.

Mental alertness: Being alert and aware of the mental components of the game, as well as being 100% focused on exactly what you need to do and the repercussion of playing against your opponent in real match conditions, where 100s of factors contribute toward your success.

Mr dependable: A batter or bowler who can be relied upon in pressure sitautions to play his natural game and do what is required for the team without much risk of failing

Offie: An offspin bowler or a stock off break delivery bowled by an off spin bowler.

Pick the length: The act of watching the ball out the bowler's hand and being able to judge and predict where the ball will bounce and how high it will bounce.

Pinch hitter: a batsman who is not a specialist or recognized batsman and who is sent in to simply accelerate the scoring rate through taking risks and potentially hitting boundaries

Played-himself-in: when a batsman has done the initial hard work of gauging the pitch and bowling and is now seeing the ball well and playing fluently

Played-in: When a batsman is seeing the ball well and has gotten used to the pitch and the bowling.

Playing in-the-V: playing only straight drives in the gap between mid-on and mid-off, usually involves a straight bat, elbow up, head down and vertical backlift

Playing your cards right: using the right combinations/permutations in regard your batting and bowling orders

Predetermined protocol: A plan or strategy which has been formulated and decided upon before the match has started or one which ignores the changing situation of the game.

Purchase: the amount of turn a spinner can get upon the ball pitching and hitting the pitch – usually varies according to type of pitch as well as skill of the bowler.

Resultant trajectory: what the final shape of the ball will be upon pitching and hitting the pitch – we must allow for the topspin and the resulting path being different and varied from a standard parabola.

Resultant vector: the shape the ball takes after bouncing and pitching. The resultant vector is always of the same or similar shape as the initial vector or source vector.

Revs: The amount of spin and revolutions a spin bowler is able to impart on his deliveries.

Rhythm: When the bowler is bowling smoothly and everything, biomechanically speaking is in full flow and perfection.

Rig Veda: An auspicious scripture containing many anecdotes, quotes, sayings and words of advice by religious gurus.

Round arm: When a bowler bowls the ball and upon release his arm is closer to being horizontal as opposed to being close to his ears – usually applies to leg spin bowlers

Scalar: a physically measurable quantity, such as weight, velocity or direction.

Scoring rate: The run rate at which the batting side is batting at, or the required run-rate by the batting team necessary for victory

Side-on-sport: cricket is a side-on-sport – batsmen are take guard side on, spinners try to get side-on before they pivot, and fast bowlers use an element of side-on in their action in order to generate swing in both directions.

Straight arm: when the arm upon delivery stride is close to the ear – contrast this with round arm

Strong bottom hand: where the bottom hand or right hand for a right hander generates all the power and bat speed for the stroke.

Toppie: a ball bowled by a spinner which has great amounts of over spin on it and bounces up higher upon pitching.

Tossing the ball up: When a spin bowler bowls higher and slower and with greater flight in the air, in the hope of getting a wicket or a miscued drive

Touch player: A batsman who relies more on timing and wrist-work as opposed to bottom hand and power

Turnover: The reason why businesses, companies and organisations exist. The money made each year from any academy or business.

Typical sport: One with hard knocks and physical moves

Vector force: The final forces imparted or created by a physical vector, or the sum of the two scalars.

Vector: The sum of two scalars, one being direction and the other being magnitude.

Wicket-taking-option: A bowler who is a strike bowler and who has the skills and abilities to get the batsman out as opposed to just containing the scoring rate.

Zip through: when the ball pushes through fast and straight and generally without any sideways deviation.

A Note By The Author

At no time during the making of this book do we advocate the emulation or copying of any figure or player, through the making of this book we seek to merely explain the concepts and scientific theory involved in batting, bowling and captaincy and justify this through written word and discussion. Just as if like a batsman playing the man and not the ball, or a bowler trying to emulate the action of an idol or a cricketing great, through the understanding and reading of this book we are not here to foster this approach in any sense even miniscule. Instead we are here to encourage you to get a proper education about cricket, and encourage you to understand the theory and science behind what we do in cricket and why. We are here to merely educate you and point you in the right direction, and encourage you to base your game and learning of the game on solid and acceptable scientific cricketing fundamentals. Anything I have explained in this book is purely a theory or a concept which I believe is important to your cricketing education as a bowler or a batsman, and is not promulgated as simply an attempt to copy or mimic what the greats do. I have shown you a certain technique to footwork which my coach has explained to be superior, not because Tendulkar and Waugh also uses it – this is purely a coincidence. I have explained to you about the pace of a good run-up based on my own experience and personal coaching, not because Warne and Murali also use it – this is because they are the greatest exponents of their chosen field and have also based their movements around a scientific and proper education and guidance on the game. We encourage you to listen, take everything on board and between your ears; and then after finishing this, go out and see what works best for you and try develop your own style whilst at the same time using and religiously following the fundamentals of the sport I have shared with you.

We appreciate you reading, do recommend to others if you found it useful, and we hope your education on the game is complete or near complete, and you are now ready to go out and practice hard with a more confident approach.

Thankyou

All the best,

Nikhil Jain
(Aust. State level legspinner/offspinner, Canberra)

Here are our final words on the game of cricket which we think sums up the book and is important for your cricketing education to continue and for you to grow as a player:

"Cricket is an off stump game, a side on game and a game of length, not to mention a game of mental toughness. Mental toughness can be defined as: Strategy, tactics, concentration, shot-selection, assessing the situation and the requirements at the time, adjusting your technique to fit the moment, and adapting and changing your calculation for victory, both on a team basis and individual basis."

...Nikhil Jain

"Mental toughness, strategy and 'out cricket' can contribute as much as 50% to our performance on match day in limited-overs cricket formats"

.....Nikhil Jain